Praise for
THE RACE FOR A NEW GAM

"It is not often we get to read the real story of a
with doing the impossible. When we do, the heroes are usually
something like historical or maybe modern-day adventurers or rescue
personnel. But in *The Race for a New Game Machine*, we see the hard
work and the intellectual and interpersonal frustrations of a group of
top engineers who are tasked with doing something that no one has
ever done before. And along the way, we are both educated in a
dozen important principles of creative change, and challenged to do
something equally important in our own businesses."

> —John C. Beck, author of *Got Game: How the Gamer Generation
> Is Reshaping Business Forever* and *The Kids Are Alright:
> How the Gamer Generation Is Changing the Workplace*

"The book is fascinating because it's written by one of the few people
who had insight both into the creation of the groundbreaking Sony-
Toshiba-IBM Cell chip for the PlayStation 3 and the code-named
Waternoose microprocessor that IBM created for Microsoft's Xbox
360. When I tried to get such an interview in the past, IBM turned me
down flat and gave me a bland interview with someone several layers
above Shippy. I got a sanitized version of the story, but Shippy gives us
the contaminated version. For contaminated is exactly how he felt
when he was essentially asked to be a double agent in the chip design
process."

> —Dean Takahashi, author of *Opening the Xbox*
> and *The Xbox 360 Uncloaked*

"One of the great business stories of our young century lies buried
within the 74 million videogame machines sold in the past three years.
This fast-paced tell-all follows the model of Tracy Kidder's classic book
about computer development, letting the chips fall where they may."

> —Steven Cherry, editor, *IEEE Spectrum* magazine

"The authors give readers a seldom seen view into the demanding
world of technology creation on the bleeding edge. Gripping, intense,
and a bit of intrigue to boot, *The Race for a New Game Machine*
reveals that the video game industry is anything but a game.
Absolutely fascinating!"

> —Chris Melissinos, Chief Gaming Officer, Sun Microsystems

"Shippy and Phipps expose the drama and secret deals that rock the mega-billion-dollar world of bleeding-edge computer chip design. This is the real deal."
—Bob Molyneaux, president and CEO, ChipBridge

"Shippy takes us on a journey that one would have never imagined— starting from scratch, facing significant obstacles while serving three masters to deliver the goods. And deliver the goods they did. David and his team gave us the 'brains' behind two of the most unbelievable gaming systems the world has ever seen, in the Xbox360 and the PlayStation 3. Their effort was truly game changing! It was educational, intriguing, and unexpected."
—J. Jolly Hayden, vice president, FPL Energy, LLC;
    president, Lone Star Transmission, LLC

"David Shippy and Mickie Phipps' book has all the videogames industry drama that a person could ask for. . . This book doesn't have spies, ninjas, Master Chief, or pictures of cats in precarious positions with hilariously misspelled captions to explain the predicament. It does have an awesome story to tell, though."
—Brad Nicholson, Destructoid.com

"David Shippy and Mickie Phipps take readers on an impressive journey through the design and development of what would become the famed Cell processor . . . The book that's lighting up the tech world and in the process helps shine a light into the secretive world of processor development and industrial intrigue . . . With its intriguing blend of historical narrative and a unique look at management, *The Race for a New Game Machine* is sure to please those wanting an in-depth look into the creation of the PlayStation 3 and Xbox 360 gaming consoles during one of the most unique moments in the history of interactive entertainment."
—Nathan Evans, Popzara.com

THE RACE FOR A NEW GAME MACHINE

Creating the Chips
Inside the Xbox 360 and the PlayStation 3

David Shippy and Mickie Phipps

CITADEL PRESS
Kensington Publishing Corp.
www.kensingtonbooks.com

CITADEL PRESS BOOKS are published by

Kensington Publishing Corp.
119 West 40th Street
New York, NY 10018

All Kensington titles, imprints, and distributed lines are available at special quantity discounts for bulk purchases for sales promotions, premiums, fund-raising, educational, or institutional use. Special book excerpts or customized printings can also be created to fit specific needs. For details, write or phone the office of the Kensington special sales manager: Kensington Publishing Corp., 119 West 40th Street, New York, NY 10018, attn: Special Sales Department; phone 1-800-221-2647.

CITADEL PRESS and the Citadel logo are Reg. U.S. Pat. & TM Off.

First trade paperback printing: January 2010

10 9 8 7 6 5 4 3 2 1

Printed in the United States of America

Library of Congress Control Number: 2008936686

ISBN-13: 978-0-8065-3142-7
ISBN-10: 0-8065-3142-8

To my wife, Leslie, and children, Grant and Reed,
I love you more than words can express.
You are my joy and inspiration.

—D.S.

To my husband, Jerry, the love and light of my life
—until there is no more.

—M.P.

CONTENTS

Contents

INTRODUCTION

Many years ago, I read a thrilling true story about Tom West and his band of adventurous engineers, the men and women from Data General who invented a new minicomputer. Tracy Kidder chronicled their arduous journey in his 1981 Pulitzer Prize–winning national bestseller, *The Soul of a New Machine*. He inspired me with his fascinating saga of the people and their machines that revolutionized the world. A typical rebellious teenager at that time, I was still contemplating a possible future as an astronaut, an Indiana Jones clone, a basketball superstar, or a professional surfer, but Kidder gave me a glimpse of a different world. As I read about the rebellious Tom West, I suddenly saw through the eerie and frightening scientific mumbo-jumbo, and I could think of nothing I wanted more than to be a part of that emerging high-tech world.

We've come a long way from the time of Kidder's tale, and the computer he described is a prehistoric relic compared to the chips that give life to today's PCs, laptops, and game consoles. Now CEOs, grandmothers, farmers, teenagers, and people from every walk of life, demographic niche, and geographic region are computer-savvy. Attention spans are short, and expectations for the next latest-and-greatest product are high. When a kid drops $59.95 at Circuit City on Microsoft's *Halo 3* interactive shoot-em-up and launches the game on an Xbox 360, more is demanded from this game console than has ever been demanded from any other game machine. When the player swings the joystick and levels a weapon at a charging alien beast, then presses the button and showers it with lead, splattering it straight back to hell, the quality of the experience depends less on the fancy code written by the people at Microsoft than on the processor brains in the chip inside the box.

Anyone who dares to look under the hood of that game console will find my fingerprints, for I am one of the "computer neurosurgeons" who infused the spark of life into that brain. From 2001 to 2005, I joined my friends from IBM, Sony, and Toshiba to form a partnership, a melting pot of the best chip-making talent in the business who revolutionized the home entertainment industry. We enlisted the smartest IBM chip veterans from Texas, New York, North Carolina, Minnesota, and also Germany, beefed up that team with young hotshot grads from top universities like Duke and Purdue, and then added the best PlayStation 2 engineers from Sony and Toshiba. We were hot, and we pushed the leading edge of technology further than anybody dared to hope. We designed the fastest microprocessors in the world, the brains of both the Microsoft Xbox 360 and the Sony PlayStation 3.

Microsoft and Sony dreamed of far more than just another game machine. Separately, they devised competitive plans to take over not only the game market but also the entire home-computing environment, replacing every household's PC with a machine based on a new game chip. These revolutionary chips have all the capabilities of a personal computer or a notebook computer, with the turbo-boosted supercomputer power made possible by our microprocessor technology. The next step in their grand scheme was to power broadband home servers, high-definition televisions, and handheld devices. As a veteran IBMer, I was extremely fortunate to be on this multicorporate team that introduced a major paradigm shift in home computing, the kind that only comes around once every twenty years or so.

While this is an amazing true story of high-tech innovation in a complex business environment, it is primarily a story of the extraordinary individual heroes—the microprocessor design engineers—who delivered the fastest microprocessor in the industry in record time. We worked hard, we played hard. Behind the scenes, the corporate intrigue that swirled around the development of these chips was so startling it was almost unbelievable. Through a series of secretive business deals and design decisions, my diverse multicorporate team ended up designing a single common microprocessor core that became the heart and soul of both game machines. The Sony and Toshiba employees who lived, worked, and played side by side with my IBM team ultimately participated in the design of the microprocessor core that now powers not only the Sony PlayStation 3 but also their archrival's machine, the Microsoft Xbox 360.

We dumped a few hundred highly skilled engineers into this secretive, complex work environment and the result was sometimes fun, often intense, and always challenging. Against all odds, in spite of significant trials and risks, this team achieved record-breaking success. They did it through strength of commitment, technical prowess, and effective leadership. Here are some of the key leadership principles highlighted in the story.

Inspire a bold vision. Combine a deep and abiding passion with a vivid imagination and extraordinary expertise, and you have the makings of a visionary. There were more than one such rare individuals on this project, and it was their grand dream of challenge and glory that enticed our team to work harder than ever. We were energized by a future lined with possibilities never before imagined.

Build a team for success. Through these pages, you'll meet a highly diverse team of talented engineers who devoted a big chunk of their lives to creating the chips for the Xbox 360 and PlayStation 3 game consoles. It was not chance or coincidence that brought this phenomenal group together. It took a concerted effort of managers and technical leaders who understood that assembling the team was only the beginning. We gave constant attention to the mix of skills and personalities, tweaking assignments, building proficiency, and shuffling people to optimize performance. It took absolute focus and die-hard persistence.

Know your competition and do your homework. Each player in this saga—Sony, Toshiba, IBM, and Microsoft—had a different race to run, a different set of rivals to beat. The strengths and accomplishments of the competition helped shape our project goals. Even at a personal level, this axiom applied.

Inspire innovation. We couldn't reach those lofty chip design goals without flying there on the wings of invention. No one had ever done the things we set out to do and, contrary to popular belief, creative juices don't just flow from a spigot with an on/off knob. Inspiration comes from the challenge of solving problems. You have to coax novel ideas into the light, then carefully dissect and analyze them. It takes a coach with finesse and expertise, and an inventor with thick skin.

Work hard, play hard, celebrate success. Chip design is exhausting, intense, complicated work, and we couldn't survive it without a way to reenergize. Our playtime reinforced the interpersonal relationships, those priceless intangibles that made us want to come to work every day. Our celebrations put a spotlight on our accomplishments and helped us recognize real progress. It made us feel like winners.

Enable risk taking. The satisfaction that came from winning, the certainty we were on the right path, and the strength and support we gained from our fellow engineers and leaders— with these things, we believed we were invincible. We could step out on a limb with a new idea, challenge an outdated technological truism, or commit to a near impossible schedule.

Stay positive, even in the swirl of controversy. Of course, on the heels of invincibility comes the inevitable reality check. We had a huge load of work, very little time to do it, and many eyes watching us. Staying positive kept our focus on the desired results, even when it was so tempting to surrender to the naysayers.

Be proactive, anticipate problems, hold everyone accountable. Engineering problems that hit you out of the blue can crater a project. Utilizing proactive project management and anticipating the tough problems before they spiral out of control allows projects to stay on schedule and be delivered with high quality.

Stay laser focused on the end result. It is a common pitfall to focus on the obstacles and challenges we face in life. Staying focused on the fruits of the end result is what ultimately leads us to success.

The battle for supremacy over the gaming world will continue, and whichever side wins, that success will have been powered by the work of our team of brilliant designers. Mickie and I present the inside story of this chip development experience with two hopes: one, that it will inspire other engineers to reach for the stars and, two, that it will provide some valuable leadership lessons for other leaders and managers.

We feel compelled to offer this disclaimer. Although we did our utmost best to stay true to the story and the way we remember it unfolding, we recognize that memory is ultimately fallible. There are certain to be errors in our story, and we apologize in advance for any discrepancies that disturb or offend those most familiar with these events. We changed the names of some of the people in the story in order to protect their privacy. We hope you will enjoy this tale of human toil and triumph in the workplace the way we remember it.

ACKNOWLEDGMENTS

There are so many people we must thank for their support of our work and for their contributions (both intentional and unintentional) to this story.

First, our deepest and most sincere gratitude to our mentor, Chekib Akrout, for all the many things he taught us, for the doors he opened for us, and for his friendship. His optimism and enthusiastic leadership lifted us up to the challenges encountered during this chip-building effort. His truthfulness set the standard that we try to follow even today.

Secondly, we owe many thanks to the fearless Jim Kahle for his willingness to hold a hard line, his blistering drive, and the abundance of technical skills he shared with us.

Many thanks to the four extraordinary companies that made this technology possible: IBM, Sony, Toshiba, and Microsoft.

Our gifted coworkers from the four companies featured in this book are the true heroes who strive for perfection in their creations. We sincerely hope that the rewards of this challenging work continue to fulfill their dreams.

We will always be indebted to Darlene Dean and Ann Hatton for superb and timely editorial comments. Their touch made this a much better book.

We'd also like to thank our editor, Richard Ember. Richard "got it" the minute he heard our story. He is a great editor and his enthusiasm has been contagious. Thank you, Richard, for everything.

And last but not least, from the bottom of our hearts, we thank our families for their positive encouragement and rock-solid support on this exciting adventure. They were and still are our most trusted confidants, our patient and insightful first readers, and always our source of joy. Jerry, Leslie, Reed, and Grant—God bless you.

NOTE TO THE READER

Co-authors David Shippy and Mickie Phipps experienced this journey through the pressure-cooker world of technology development while working side by side at IBM in Austin, Texas. To bring their extraordinary story alive for you, they present it as a chip designer's memoir written in first person in David Shippy's voice. We hope you will enjoy their adventure.

PROLOGUE

THE EXCITEMENT BEGAN in the summer of 2003. My team and I had worked tirelessly at IBM for two and a half years, breathing life into the Sony PlayStation 3 "Cell" central processing chip. My team was responsible for the PowerPC microprocessor core in the central processing chip. It was an important subcomponent in the overall chip that performed the function of the "brains" for the entire PlayStation 3 game console. Our microprocessor core executed the instructions of the game console operating system and controlled the flow of information just like a traffic cop in a busy intersection. We ordered our lives around the idea of beating Microsoft to market with a Christmas 2005 launch of a revolutionary new game machine certain to soar to new heights of computing power and market share. Gamers worldwide would flock to this platform to blow away ghouls, race speedboats, and seduce bikini-clad vampiresses. With Sony's dream to extend its empire to take over the home-computing business, a second and almost as consuming focus was the race with Intel and Advanced Micro Devices (AMD) to develop the chip that would surpass the world's current performance record.

Then Dr. Chekib Akrout, IBM's senior vice president responsible for the PlayStation's chip team, told me another customer wanted our secret-weapon, record-smashing PowerPC microprocessor core. It was Microsoft.

We sat alone in his office, a barren, windowless hole on the sixth floor of an IBM building in Austin, Texas. Akrout leaned forward in his big leather executive chair and watched me, tapping his pen on his desk, waiting for my reaction to this shocking news. I was confused. Sony had agreed that IBM could use the PlayStation 3 PowerPC microprocessor core in other applications in the future, so IBM was on solid legal ground. Nevertheless, this new deal raised some sticky ethical questions in my mind. Wouldn't we be competing against ourselves? Two-timing? Sleeping with the enemy? Sony was my partner! My temples pounded. Fury gripped my throat.

I was so angry I didn't dare look at Akrout, so I swiveled my chair to the side and glared at the drab, bare wall instead. I wanted to make a competitive difference for Sony, who commissioned this little work of art. I spent years building a chip for them that would power their game machine to crushing victory in the marketplace, and it was a dream I was not ready to relinquish. While I fully expected our breakthrough chip to continue into future products in some derivative form, I never imagined it would happen before the current job for Sony was finished. I wasn't ready to consider the demands of an additional customer, especially one that presented such a vast conflict of interest.

"How did this happen?" I grumbled through gritted teeth, still looking at the cracks in the yellowed wall. Fluorescent lights buzzed and flickered above me, creating weird shadows that bumped into each other in the corners of the room.

"Let's just say it was a blockbuster, an offer IBM couldn't refuse," he answered. Lest I think the stakes of the enterprise were small, Akrout told me that over a billion dollars was involved, spanning the entire spectrum from development to chip manufacturing. Microsoft's Bill Gates approached Sam Palmisano, IBM's CEO, about designing the next generation Xbox microprocessor chip. The IBM sales team laid out every other chip option they possessed or could dream up, but nothing caught the interest of Gates's team. Then a senior IBM engineer from another division disclosed to Microsoft some of the most sensitive details of the microprocessor core I was designing for the Sony chip.

My jaw dropped at this news, and I spun around to face Akrout. That was my baby! It was as if they had snuck an unauthorized Polaroid out of the labor and delivery room and posted it on the Internet. This was personal. IBM is a big company, spread across many locations and organized into a complicated web of semi-related divisions, each with its own mission, its own independent team. Even so, I had a reasonable expectation to be included in any discussions with potential clients for my processor. I fumed and raged about the subterfuge, but in the undercurrents beneath my anger, a more familiar beast took a deep, satisfying breath—my pride. Microsoft's interest was flattering, a high compliment to my team's virtuosity. We designed the fastest microprocessor in the industry, one that broke numerous performance records. It was tiny, and it consumed very little power. We gave Sony's little game box the performance of a supercomputer, driving a deep shaft into a goldmine of riches for IBM that would endure for years.

"Dave, you and your team have done an amazing job. I'm proud of your work." Akrout was quick and generous with his praise, and because of my respect for him, his approval meant a great deal. Grinning, he added, "It was your team's microprocessor that turned Microsoft's head and convinced them to strike a deal with us."

"Of course it did," I retorted, rocking forward in my chair. That's the only thing he'd said that hadn't surprised me. "Given all the bad blood between IBM and Microsoft, I'll bet they considered every other option before they came to us, didn't they? And I can tell you what they discovered. The folks at Intel and AMD can't deliver anything like this."

Did I mention that we chip designers are as competitive as *Top Gun* pilots?

"There's more," Akrout said. He sank back into his chair, a subtle shift of body language, but enough to tell me he didn't like relaying the next tidbit of news any more than he had the first. He ran a hand across his thinning black hair and sighed. "Microsoft wants something very similar to what you designed for Sony but with some unique enhancements, and they want it on the same schedule." He then described the design changes Microsoft needed for a super-aggressive, market-shaking Christmas 2005 launch.

"That's crazy!" I shouted, and slapped a hand down on the table. "It's practically a total redesign. It took us two and a half years to get to this point on the PlayStation 3, so how does Microsoft think they're going to hit the same schedule? I mean, even if we could do our part and deliver a chip to them on time . . . and I'm extremely doubtful we could . . . how can they possibly do all the stuff they have to do to get a console ready by then and also have games available to play on it?"

Akrout didn't blink. It took me a second, but I got the message. He was such an optimist, he actually thought Gates's people might just pull it off, with our help.

I slumped into my chair again, waiting for the next shoe to drop, while Akrout morphed into a used-car salesman—his sly grin, a smooth-as-silk voice, that sophisticated French accent. "In addition to your role on the PlayStation 3 chip, I want you to take the technical lead position for the Microsoft microprocessor project," he said. "You're the only person with the knowledge and skills to pull it off on this insanely aggressive schedule."

I had extremely mixed feelings about the offer. I was flattered but still felt like a two-timer. I loved Akrout. In his finest moments, he was completely capable of convincing his people to follow him over a cliff. He knew exactly where my buttons were, knew I couldn't resist a high-flying challenge. I was such a sucker. My plate was already full, as was that of my team. I rarely got home in time to tuck my little boys into bed at night. Piling on more work, especially work that approached the shady side of impossible, would not be smart.

After some internal debate, my pride delivered a deathblow to my anger and perhaps to my common sense. "I'm pretty sure one of us is going to regret this," I said as I shook Akrout's extended hand. "I accept your offer."

My goals were very clear when I joined IBM in the mid-1980s. I wanted cutting-edge microprocessor design projects that really pushed the state of the art. I wanted to lead design teams and leave my mark on the industry. This vision was the focal point of my whole career. Akrout handed me one of the top technology leadership positions in the entire industry and, for one brief moment, I saw the top of the mountain, everything I wanted. Would I have to stake my claim by screwing Sony and extending Microsoft's dominance of digital life? Or could I help them both succeed?

CHAPTER 1

The Holy Grail Vision

At the heart of every successful
technical accomplishment,
there first existed a
bold vision that inspired the team.

*Onward Through the Fog. Live Music Capital of the World.
Hillary Is Hot! You're just jealous because the voices only talk to
me. Save the Giant Flying Vampire Armadillos.*

THIS STRANGE ARRAY OF BUMPER STICKERS on
the Volkswagen van in front of me held my attention a moment too
long, and I almost missed my turn. I take pride in being a nonconformist,
but in Austin, Texas, where "Keep Austin Weird" is the city slogan, I
clearly reside deep in "normal" territory. It was February of 2001, and
little did I know that I was about to jump on board the ride of my life.

I parked in front of the Gingerman Bar, the epitome of Austin's
funky hippie-yuppie lifestyle. It was once a favorite hangout of mine,
and I hadn't been there in years. I came to meet an old friend who
wanted to discuss a job with me. A secret interview, he'd cautioned
seriously when he phoned. I came mostly out of curiosity, for I was not

in the job market. I glanced around the parking lot but didn't see anyone I knew, no one to break my cover—I already disliked all this cloak and dagger stuff.

A cool breeze cut through me when I stepped out of my car, making me glad I'd swapped my baggy cargo shorts for a pair of faded jeans. Sandals flapped against my heels as I walked. No suit, tie, and spit-shined shoes, no well-crafted resume in hand. I heaved open the massive door, pulling against the wind. I barely squeezed inside before the door sucked closed behind me with a bang, nearly hitting me in the heels. I glanced into the entryway mirror and brushed a hand across my hair, but it was stubborn and chose to stick straight up despite my best efforts. Good enough, I thought, as I flapped a hand at my disheveled reflection.

Dim overhead lights and meager sunlight from the grimy windows did little to brighten the spacious bar. I snagged my Oakley sunglasses into the top buttonhole of my Hawaiian shirt.

"Shippy!"

I turned and moved in the general direction of the voice. Even though I couldn't see well enough to identify the speaker, I knew who it was: the man I came to see. My eyes adjusted, and I spotted Jim Kahle in a corner booth. I lifted a hand in recognition and headed that way, weaving between a jumble of mismatched tables and chairs where a handful of patrons sipped tall glasses of beer.

I studied my old friend as I approached. He was fortyish, but he looked as lean and athletic as ever. Yellow polo shirt tucked into faded blue jeans. Well-worn running shoes. He still brushed his wavy sandy-blond hair straight back, but now it revealed a deeply receding hairline and a sunburned forehead.

He stood up to greet me, and we shook hands and patted each other on the back. Two years had passed since the last time we met, so all week I'd looked forward to seeing him again.

Kahle and I shared a long intertwined history as microprocessor designers at IBM. We first met in the fall of 1989 when I transferred from Endicott, New York, to Austin, where Kahle became my manager. We clicked right away. We both possessed an aggressive style, a hard work ethic, and a "victory or death" attitude about work and life in general. We found common interests outside of the office including soccer, water skiing, and drinking beer. Ten years later, at the height of the technology boom, I left IBM to seek my own mythical dot-com fame and fortune at a local startup company. Kahle stayed on at IBM, diligently climbing the corporate ladder, becoming a Distinguished Engineer, a recognized force throughout the company. His team produced the microprocessor chips that put IBM in the lead in high-performance Unix servers and powered Apple's resurgence in the personal computer market.

I slipped into the opposite side of the booth, sinking into well-worn burgundy leather. I teased him about the need for secrecy. "What's up with that?" I asked. "Don't tell me . . . the CIA wants us to solve the problems with global security, right?"

Kahle just smiled, looking every bit like the cat that swallowed the canary. "We'll get to that," he said. He had a secret worth sharing, but he was going to play it for all it was worth. He bought the beer, so I didn't mind waiting.

We talked about our families, caught up on personal events of the past few years, sipped on frosty mugs of dark beer. Kahle's three children were a couple of years older than my two sons, but still close enough in age that we had a lot in common. Parenting can be the universal leveler.

A half-hour passed, and I glanced at my watch. When would Kahle get to the heart of the matter? Silence settled heavily into a momentary gap in our conversation, and the polite pleasantries ended abruptly.

Kahle leaned across the table, whispering inspired words charged with intensity, filled with passion. He described a powerful partnership recently formed between Sony, Toshiba, and IBM to build the processor for the next version of the PlayStation game console. Sony was the biggest game player in town, with over 55 million PlayStation and PlayStation 2 units sold worldwide. Game developers flooded the shelves with over 430 million copies of game software for the PlayStation line. There were no official announcements of the partnership yet, and Sony insisted on keeping it quiet for as long as possible. Hence the need for secrecy.

"With this project," Kahle said, "we have the potential to hit a home run and take over the entire home computing market. Or"—he paused and shrugged his shoulders—"we could just hit a single and go build a cool chip for a game machine the whole world loves. At the very worst, we'd have some fun."

Both prospects intrigued me.

I took a long pull from my beer. These babies weren't just toys—they were high-performance computing engines. Music to my ears. I'd worked on microprocessors for everything from mainframes all the way down to notebook computers. Designing a game machine would be a welcome change, and the software would be much sexier than the corporate stuff running on most of my previous designs.

"Okay. You've got my attention," I said.

Kahle squirmed and continued with his story, setting the bait. He represented IBM when these three high-tech giants collaborated on an idea for the PlayStation 3, a revolutionary game machine intended to turn the electronic games industry upside down. I was shocked at the extraordinary amount of money involved in this endeavor. Sony, Toshiba, and IBM agreed to spend $400 million over five years to develop the processor for this machine. Kahle's eyes gleamed as he told me that this path-breaking, joint development venture, dubbed the STI Design Center, would be located right here in Austin. On top of that, this powerful threesome planned to spend billions of dollars for two state-of-the-art chip fabrication facilities. Sony also agreed to pay IBM hundreds of millions to set up a production line at their new facility in Fishkill, New York. That's a lot of money to spend before a single chip rolls off the line.

"Sony's Ken Kutaragi was the instigator who brought the three companies together for this adventure," Kahle said with just a hint of triumph in his voice. He looked disappointed when I failed to respond with appropriate awe. "Kutaragi is president and CEO of SCEI, Sony's video games division."

"Oh." I wiped off some of the gathering condensation on my mug, stalling for a moment while I considered this. "I've been a little busy the last few years."

"But he's known everywhere as the father of the PlayStation." Jim emphasized his words with extended arms, palms up. He studied my face, apparently looking for some *aha* moment, some sign that I recognized this famous man.

"Jim, I barely know what a PlayStation is."

"Hmph," he said, shaking his head, still unable to fathom the depths of my ignorance. "Okay. So I'll give you a quick education. Kutaragi single-handedly led Sony into the game world, and the PlayStation game machines and software became the heart and soul of Sony's business model. It's their most successful product ever. With the PlayStation 1 and PlayStation 2's phenomenal success in his pocket, Kutaragi felt he must and could realize a grander dream for the broadband market looming on the horizon. He wanted the PlayStation 3 to be a personal computer that also played games, with a chip that could take on roles in many broadband applications, from on-demand television to online gaming to real-time video chats."

As J. R. R. Tolkien might have put it, I thought, "One chip to rule them all / One chip to find them / One chip to bring them all / And in the darkness bind them."

"Remarkable," I said, struck more by Kahle's admiration for this man than by the story itself. Kahle is not one who is easily impressed.

Kahle was on a roll and went on to describe Kutaragi's reputation as an excellent problem solver and a forward-thinking engineer. "That proved true enough during the project planning stages, though I also found him to be demanding and unyielding. To achieve his vision, Kutaragi needed help from experts in processor development and silicon manufacturing. Sony brought expertise in consumer markets, Toshiba in high-volume products and we, IBM, brought microprocessor and system design experience."

"That's a pretty high-powered partnership for just one chip-development effort," I mused.

"Oh, it may be just one chip, but it's much more than just one product," Kahle replied. "The building-block potential of this processor inspired each company to nurture visions of using this design in their traditional product lines. Toshiba plans to incorporate it in high-end televisions, and IBM is contemplating using the new chips in high-performance servers."

Maybe I didn't know Kutaragi, but I still recognized the rare opportunity this partnership represented. When Kahle took a breath, I reached across the table and shook his hand, congratulating him on his accomplishment. "It's a well-deserved honor for you to serve as IBM's point man for negotiations with Sony. Outstanding!"

Kahle modestly claimed he was just lucky, but I knew differently. He was bright, maybe even brilliant. After graduating from Houston's Rice University, he accepted an assignment with IBM's research group, the beginning of a career-long tie to the folks in Yorktown, New York. His first assignment took him into design tools—money-saving, software-based programs that improved the quality of a design by automatically checking for errors, cross talk in the wires, and other design points that exceeded acceptable limits. He integrated those cutting-edge tools into the design process for the chip that eventually put IBM in the lead in high-performance Unix servers.

Kahle spent nearly twenty years of his life at IBM, serving as a key player on several highly successful development efforts including the breakthrough server chip known as the Power4 Gigaprocessor. He was very smart and very aggressive, big reasons why he was one of the most influential engineers at IBM.

I recalled the first time he invited me to play soccer. I scrounged around in my closet, found my old cleats, and brushed off the dust from a few years of neglect. Half an hour on the field and I was stiff, sore, and exhausted, but not giving up. I joined Kahle on the front line, and we tag-teamed the ball toward the goal. When we failed to score, Kahle ran across the field and screamed in my face for not hustling enough. He prided himself for being the fastest, most aggressive player on the field. He made up for any lack of ball-control skills by out-hustling his opponents. He was a bully, but I admired his competitiveness.

Whether playing soccer or designing a new chip, losing was not an option. Kahle was quick to reject those who didn't agree with him, and more than one IBMer's career suffered for crossing him. The Sony chip lay on Kahle's career path; it was his next stepping stone. Nothing would keep him from success. I was more than a little flattered that he saw me as an asset in that venture, but I remained on the fence about joining up. I enjoyed the impact I could have in a small company. Going back to a big company like IBM wasn't exactly appealing.

I drained my mug and then motioned to our waitress for another round.

Kahle described his new design center, which fell under the auspices of IBM's Microelectronics Division. "I spent the first few months of the STI partnership serving as the director in charge of both business and technical issues, even helping to write the contract. Boring stuff. As you can imagine, I was dying to get involved in chip design. The technical complexity of the chip soon consumed my interest, my energy, and my time, leaving little for the business side of things. Paperwork fell into complete disarray, I had no time for staffing, and the executives started to worry."

"I doubt anyone could handle both of those challenging jobs," I sympathized. As I well knew, Kahle was a technical wizard. He would perform much better in an engineering position than he would in a management or business role.

"Maybe not, but I quickly found out that I didn't *want* to handle both jobs. I took the title of chief engineer, focusing on what I do best, chip architecture. I let others handle the contracts, financial controls, staffing, and other adminis-trivia. Finally, I was in the right place."

I had no doubt he'd made the right decision. He wielded a strong influence over any IBM team, and they generally accepted his technical command as absolute rule.

Kahle finally zeroed in on the point of our meeting. One of the first jobs he needed to fill was that of the chief architect for the PowerPC microprocessor core, the "brains" of the chip. "That's where I need you, Shippy. You've always delivered high-quality innovative solutions for me."

I liked the sound of that. As the chief architect, I would take on the coveted role of the technical lead, defining the fundamental blueprint for the PowerPC microprocessor core. It was a once in a lifetime opportunity, the kind of job every engineer desires. It would allow me to exercise all of my creative and innovative engineering muscles and have a major influence on the design. I leaned back in the booth, ignoring the creaking of the old leather seat, and looked Kahle in the eye. Cutting-edge technology, a chance to be in the thick of things, a key leadership position, ground-floor opportunities—who wouldn't be interested?

Kahle sensed a win and immediately moved to close the deal. "This project is extremely important to the IBM Corporation, and folks like you, hired into key positions, will be heavily rewarded."

I smiled at that. He definitely knew the way to my heart. I said, "You just caught yourself a fish."

We spent another hour or so reminiscing about the good times we'd enjoyed together in the mid-1990s at the Austin-based Somerset Design Center, a joint venture between IBM, Motorola, and Apple. Somerset challenged Intel for the PC market with a sleeker, cleaner, PC version of IBM's standard Power server chip, called PowerPC. The Somerset office lay outside the main IBM campus, purposefully free of most of the bureaucracy found in industrial giants, thus creating the impression of a small, privately-run company. It was IBM's bid to give its entrepreneurs the freedom to create and to invent. Kahle's team delivered the first Somerset microprocessor, the PowerPC 603, and then Kahle brought me on board to architect the follow-on micro-processor, the PowerPC G3. Exciting times! The engineers on my team actually believed they could beat Intel, and I guess I did, too. We worked long and hard on our chip designs, and we frequently ended the day on a sand volleyball court at the design center or at the nearby Arboretum drinking beer together. We were a tight group.

Kahle threw big parties for the design team at his house, nestled on the cliffs overlooking Lake Austin. Always a savvy investor, he built his house back in the 1980s before the rest of the world discovered Austin. The folks at his parties were rowdy and consumed lots of beer and margaritas. Kahle cooked his famous "Kahle burgers," delicious, if technically inelegant—thick, hearty, and smothered in cheese. Classic rock tunes from the 1960s and '70s played in the background. There were generally two camps of folks at the parties: The first camp wanted to talk nonstop about work (shoptalk). They could pontificate ad nauseam about the details of their work. The second camp, which I belonged to, wanted to talk about anything *but* work. Both camps liked to drink a lot.

We were having so much fun, we didn't even realize we'd awakened a sleeping giant. It took several years, but ultimately Intel crushed Somerset just as they did all of their competitors. Kahle fondly referred to those days as "taking on the dark side." There was a negative perception of Intel in the engineering world due to the technology giant's monopoly of the PC microprocessor design space. On the software side, there was a similar perception of Microsoft, which dominated the software used on PCs. Microsoft and Intel, nicknamed the "Wintel" pair for their combination of the Windows operating system and the Intel microprocessor, presented a formidable foe. Even facing that serious challenge, Somerset was still a fun and intellectually stimulating environment that Kahle and I both badly wanted to re-create in the STI Design Center—but this time, we meant to win.

The landscape of high-performance microprocessor design had changed significantly since those days in Somerset. Digital Equipment Corporation (DEC) and their once formidable Alpha microprocessors had disappeared. Sun Computer had lost a lot of their market share with their SPARC architecture. Supercomputer maker Cray Research had also gone by the wayside. Other minicomputer and mainframe shops like Data General, Amdahl, and Hitachi had mostly disappeared. There were really only two horses left in the high-performance microprocessor race: the X86 architecture produced by Intel and AMD, and the PowerPC architecture produced by IBM and Motorola. These microprocessors accounted for the majority of the PC and high-performance workstation business.

The only other exciting microprocessor technology was the nimble ARM Architecture—Advanced Reduced Instruction Set Computer (RISC) Machine, which was pervasive in the emerging mobile and handheld space. Most of the rest of the electronics companies adopted a System on a Chip (SOC) philosophy, where they embedded X86, PowerPC, or ARM microprocessor cores into their own custom chips. They differentiated their products by adding their own "secret sauce" intellectual property (IP) to the chip. For example, a disk drive chip might include an embedded microprocessor core alongside a patented read channel controller. An automotive chip paired an embedded microprocessor core with a patented auto controller IP.

Three weeks after that secret meeting at the Gingerman, I found myself wearing an IBM badge . . . again. I would not have predicted it in my wildest imagination. When I resigned from IBM in 1999 to join a little startup company, I was certain I had left big company bureaucracy behind. The high-tech dot-com era was at its peak, and my pot of gold was calling. But Kahle convinced me otherwise. I walked back into IBM's familiar pink palace on Burnet Road, very happy that I had not completely burned my bridges when I left.

Jim Kahle welcomed me back with a tour of his fancy facility. IBM signed over several floors of this high-rise to house his multicorporation team, and Kahle spared no expense in remodeling the space.

"Visiting executives sometimes criticize the plush surroundings, but the investment was for the team," he said, as we strolled down a hallway lit with contemporary high-end wall sconces. "The modern uniformity bonds us together, levels the playing field, and rids all of us of petty jealousies over prime real estate."

We walked past a handful of offices on our tour. One was Kahle's, I knew. Kahle said the other four belonged to the IBM director, Chekib Akrout, his counterpart Sony and Toshiba directors, and the software leader. Everyone else on the team, including the managers, got a cubicle.

Kahle proudly ushered me past many empty cubicles to my own box, the best one in the building—a corner unit on the third floor with floor-to-ceiling windows on two sides. I turned my back to Kahle to hide my disappointment, looking instead out my new window at tall cedar trees swaying back and forth on the wooded lawn. The amount of money sunk into the modernization effort was impressive, but I would gladly have traded my new high-tech cubicle any day for an old, outdated windowless office with a door that closed. I didn't tell Kahle that.

He pulled out a sliding whiteboard to demonstrate that I could increase the privacy in my cube, but that did nothing to reduce the distraction from the high noise level. No stranger to cubicle environments, I had always found it difficult to concentrate when I could so easily hear the phone conversations of my neighbors across the partition. Even quiet conversations among my fellow engineers disturbed my thought processes. Numerous break-out rooms lined the walls of the open floor plan, providing space for private conversations and small meetings, but I worried about the negative impact on the team with the heightened scrutiny and lack of privacy.

Kahle introduced me to my Japanese partners and a handful of IBMers as we continued our tour. My stomach clenched. So few people. Who was going to help me do all that design work Kahle promised?

The second and third floors sported large break rooms with snazzy new-age green glass walls laced with zigzagging copper tubes. Modern kitchen appliances and café-style furniture matched the look.

Kahle and I returned to his office. File cabinets lined one wall, while photos of previous chip designs, various project plaques, and patent awards adorned another. I called it the "I LOVE ME" wall. Every engineer has one. His desk was a familiar mess, cluttered with stacks of technical papers and journals. We sat at his modular, natural-maple desk while he gave me a short history lesson on the Design Center.

"My first discussions with Ken Kutaragi occurred just a few months ago in a hotel in Roppongi, Japan, the location of IBM Japan's head office. I offered him every chip option we had for a potential PlayStation 3 processor. The idea I liked the best and pushed the hardest was a derivative of the Power4," Kahle said.

"Oh, man, that would've been sweet!" I said. Kahle and I had invested a great deal of our own blood, sweat, and tears into the development of the Power4, and we would have been so proud to watch this baby take over a high-volume consumer market like the PlayStation 3. This highly successful server chip was IBM's first microprocessor to break the one-gigahertz clock barrier. That long-standing performance obstacle had once seemed insurmountable. From the early 1980s—when Intel's first 8086 PC microprocessors ran in the low megahertz range—to the turn of the century, it had taken nearly twenty years of evolution to break this barrier.

"Unfortunately, that idea didn't capture Kutaragi's interest." Kahle pointed to a list of products on his whiteboard. A maze of notes and arrows swirled around the barely decipherable column of names. "So I proposed all these other IBM PowerPC derivatives, including the line of embedded cores developed by the team in Raleigh, North Carolina. By the end of the Roppongi trip, I had pitched the entire spectrum of IBM's processor cores, from the very simple and small up to the very large and complex."

I studied the list for a moment. "So Kutaragi rejected everything. Did he give you some idea of what he *does* want?" I was beginning to worry that Kutaragi had some pie-in-the-sky dream that wasn't achievable in real hardware.

"Oh, yes, he did." The excitement in Kahle's voice ramped up. "He challenged us to create something new to leapfrog Intel's technology, something like a supercomputer-on-a-chip. This is Kutaragi's bold vision. His chip will be the heart and soul of a bleeding-edge gaming console. He insists on both multigigahertz frequency and very high floating-point mathematical computation capability."

Floating-point units are included in many microprocessors, but they involve some very complex circuitry with a high transistor count, which translates into costly silicon real estate. Due to this complexity and size, they create much greater challenges for achieving high frequencies.

I nodded my head, nearly salivating over the opportunity to invent something new. This supercomputer-on-a-chip would provide high precision as the chip adds, subtracts, or multiplies very large decimal numbers. "I agree that's a deadly and difficult to beat combination. Tough to build, though," I said.

"You bet," Kahle answered. "A typical game application uses millions of floating-point computations to create animated graphics. Higher precision means that the processor can calculate the physics involved in moving, bending, jumping, crushing, colliding, bouncing, and so on, with a higher degree of accuracy, and thus provide more fluid character movement in crisp, realistic scenes."

That made a lot of sense to me. I already knew that millions of computations determine every pixel position in every scene that flashes across my computer or TV screen. The faster the position of the final pixel is calculated, the more lifelike and fluid that game becomes.

Kahle understood very well what Kutaragi wanted, but in order to get IBM to commit to a major new processor development effort, I knew he would have to engage in and win a major turf battle with IBM's Server Group, our former team. I was sure the folks that had worked with Kahle and me on the Power4 processor would fight fiercely to own this processor and would push for a Power4 derivative as the base design. "What do our friends in the Server Group have to say about all this?" I asked.

"Plenty. They argued that one of their own homegrown server chips or a derivative thereof could just as easily fulfill Sony's game machine requirements and IBM's requirements for new broadband product development. Why invest millions of dollars into something new when off-the-shelf processors fill the bill?"

"Can't argue with that line of thinking," I said.

"True, but I've already been down that path with Kutaragi, and that idea won't fly. He doesn't want what they have. As much as I dread it, a futile and time-consuming turf battle might possibly be the only way to make progress and clinch a deal with Kutaragi. Even with a corporate approval in my pocket, I have no doubt there will continue to be bloody battles over which in-house team—Server Group or Microelectronics Division—will win the job."

I sympathized with Kahle's reluctance to enter into a turf war because I carried my own scars from previous processor wars within IBM. In the mid-1980s, the IBM mainframe processors created most of the revenue in the company. These processors were inside computer products priced from hundreds of thousands of dollars to over a million dollars per system. Processor design houses located in Endicott, Kingston, and Poughkeepsie, New York, as well as Rochester, Minnesota, and Boeblegen, Germany, fought to carve off a piece of the pie and cover the broad range of computing power and cost. Each group, seriously handicapped by the "not invented here" syndrome, wanted to design processors in their own unique way while they created and protected their market niche. Eventually, market demands dictated lower volumes for these mainframes, forcing IBM to cut back on the number of processor designs they could support. This resulted in massive layoffs at some of the company's oldest established sites, from Endicott and Kingston, New York, to Rochester, Minnesota. Politics, not engineering, drove many of those decisions. The loudest and most aggressive leaders typically won.

At the end of the turf wars, the IBM locations that continued to own major processor design work could justify hiring and maintaining a large engineering staff. Those locations that did not own a major mission were forced to downsize. It was survival of the fittest. With job security in mind, I had jumped at the chance to escape Endicott and move to Austin, which soon became IBM's center of competence for processor design. Lucky I made the jump when I did. While Endicott entered a long period of instability, Austin was able to continue to hire and sustain jobs for the best and brightest.

Based on my previous experience at IBM, I realized what a prize the PlayStation 3 would be for the owning engineering organization. That organization could justify their existence for years to come, and I could see why Kahle would fight tooth and nail to secure this highly coveted processor design.

Dominique Fitzgerald, a diminutive French woman who served as an executive administrative assistant, interrupted our discussion to inform me that my presence was required in the office of Dr. Chekib Akrout, the vice president in charge of entertainment and embedded processors. Akrout took the reins from Kahle as IBM's business director for the STI Design Center when Kahle moved into the chief engineer's slot. Dominique ushered me into the executive office next door, then quietly ducked out.

Akrout immediately stood and walked around the desk to greet me with a firm handshake and a ready smile bracketed by deep dimples. We settled into our seats, one on either side of the big maple desk. My new boss looked much younger than I had expected, probably barely forty. He was well over six feet tall, rather large boned, and dressed in trendy brown slacks and a tan long-sleeved shirt that looked classy and expensive but still casual enough to blend into a blue-jean culture. He spoke with a heavy French accent, but his black hair, olive skin, and dark brown eyes made me think of Greece, or Italy, or somewhere in the Middle East.

"I've heard good things about you," he said.

As the discussion progressed, we became instant friends, sharing a similar sense of humor and a mutual respect for each other's technical ability. We quickly veered off a discussion about the project and launched into a friendly exchange of personal histories. Born in Tunisia, Akrout received a B.S. in physics and two Ph.Ds (electronics and physics) from the Université Pierre & Marie Curie in France. Astonishingly, he was fluent in no less than five very dissimilar languages.

Dominique poked her head into the office to announce that Akrout's wife was on the phone. I offered to step out for a moment to give him some privacy, but Akrout motioned for me to remain seated. He carried on a short rapid-fire phone conversation in French. I smiled and relaxed, realizing that his mastery of foreign languages provided all the privacy Akrout needed. When he hung up, he picked up his conversation with me, hardly missing a beat.

Akrout started his IBM career in 1982 as a circuit designer in the elite high-speed memory design group. These folks designed memory chips that were much faster than the standard memory chips attached to most PCs. They laid down intricate patterns of millions of transistors, leading edge work that tapped technical skills as well as artistic talent. Akrout showed a flair for management and far-reaching technical and administrative acumen, overseeing a technical smorgasbord that included everything from general-purpose microprocessors to application-specific chips to complex mixed analog/digital designs. In 2000, as director of high-speed and broadband microprocessor development at IBM's Microelectronics Division, Akrout managed the development of PowerPC processors for Apple's Macintosh desktops and for Nintendo's GameCube. In 2001, his role expanded to include responsibility for the entire STI Design Center. He was a star, and the Design Center was lucky to have him.

A man of great charisma and technical depth, Akrout inspired trust both from his own team and from the heads of other companies who wanted to do business with IBM. He was well liked and trusted by the Japanese directors within the Design Center, certainly a big advantage for IBM. Like Sony's Kutaragi, Akrout was a visionary, willing to take significant business risks. He was a breath of fresh air in the executive ranks, very unassuming and approachable, always focused on doing the "right thing" for IBM. I was generally unimpressed with IBM's new executive management chain, but Akrout was different. He had the perfect mixture of technical ability and people skills.

Other than the one phone call he took from his wife, Akrout gave me his complete and undivided attention during the afternoon. It didn't seem to be special treatment, either; I think he treated anyone who came to his office with the same focused attention. When he listened, he listened with everything in him. His positive energy raised the bar on any conversation.

As I left Akrout's office, I checked the time. The hours had flown by, and I was late to pick up my two sons. I rushed to gather up my laptop, and then zoomed out of the building.

I raced south down Mopac Highway toward my sons' school, but Austin's daily traffic snarl brought me to an abrupt halt. Taillights lined the highway as far as I could see. While I crept along, my thoughts turned to the enormous task that lay ahead of us. Akrout was unmatched in charisma and optimism, but could he convince this team, one not even completely formed yet, that they could be successful where no others had been? Would this kind and jovial man be strong enough to lock horns with Sony and Toshiba when tough calls landed on the doorstep, as they undoubtedly would? And what about the executive team above? Akrout had a grand vision for the future of this product within IBM, but I knew it would be a hard sell to the server-centric, conservative decision makers above us. Those powerful executives remained focused on the IBM server and mainframe computer systems that claimed the highest revenue. They were not interested in the emerging low-end computer space belonging to the PC and the game machine. I smiled. Worried or not, I liked this kind of challenge. I looked forward to being on Akrout's team and to being IBM's rebellious stepchild once again.

I looked at the bumper-to-bumper cars around me. A huge number of those drivers were involved in one way or another in Austin's booming high-tech industry. IBM, Motorola, Dell, Sun, AMD, Applied Materials, Samsung, Solectron, National Instruments, 3M, and a host of smaller businesses called Austin home. With the momentum of all these high-tech companies, Austin was becoming a smaller version of the oft-publicized "Silicon Valley" in California. We called our town "Silicon Hills." Big things were happening in computer chips all over and Austin was right in the thick of the action. It's a self-perpetuating cycle, or maybe a chicken-and-egg scenario. Did the high-tech companies come to Austin because of low tax and economic considerations found in Texas, and then the engineers followed? Or did the growing pool of engineers draw the companies here by offering the necessary resources for corporate or project growth? With the prestigious University of Texas here, a steady stream of new graduates were readily available to infuse fresh ideas and new learning into the creative process.

Computer chips were an integral part of nearly every facet of life in the civilized world, from home appliances to automobiles, cell phones to soda machines, TVs to pacemakers. Technological advances arrived at hypersonic speed, making most electronic devices obsolete within just a couple of years. Demand for the latest and greatest digital gadget was unprecedented. Austin was a high-tech oasis, ideally positioned to take advantage of the new markets spawned by the widespread use of the Internet. I joined the throngs in the enormous turnover in the Austin workforce as engineers moved from one startup company to the other in search of a rocket ride to riches via an initial product offering. The dot-com explosion was on the decline, and those same engineers were now looking for more stable employment.

The line of cars crawled past the exits for the University of Texas and then downtown and its famous Sixth Street. We rolled across the Town Lake Bridge. It was still hard for me to believe I was working for IBM again, and under heavy veils of secrecy, helping create the PlayStation 3 Cell processor. I had one goal: create a world-class, leading-edge processor chip and deliver it in time for a Christmas 2005 product launch.

Not since the invention of the PC more than twenty years ago had chip engineers been asked to start a design of this magnitude from scratch. Truth be told, this was the mouth-watering opportunity that enticed me to return to Big Blue. Chip designers seldom get to start with a clean sheet of paper, primarily because the PC and server markets demand absolute backward compatibility with previous generations of hardware and software. Heaven help us all if the new version of Microsoft Word doesn't open old Word files. It's even more vital in applications that are more sophisticated. Given the high cost of a skilled workforce, lengthy time to market cycles, increasing design complexity, and the exorbitant cost of specialized design tools, we always had plenty of incentive to lean on previous designs. A clean sheet of paper excited every engineer who grew weary of working on derivatives and spin-offs from someone else's design. It was our chance to *create*. Success could bring a paradigm shift in home computing.

Thoughts of fame and glory danced in my head, and I felt pretty good by the time I pulled up in front of my sons' school. With Kutaragi's grand vision as inspiration, Akrout, Kahle, and I were about to set out to design the Holy Grail of computing: the highest frequency, highest performing microprocessor in the industry—better than anything any PC had ever offered. We were going to make a supercomputer on a single chip.

If we could pull it off, a whole generation of gamers worldwide would pay us tribute, with their bloody digital broadswords raised on high.

CHAPTER 2

Building a Team for Success

*The first step to building a highly successful team
is to recruit top talent and seed the team with true
leaders. The next step is to organize the various
disciplines and leaders to maximize success.*

DURING MY FIRST WEEK ON THE JOB, I got a good look
at the towering mountain of work ahead of us. My coworkers consisted of Chekib Akrout, Jim Kahle, one or two managers, a handful of
high-powered engineers, and a few administrative assistants. That was
the whole team! Woefully understaffed, we plowed through heaps of
resumes, scheduled interviews, and, in between, tried to arrange office space, develop org charts, and write job descriptions. The technical work was still in its infancy. I figured I'd better get some other
engineers on board quick, or I was going to be one tired puppy. I
wanted some help with all that design work Kahle promised. Finding
top-notch technical leads was my highest priority.

While I was head down trying to staff my team, Kahle dragged
me into the politics of IBM's latest processor war. The battle for chip
development funding between the Server Group and the Microelectronics Division, where the STI Design Center resided, still raged.

Great ideas, of which there is never a shortage, require significant monetary investment—top-notch salaries, employee benefits, office space, silicon test chips, lab space and equipment—in order to mature into hardware. Sharing that finite pot of gold with its sister division simply reduced either's ability to pursue homegrown innovation. Parochialism was indeed entrenched in the IBM culture and presented a never-ending source of contention. As with the mainframe processor wars of the 1980s, the group awarded the PlayStation 3 processor would secure funding from corporate IBM to staff up a large engineering team. So it all came down to job security again.

An IBM Fellow (the highest rank on IBM's technical career ladder), Rick Baum, drove a task force to resolve the processor roadmap for the entire IBM corporation. The words "task force" made me cringe. This method of problem solving was a relic from the old IBM culture, and I felt it was a huge waste of time and money. It's a committee of high-level engineering experts, pulled from various disciplines within IBM for the express purpose of solving some problem du jour. They would meet on a regular basis, with each member reporting the results of their various homework assignments. Grouped into opposing camps, each side would attempt to persuade the other that their engineering position was the right one, and it was next to impossible to reach a consensus. As I met with Baum's task force, I wondered once again if jumping back into a big corporate environment had been the right decision.

The conclusion, if there was to be one, could be very important to the STI Design Center, so I tried to stay focused. Some members of the task force lobbied for one common processor core to cover both the high-end server space as well as the high-end game space. Kahle was pushing hard for a separate game core.

Kahle presented his case to Baum and the task force: "The server requires something entirely different than the game console does. I need a small, simple core that focuses on high frequency, without all of the baggage that the server core will require."

The Server folks presented their own arguments, though they didn't appear to have any good technical data. They just wanted to own the core for bragging rights, and they wanted funds to sustain future engineering jobs. Kahle told me later, "Baum doesn't really like me much, but I've got money coming in from Sony and Toshiba. I've also got some important executives backing me because I'm going to help pay for our new fabrication facilities by filling them with high-volume chips."

The task force fizzled out, as I predicted, and Kahle got the green light to develop a new PowerPC game core. I was glad the task force didn't last too long because I desperately needed to fill some of the key leadership positions on my team.

I called some of my old buddies from my Power4 experience. Most folks were already committed to other critical IBM server chips. However, I lucked onto one veteran engineer, David Ray, who was willing to talk to me. David and I worked together on several previous IBM microprocessor designs. He owned a small piece of property in the hill country outside of Austin, so I teasingly called him "Farmer Dave." Everyone knew he would rather be building a barn than building computer chips. He was a quiet, crusty engineer who never seemed particularly happy and who especially hated managers; however, he was sharp and always delivered high-quality designs ahead of schedule. He earned the highest respect from his peers and from the people he led. Thankfully, David was in-between projects right then and was fairly unhappy with the Server Group management, so I invited him to meet me for lunch in the cafeteria.

As soon as we went through the food line and found a table, I jumped right in. I told him the truth: "Dave, I've got the deal of a lifetime for you. How'd you like to work on a start-from-scratch design for a supercomputer-on-a-chip for a game machine? It's going to be extremely difficult work, we're severely understaffed, so we'll be running lean and mean for a while, and it's all sort of top secret. How's that sound?" I laughed, half expecting him to respond with *Are you crazy?*

Instead, his eyes lit up. He leaned forward, rested his elbows on the formica-topped table, and said, "When do I start?"

He looked serious, but my proposal sounded so ludicrous to my own ears, I wasn't sure if he was just pulling my leg. "Well, you'll be my first technical leader, so the sooner the better," I said.

Turned out Farmer Dave was serious. The challenge hooked him as much as the start-from-scratch opportunity. Before lunch was over, he accepted the position, and we made plans for his transition from the Server Group.

David Ray also pointed me to my second technical lead, Jim Van Norstrand. David and Jim worked together on the Power3 microprocessor. Jim was another twenty-year veteran with a wealth of design and management experience under his belt. I knew I was lucky to have him on the team. He was an expert logic designer who was intimately familiar with the instruction unit, the most complex and critical subcomponent of a microprocessor. An instruction unit is responsible for handling low-level software instructions running on the processor. It fetches the instructions from memory, decodes them, and issues them to functional units, which then execute the operations specified by the instructions. The instruction unit is like the head cook in the kitchen who fetches and reads the recipe, while the kitchen staff (the functional units) executes the instructions handed down by the cook. An inefficient instruction unit could break the back of an otherwise reasonably designed processor and limit the ultimate speed it could achieve. Van Norstrand became my second in command, assuming a significant share of the technical responsibility for the entire microprocessor core.

Jim Kahle recruited Tony Truong (pronounced *Trong*) back into the IBM fold before I got there, so I inherited Tony as my third technical lead. We had worked together on a previous project in the Server Group, but he left IBM in the late '90s about the same time I did. I was glad to see he had also returned, and I knew I was lucky to have him lead the design of the PowerPC's memory subsystem. Tony's strengths lay in his work ethic and his deep knowledge of memory subsystems. He could hone in on a troublesome area of the design that was difficult to verify, and come up with a way to test it. It might take him several grueling twenty-hour days in a row, but he would finish it, and we would end up with a stronger design because of his work. One of the things I loved about working at IBM was the cultural mixture. Tony was from Vietnam, and I could always count on him to find the best Vietnamese food in Austin.

With these strong team leaders in place to help me, I turned my focus to the organizational configuration. I created a two-in-the-box structure to lead the team. With this two-leader configuration, an IBM second-line manager and I ran the large PowerPC team together. I focused on the day-to-day technical work as well as some of the project management aspects of the project. The second-line manager focused on personnel and administrative issues as well as the remaining project management issues. It was a divide-and-conquer approach.

Previous project leaders at IBM had organized their teams around interdependent functional disciplines—for example, logic design, verification, or circuit design. Experience already taught me that this type of organization created too much of a "throw it over the wall" mentality when problems created by one team were passed on to another to solve. I wanted self-contained entities responsible for all aspects of the design from start to finish. I carved up the microprocessor core into functional units and created teams around those units. Each team was responsible for delivering a final physical piece of silicon (hardware), which was logically and physically verified and complete. Each member of that team worked toward one common goal—functional silicon. It was not acceptable for anyone to say, "Well, I did my piece"—meaning they washed their hands of any problems—because they were all responsible for the end goal. The structure created accountability for everyone on the team. I also created a two-in-the-box leadership configuration for these teams. In most cases, one leader focused on logic design and verification, while the other focused on circuit design and physical design.

I was well on my way to creating a high-performance team.

While I was elated that all three STI partners vowed to provide their very best architects and designers to meet the challenging project goals, I knew it was a promise they would find difficult to keep. Sony and Toshiba faced the larger problem of convincing their top designers to take a two- to three-year tour of duty in the United States. IBM's problem had more to do with balancing projects and earnings. While they could draw from a vast pool of engineers, they were on the cliff's edge of the post-dot-com technology bust and were drawing up plans to downsize. In addition, most of the top IBM microprocessor designers were committed to critical IBM server chips, the bread and butter of the company. "Not available" was the line Kahle heard over and over when he attempted to recruit his pals from former projects.

This opened up an opportunity for external hiring.

One human resources representative explained that IBM's hiring practices moved in cycles, and she warned us it was best to take rapid action as soon as the external hiring window opened, because it could close at any moment. When Kahle pulled me through that window, no one was sure how many others were going to follow.

Microprocessor design demands a team with highly specialized skills. While Jim Kahle and others focused on luring experienced engineers away from other high-tech companies, I withdrew to my sunny new cubicle to comb through a stack of resumes from engineers who expected to graduate from college in 2001. With the shape of the current economy, I knew I could afford to be picky and select only the best and the brightest from top-notch engineering schools. The lifeblood of the project as well as that of IBM rested on hiring top college grads who would bring fresh energy and insight to the company. I liked them because they were fearless. They didn't know the meaning of the word impossible.

Although IBMers historically conducted very polite, unobtrusive interviews, this did not always lead to finding the most qualified candidates. At Somerset, we brought young engineers before a committee of several interviewers at once and pounded the potential candidates with tough, hard-to-solve engineering problems. It was an effective method, but a bit ruthless. More than one contender left the room on the verge of tears.

For the STI candidates, I adopted a toned down version of that style. I brought each one in for a series of individual forty-five-minute interviews with four or five technical leads and managers. Some of the interviewers conducted the same old traditional polite IBM interview, smiling while they struggled to glean hints of the candidate's technical capabilities.

I confronted my too mild fellow IBMers: "Come on! Challenge these guys! Your butts will be on the line if we hire nonperformers. We have to be looking for the cream of the crop."

When it was my turn, I grilled each applicant with several problem-solving exercises and asked specific engineering questions. While I listened to the responses, I tried to decide if I would enjoy working with the engineer on a daily basis. Better yet, would I enjoy drinking beer with him or her? Always an important criteria.

After we completed each day's interviews, the IBM team met for a lively discussion to sort through the results. Each one of us presented our impressions of the candidates and argued about their strengths and weaknesses.

"Don't the schools today teach these guys anything?" one interviewer complained after interviewing an inexperienced candidate.

"Did you talk to the woman from Princeton? Or that youngster from Cal Tech?" another crowed, obviously in awe of the pedigrees.

"Oh, yeah, I did. How about the one with the Ph.D. from Duke?" responded another like-minded fan of prestigious schools.

I just wanted smart engineers who worked hard and fit in. With a thumbs-up or thumbs-down vote, we made the hiring decisions. When we disagreed, the discussions tended to drag on. Whenever I could, I shut down these arguments. "If you have any doubts about this candidate, let's just pass," I said, sliding the questionable resume into the trash. "Let's move on." There was too much other work to do.

I really didn't care which prestigious high-browed university they attended, though I did handpick a few graduates from prestigious universities such as Duke, Purdue, Carnegie Mellon, and the University of Texas. We even hired a couple from my alma mater, the University of Kentucky. Where someone went to school is not as important as the person's commitment to an education. You get out of it what you put into it. With the draw of the opportunity to work on the next PlayStation 3 chip, I was able to attract engineers from the very top of their classes. These young techies were born in the late 1970s or early 1980s, and they grew up playing video games. To many of the seasoned veterans on the team, these grads were just youngsters, barely older than some of their own kids. But they brought a new dynamic and energy to the team that couldn't be created any other way. They were proud, outspoken, egotistical, very confident in their skills, and convinced that they had something unique to contribute. As lean as we were, several of these wonder kids quickly moved into critical roles, taking on far more responsibility and workload than some of their more senior colleagues. These youngsters may have held some totally unrealistic expectations of their careers—like believing they would move from junior engineer to CEO in a mere handful of years—but they remained resilient, willing to learn, and highly competitive.

In addition to college graduates, another very attractive talent pool was the significant number of experienced engineers, like me, who left IBM at the height of the technology boom of 1998–2000 to find fame and fortune in the startups. Kahle and I conspired to hunt down some key former colleagues and make offers they couldn't refuse. It was something of an uphill battle, because even if we could entice one of our buddies to return to the ship, it was always possible that the IBM executives would reject the request for authorization to hire. Many true-blue executives flatly disagreed with the practice of rehiring former employees, believing them to have been disloyal in their previous abandonment of the company. Fortunately, Akrout was not so adamantly opposed. He couldn't afford to be.

If we were to have any hope of filling out a team in time to meet Sony's goal for a product launch in 2005, we were going to have to do whatever it took to bring in the talent. I leaned back in my chair and propped one sandaled foot on my desk, while I casually phoned a former IBMer, a guy I worked with several years before. We chatted for a while, bemoaning the demise of the startups, remembering the excitement and the dream we shared of the pot of gold just waiting for us to claim it. The potential certainly existed, and a few people we knew landed in startups that went public or were purchased by some bigger corporations.

My friend sighed. "Some people got lucky, but most of us just got worn out. It was hard work, long hours, and, in the end, all you wanted was your paycheck, which was two months late." He was more than happy to come in for an interview.

The startups were drying up, innovative work was suddenly scarce in the industry, and the economy in general had tanked. Everyone was hungry for something exciting—and stable—to work on, and they recognized the game processor as a once-in-a-career opportunity. We had no trouble lining up eager engineers to interview. The promise of a new high-performance microprocessor design team allowed IBM to cherry-pick top talent from some of their competitors. Given the right incentives, good engineers were willing to go wherever the best work existed. Company loyalties didn't have a chance against the spectrum of design work we offered.

Each new addition to the STI team, whether an internally transferred loyal IBMer or a prodigal son/daughter returning to the fold, brought with them priceless contacts with other engineers who might be interested in hearing from IBM. It was always easier to convince potential candidates to join a team of old friends.

Sony and Toshiba did not have as much luck filling out their part of the STI team and, like IBM, they were hampered by the staffing demands of other high-priority projects within their companies. Ongoing work on PlayStation 2 derivatives consumed a significant number of Sony's workforce, while Toshiba was busy with their own products. Out of necessity, Akrout gave the order to continue bringing in IBMers to achieve the critical mass necessary for the STI team to achieve their goals.

This led to an unequal split in the team, with IBM having approximately three-fourths of the resources. Akrout predicted the occurrence of this situation, but kept a low profile in front of his Japanese peers. Since each company contributed one-third of the funding, this resulted in a lucrative deal for IBM (three-fourths of the resources, but only one-third of the salary bill), and a good means for Akrout to continue to hold onto a larger pool of talent for any future IBM needs.

While Sony and Toshiba did not contribute as many engineers as IBM, the ones they did bring into the Design Center were top notch. The problem, as might be expected with this international mix of players, was communication. My first close encounter with the Japanese engineers came at a lunchtime gathering that Tony Truong organized. Tony rounded up eight of us, and we headed off to his favorite Vietnamese noodle shop in North Austin. The place was a hole in the wall, but the food was excellent. I always deferred to Tony to order for me, and that day he chose a large bowl of rice noodles with spicy meatballs for me. I was never sure how to eat this tasty mixture of chicken broth, rice noodles, and meat. Should I use a spoon, a fork, or chopsticks? Or should I just pick up the bowl and slurp? I mostly chose the latter.

As we ate, I tried to make casual conversation with one of my Japanese lunch mates, Takeshi Yamazaki, who Tony introduced as one of Sony's chief engineers on the project. What Tony had not told me was that Yamazaki spoke very little English. I muddled through several attempts at conversation, but Yamazaki returned only blank stares. He said nothing.

At first, I thought he was one rude fellow, but then I finally figured out the problem. I thought to myself, "This is going to be an interesting project if none of my partners can speak English!" I certainly couldn't speak Japanese.

At just about the same time, IBM halted all external hiring, proving true the predictions of that wise human resources representative. Corporate management informed us there was a surplus of design engineers in the company who we must re-deploy before considering any more external applications. I can be as true-Blue as the next IBMer, but I knew right away that this was not going to be any easier for us than hiring off the street. In fact, it would probably be harder. As in any large family, our remote cousins were not enthused about letting us take charge of the family fortune.

First, we looked to Rochester, Minnesota, the hotbed of high-performance microprocessor design in the mid-1990s. Their AS/400 minicomputers had been popular business and accounting computers, but those machines relied on proprietary operating systems and software. They eventually lost market share to the more popular open source Unix computer systems. With this erosion in the customer base, IBM corporate offices pulled a sizeable chunk of funding from Rochester, forcing a downsizing. Despite the reductions, some top engineering talent remained in Rochester.

My first task was to figure out how to integrate a large group of engineers into my Austin-based design team and keep them motivated and happy while working remotely from Rochester. After several brainstorming sessions, I decided we needed to partition the microprocessor core in such a way that we could give the Rochester team a self-contained, "meaty" portion of the design, sort of a mini-project. This would serve two purposes: first, it would minimize the interaction required with the rest of the core team in Austin and, second, it would build pride of ownership at the Rochester site. The alternative was to give them responsibility for bits and pieces of the design work scattered throughout the core, a choice that was far more likely to complicate communications and make the Rochester team feel like hired guns.

I deployed a similar technique with a team from the Research Center in Yorktown, New York. The Yorktown folks were some of the best engineers in the company, who had made major contributions to the Power4 microprocessor design. I was counting on a similar performance from them for this new design. I gave them a self-contained piece of the design so that the Yorktown contingent could work on their own mini-project.

Since external hiring for IBM was no longer an option, we worked out a one-time good deal with Toshiba where they agreed to hire a hotshot ex-IBMer, Jack Bell, who we desperately needed for our verification team. It sounded like a great idea to everyone, and we all got what we wanted. The reality was very messy, though. Bell was looked upon by IBMers as "one of us," so he was privy to lots of secrets that we didn't necessarily want to share with our Japanese partners. We conveniently forgot he was in the room when we discussed IBM-only topics. Thankfully, he didn't report everything he heard to Toshiba, because in truth, at the beginning at least, his loyalty was still to IBM. Meanwhile, Toshiba engineers didn't fully trust Bell and probably viewed him as a spy in their Toshiba-only meetings. What an awkward situation.

As the team grew, the management structure grew, too. Eventually, there were six second-line managers and one project manager working under Jim Kahle and Chekib Akrout in the Design Center. Technology and engineering as a whole were still overwhelmingly male-dominated fields, so it was somewhat surprising when the Design Center ended up filling five of these top leadership positions with women. The STI project was not a proving ground for gender equality, nor was it a traditional engineering team where men ruled the roost. It was simply proof positive that IBM's long-held policy of hiring, developing, and promoting women engineers was effective. It functioned exactly as intended by providing IBM with a strong, capable, and diverse workforce. The STI project's diversity is a tribute to Chekib Akrout, who selected leaders based on capabilities, not gender or race. At STI, the two or three dozen female engineers on the team gained a real vision for their own advancement potential by looking at the good role models these women in leadership positions provided. This coalition of powerful women created a climate of cooperation in the workplace, making it a place where teamwork ruled.

Second-line managers were responsible for the technical goals, schedules, and performance for their respective teams, as well as all the personnel issues. Their teams came in sizes ranging from 30 to 240 people. Linda Van Grinsven was the first woman recruited for one of the coveted second-line management positions. She and her husband, Gene, both engineers, had been with IBM for nearly twenty years, mostly at the Rochester, Minnesota site. They relocated to Austin for a two-year temporary assignment, and Linda led the group responsible for the design of the Synergistic core, which you'll read more about later. This core, slated to be used multiple times on the chip, was the brainchild of Ken Kutaragi and Jim Kahle. The forty-five people on Linda's team were almost all located in Austin, but many of them were Japanese employees of Sony or Toshiba. Consequently, she tackled the language barrier early on and was instrumental in forming many of the practices that helped the Design Center function effectively in a multicultural environment. With a couple of hothead technical leads under her, Linda had her hands full keeping the peace in her team.

My co-author, Mickie Phipps, a relative newcomer to IBM, came in as a first-line manager in 1999 from Eaton Corporation. Prior to that, during her 20 years in active duty and reserve service with the United States Air Force, Mickie's resume spanned such jobs as aircraft mechanic, intelligence officer, and research and development engineer for air-to-air missiles. She joined the STI Design Center in September 2001 as Chekib Akrout's technical assistant. This was a period of uncertainty for her as our country recalled military reservists in great numbers to fight the war on terror. She had been expecting to retire from the Air Force that year, but the attack on the Twin Towers in New York City changed everything. Twice, Mickie received orders to report for active duty with the Air Force, and both times those orders were cancelled at the last minute. Her position with Akrout was meant to be a gap-filler while she waited for her date to report. Months later, the Air Force released Mickie from service and in the summer of 2002, Akrout promoted her to second-line manager for the PowerPC team. I knew her well from her work with Akrout and was very pleased that we were now partners. Our team, located at seven different IBM sites in time zones that stretched from Germany to California, eventually grew to 240 people. Technical complexity, size of the team, geography, and language and cultural differences presented rocky challenges that we worked through together

Kathy Papermaster led the Convergence team for a short time in late 2001 and early 2002. Her team was responsible for functions that were more global in nature or were more focused at the chip level, like design tools which had to be common throughout the team, chip verification, and chip integration. Kathy definitely had her heart set on becoming an IBM executive and soon left the Design Center to take a position as an executive assistant to a vice president, Michel Mayer. To replace her, Chekib Akrout brought out the big guns and lured former IBMer Dac Pham away from a very high-level position at Intel. Dac was high-energy, enthusiastic, and optimistic.

After more than fifteen years of service with IBM, Pam Spann had resigned (along with many others) following the infamous retirement plan debacle in 1999. In one fell swoop, IBM had adjusted their benefit plan to fit a younger, more mobile workforce, drastically altering the retirement plans for a significant number of long-term, dedicated employees. IBM's new plan no longer offered benefits that provided retired workers with a monthly check, and instead offered a cash-balance plan that would pay employees a lump sum when they left the company. One result of this change was that many of those long-term employees no longer felt obliged to hang in there for that payout during their golden years; they could take their money (what little was offered) and run. And many did. It was, after all, a boom time in the high-tech industry. However, Pam's gamble on one of the dot-com startup companies wasn't altogether a pleasant experience, and she quickly accepted when STI called her home to IBM. In late 2001, Chekib Akrout rehired Pam to manage the Design Center's business operations, including all the finances, staffing, and personnel issues. Even during the darkest of days in the Design Center, Pam would always say she was glad she had come back. She tried to encourage the team and to help them work through any problems they encountered. She knew from experience that the grass is not always greener on the other side.

Almost from day one, Keryn Mills was the project manager, responsible for the entire schedule for the design, test, and manufacture of the chips. Keryn had been with IBM for more than thirty-five years and was a formidable force, running "her" projects with an iron fist. She was like a dog on a bone. Nothing could shake her loose from something she believed in, even if it was at the expense of the morale of the team. She worked an unbelievable number of hours, often going home only for a few short hours of sleep. She was famous for her successful projects, and many executives and managers respected and trusted her, and listened to her opinions. The trick was to know when to turn her loose and when to rein her in. Most of the technical team dreaded being in her spotlight, and managers tried to shield them from her wrath. It wasn't always easy to stay on her good side.

Over time, the team of engineers I shared with Mickie, who worked on the PowerPC core, continued to grow, expanding into a huge team justified only by the fact that we were starting our design from scratch instead of doing a derivative design based on an existing IBM microprocessor. At our home base in Austin, there were approximately twenty partners from Sony, eighty from Toshiba, and more than a hundred from IBM. The remaining IBMers were scattered across seven sites worldwide, including Raleigh, North Carolina; Rochester, Minnesota; Yorktown, New York; Endicott, New York; Boebligen, Germany; San Jose, California; and Burlington, Vermont.

CHAPTER 3

Know Your Competition

It is competition that drives us to higher levels of
excellence and, therefore, to more opportunity.
An accurate assessment of our competition's
capabilities is what enables us to refine the
boundaries of our bold vision. We must
make sure we shoot high enough.

JIM KAHLE, CHEKIB AKROUT, AND I relaxed on Kahle's
deck. A spectacular peach and purple sunset clung to the sky over the
Texas Hill Country beyond Lake Austin. Just for a moment, the conversation lulled, got whisper quiet. Hummingbirds darted in and out
of colorful flower beds, ruby throats glistening in the last of the sunlight. Bees buzzed in the trumpet vine. Heavy summer air and the
sweet smell of gardenias wafted over us. I tipped back in my chair,
propped my feet on the deck's sun-weathered railing, and watched as
a lone water-skier carved out one rooster tail after another on the
placid lake below. Contentment flowed over me like warm honey . . .
or maybe it was the Scotch. Very old, very good, single malt. Kahle's
favorite.

It was late summer in 2001 and after six months of startup work, things were going so well at the Design Center—the team was finally approaching critical mass, and a concept of the chip was coming together—that we decided to have our own little private celebration. "To success," I toasted. We clinked glasses and smiled like silly old fools.

Darkness crept across the sky, pushing the last of the golden glow below the horizon. Kahle lit tiki torches and citronella candles to keep the mosquitoes at bay. Akrout was in particularly high spirits, and the more he drank, the more he unconsciously slipped French or Arabic words into the conversation—something Kahle and I affectionately called Chekib-speak. Every once in a while, something got lost in translation, and Akrout backed up to explain. After about the fifth time, I laughed so hard I nearly fell out of my chair. I guess we were pretty loud, because Mary, Kahle's wife, came out to tell us to quiet down. The kids were in bed.

The silence might have lasted a full two seconds after she went back inside, then Akrout picked up right where he'd left off. He and Kahle took off on a tangent, fiercely debating some minute technical feature of the chip. No detail was too insignificant, for Akrout was such a geek at heart. Even as a successful vice president of one of the most powerful corporations in America, he could still hold his own against our top circuit designers. He loved technology; he was on fire about it.

Akrout could argue with Kahle all night long, but I didn't want to squander this opportunity. We weren't alone all that often. There was just one thing I wanted to hear from him. "What's keeping you awake at night?" I asked, interrupting the friendly banter. "What's the bottom line? The worst fear?"

Akrout replied without hesitation: "We don't have any idea what Intel has up their sleeves, what they might bring out of the shadows in response to STI's challenge. The home computing environment, not just games, is the ultimate target for all three STI partners, but Intel still dominates the PC market with over eighty-five percent of the market share. Intel also provided the chip for Microsoft's Xbox, the most significant threat to the PlayStation line. We need to know what to expect next in their products."

Intel was and still is, the number one semiconductor chip manufacturing company in the world. They had a yearly revenue of $40 billion, giving them both the dollars and the engineering talent to go head-to-head with any company in the industry.

We sipped our Scotch—had a nice buzz going—and discussed Intel's potential for a while. Akrout was right. We didn't really know our enemy anymore. The excitement in the Design Center was almost palpable, and my team was revving up for a serious race, but did they know where the finish line was? What could we offer that would beat Intel? That was really the question of the day. We had to know where our competition was heading.

I drove into the parking garage right behind Akrout the next morning. I wasn't normally an early bird, but he was. I glanced at my watch just to double check. Yes, his routine changed, not mine. He usually arrived early enough to park his BMW sedan in the same convenient first-floor spot in a nearly empty garage, but today I followed him to the fourth level before we came upon some empty slots. Maybe he felt as rough as I did after our night with Kahle and got a late start. It made me feel better to think that he was no more Superman than I was.

Then I watched him climb out of his car. He was practically wrinkle-free, all crisp and neat and bright eyed. On second thought, I decided, he had probably already attended two business meetings by phone, sent twenty e-mails from home, and made a dozen phone calls while he drove into work. He grinned at me, and we walked together from the garage to the office building, though I had to pour on a little speed to keep up with his jaunty pace. He chattered cheerfully about the beautiful weather, and I grunted occasional responses. Obviously, the Scotch affected us differently. Maybe he was Superman after all.

Akrout always came in with that sunny smile on his face, patting the backs of the engineers he met along the way to his office, stopping to chat with someone by the coffee machine. Junior engineers were utterly stunned when Akrout called them by name and asked questions about their specific design work. His interest was genuine, and every engineer sensed the sincerity in his words.

Most days I saw little of Akrout. He spent his time framing the big picture, getting support from his peer executives, clearing away the barriers that threatened the Design Center. He assessed and re-assessed the strengths and weaknesses of the STI partnerships. He dissected and studied the assumptions behind the business case that told us this venture made good financial sense. He queried experts on the future market potential for this breakthrough product. He placated customers. On top of that, he directed all chip development for Apple's desktops and laptops, and Nintendo's GameCube. A very busy man indeed.

We parted at the elevators on the third floor, but as Akrout stepped away, he grinned and said over his shoulder, "What is Intel thinking, and what are you going to do about it?" I nodded and kept walking toward my cubicle. It was too big a question to answer that early in the morning.

Akrout enjoyed a very close partnership with Apple, so he was keenly aware of how difficult it was to unseat Intel, the reigning king in the PC business. He stood at Apple's side for years, loyally working with them to create the perfect product roadmap that would propel them ahead of the competition. It was hard, demanding work, and they had not won yet. Though Apple (with IBM chips) had at times outdistanced Intel in terms of processor performance, they were still behind in terms of raw chip speed. Akrout hoped he might finally have the right ingredients to put both Apple and the STI partners ahead of his old enemy. He was the eternal optimist, and I prayed we wouldn't disappoint him.

To get an answer for his concerns about Intel, Akrout enlisted Dr. Peter Hofstee, one of IBM's top research engineers, to explore the competition for our next-generation microprocessor and help define project goals to ensure a win. Hofstee's claim to fame came from his involvement in inventing the first chip in the industry to break the one-gigahertz processor speed barrier, the ultimate Mt. Everest challenge to a chip designer pushing the leading edge of technology in the late 1990s. Hofstee, a brilliant researcher, obtained his Ph.D. in computer science from the California Institute of Technology, a school that produces some of the best computer engineers in the country. Originally from the Netherlands, he decided to stay in the United States after he finished his studies and even accepted a faculty position teaching computer science and chip design at CalTech from 1995 to 1996.

After sending Hofstee off to get the scoop on Intel, Akrout instructed Jim Kahle and me to define what we thought would be the most aggressive design parameters we could possibly achieve, and then to stretch beyond that. He wanted the STI product to beat all existing records, and then when Hofstee returned with his projections for Intel, we would see that our stretch design would trounce the enemy.

Kahle and I had confronted Intel during our days at the Somerset Design Center. Back then, a new computer architecture referred to as a RISC architecture was the kicker for our product, the thing that made our chip stand out among the competition. Instructions are the fundamental directions, the recipe, that tell the hardware what to do. We all believed a highly efficient RISC machine could be Apple's wedge into Intel's domination of the PC market. It was supposed to provide higher performance and higher frequency at a lower cost. Up until that time, Intel retained the top spot with their tried and true X86 Complex Instruction Set Computer (CISC) chips, the brains for virtually all PCs. The RISC approach relied on the fact that most software applications actually use only a small subset of basic instructions. Our work at Somerset focused on optimizing this reduced set of instructions to run faster than the older CISC architecture. The problem was that PC owners needed to port all their old legacy software programs from their old systems to their new ones, giving Intel a definite advantage with every upgrade.

In my first job assignment at IBM, I got a nice exposure to both the older CISC approach and the newer RISC approach while I cut my teeth on computer architecture and logic design. IBM hired me in June of 1985 in Endicott, New York, the birthplace of the company and much of the corporate tradition. In the 1960s and 1970s, IBM staked its claim to fame on the s/360 and s/370 mainframe computers designed and built in New York. However, in the 1980s, DEC and their popular VAX minicomputers started eating away at the low end of the mainframe market. Endicott's Glendale Lab was responsible for delivering a crushing response to this threat with a product called the 9370.

The main central processing unit (CPU) in the 9370 was a complex CISC processor, because they needed something that was code compatible with the mainframe s/370. I landed the job of designing the specialized input/output processor (IOP) that handled all of the traffic in and out of the computer. This IOP was just a very simple RISC design, but I was thrilled to be working on an actual microprocessor core.

When I signed on with IBM, my buddies laughed at me and said, "Why do you want to go there? They won't give a rookie like you any good design work."

With confidence, I replied, "They will if I'm a good designer."

How wrong my buddies were. IBM happened to be in an expansion stage just then and was willing to risk putting new hires into key roles. This product never saw the light of day, but it gave me valuable lessons in computer design.

I also learned to make homebrew and to snow ski while in Endicott. I sometimes think those skills have served me almost as well as my computer design experience. My cube mate in Endicott was Brice Feal. Brice was a zany bachelor with a wide variety of interests. He invited me over to his house after work and took me to his cellar, where several hundred bottles of beer filled the shelves. He blew the dust off one of them, cracked it open, and filled two frosty mugs.

"Give it a try," he said with a smile, and we clinked our mugs together in a silent toast.

It was the smoothest, best beer I'd ever tasted. "Wow, Brice!" I exclaimed. "Where can I buy this stuff?"

He replied, "You can't get this in stores. I make it."

His particular brand of beer was really a barley wine with a smooth flavor and high alcohol content. I was hooked, so Brice taught me all of the tricks and soon I was brewing my own beer.

Brice also introduced me to another passion—snow skiing. There was a local ski resort called Greek Peak. Many Friday afternoons we skipped out of work early and hit the slopes. The ski resort lit the runs with spotlights, so we skied until very late at night.

RISC computer design, homebrewing, and skiing. Life wasn't too bad in Endicott for a young engineer. However, I heard about a new development project at the IBM site in Austin, Texas, and the central processor was RISC rather than CISC. From everything I knew, this seemed like the way to go. Exposed to both methods, I could see that the RISC approach would deliver simpler, higher performance hardware. If I stayed in Endicott, the sexier computer design assignments would be on a messy CISC design. I wanted an opportunity to create streamlined fast microprocessors using the RISC techniques.

So in 1989, I went to the office of my third-line manager, Bobby Dunbar, and told him I was going to Austin to work on a RISC micro-processor. Bobby was just a good ol' boy, content to ride the success of the s/370 computers he'd come to know and love. He propped his boots on the desk and laughed at me. "Nothing will ever come of that RISC architecture," he said.

His predictions did not prove true. Today, the highest volume chips produced at IBM and at Freescale (Motorola's spin-off) carry the PowerPC RISC architecture. PowerPC is the architecture of choice at IBM for everything from game chips to supercomputer server chips. The PowerPC and Intel's X86 are the two primary architectures that stood the test of time. I knew a good thing when I saw it.

Intel stayed with their proven architecture, but they adopted virtu-ally all the RISC techniques developed by our Somerset team. They employed a brute force approach to microprocessor design. They ap-plied a team of thousands of engineers to streamline the instructions, and then to optimize and tweak those X86 microprocessors until they could offer as good or better performance at higher frequencies than we could with our designs.

Intel capitalized on parallel processing techniques invented by IBM and other companies, such as superscalar and out-of-order pro-cessing. A superscalar design gains efficiencies by having multiple par-allel execution units that operate in parallel on groups of instructions. It was like the difference between having multiple checkout lines at the grocery store versus a single checkout line. An out-of-order design gains efficiencies by scheduling instructions when they are ready to ex-ecute. This meant when even one long instruction stalled, other shorter instructions could be routed around it. Idle time is wasted time.

Intel remained the only game in town when it came to the PC, in spite of our best efforts at Somerset. Of course, it didn't help that IBM experienced various software failures around the same time.

This early defeat at the hands of Intel was in the back of my mind as I walked beside the snazzy glass wall that separated cube-city from the STI war room, the place where Kahle held his daily architecture meetings. Another engineer beat me into the room and snagged the last available Ethernet port for his laptop. There were never enough outlets for everyone at the table, and the security team had recently disabled the wireless capabilities in the building as a defensive security measure. I sat near the back of the room and opened my laptop, intending to work offline while we waited for the meeting to start. But a swirl of thoughts about Intel grabbed my attention. I knew Intel wasn't sitting on its hands; their people were working, just as we were, to push the limits of technology. They had thousands of engineers working on their next chip, while we had a few dozen. I knew several former IBMers, smart guys, who moved to Intel, and I knew they were inventing cool new stuff for our enemy. How could we compete?

Kahle waited for a quorum to gather, then stood and explained Hofstee's mission and our job. He said, "You have to be paranoid when it comes to beating Intel. Basically, we need to attack with multiple weapons, because just having a higher frequency will not be enough to make Intel's customers switch. This calls for an extraordinary new design offering an order-of-magnitude improvement in performance."

It wasn't quite a battle cry, but it generated the right discussions. We batted around various strategies, scribbled ideas on the board, and argued about competing technologies, all the while lacing our language with words like frequency, throughput, process, and performance. Also, there was a new term in the industry to describe the raw frequency of a processor. It was called "fanout-of-four" (FO4), which described the number of gate delays in each pipeline stage or, more specifically, the number of simple inverter gates connected in series, each having a fanout or load of four gates connected to them. A smaller FO4 gate delay translates to a faster frequency. This new term provided us with a way to describe and compare processor speeds across multiple manufacturing technologies. Therefore, when a processor design migrated from, say, a 90 nanometer manufacturing process to the newer generation 65 nanometer technology, the FO4 gate delay would stay the same while the frequency (gigahertz) could increase. The Power4 processor I worked on had a 24 FO4 gate delay, which translated into a 1.1 gigahertz clock speed. That was the fastest in IBM. Intel had the current speed record in 2001 with an 18 FO4 gate delay, which translated into 1.5 gigahertz.

The pressure was on.

The need for low power really tied our hands. For the compact cost-conscious PlayStation 3, achieving the frequency of a PC with the reduced power budget of the game console would be a huge challenge. Game consoles are smaller than PCs and have less capacity to keep the chips cool, and games are very compute-intensive functions that tend to max out the processor usage. Higher power on the PlayStation 3 would lead to more costly thermal control techniques like fans and heat sinks, and the costs for those components were very hard to reduce over time. Kahle explained that Kutaragi's aggressive cost-cutting strategy proved to be a huge money maker for Sony on previous products, so of course that would be the plan for this product too.

The Sony architect, Takeski Yamazaki, said in broken English, "Seventy-five watts is the highest power the console can physically tolerate." Heads nodded in agreement, all Sony engineers.

I was skeptical. Most of the server chips and PCs I had worked on in the past were well over this 75 watt budget. We set our sights on designing the fastest microprocessor in the world, but could we still do it knowing that we faced this ridiculously low power budget? We didn't know yet what raw frequency (measured in gigahertz) would describe the top speed of our microprocessor, but now we knew that, at least for the game console application, it would be constrained by this maximum operating power. What would happen if we failed to meet the power goal? Major malfunction resulting in either a hang or an automatic shutdown. Or picture little Johnny game-player running to Mom when his game console burned a hole in his desk. Or worse, console meltdown. The images weren't pretty. The faster a chip runs, the more heat it generates, so to avoid a meltdown, we have to either remove all that heat, or run it at a slower speed. Two terms that don't normally go hand in hand are high speed and low power. Seventy-five watts was going to be really tough.

Still, I wanted to believe Kahle when he encouraged the team as we adjourned: "Guys, I don't know how we're going to get there, but we're going to do it."

Dr. Hofstee was finally ready to present his competitive analysis to Akrout and the team. I had previewed the data during the course of his research, and I was anxious to hear the most recent stuff. He had studied the trends for chip frequencies, primarily dictated by Intel. Detailed graphs showed his predictions of what current and future technologies could achieve. Part science and part science fiction, his analysis was a combination of what the physics of technology could deliver and what smart engineering could achieve. Intel was always the benchmark. There was no other game in town.

I had done some comparison studies in the past, much like Hofstee's task, so I was well aware of what a struggle it was to compare the different microprocessor designs (apples and oranges) on the market. Each one, shrouded in secrecy, manufactured in a different fabrication facility, used a different process. Details were scarce. As much as the efficiency of the design, the silicon manufacturing technology also determined the achievable frequency for the chip. It defined the minimum size of the transistor, the fundamental switching device in a design. Transistors became smaller and smaller as technologies evolved, and smaller meant faster.

We gathered in Akrout's executive conference room with its subdued sage green against natural maple, smoky shaded windows, automatically dimming recessed lighting, and luxuriously upholstered chairs that swiveled, tilted, adjusted, and rocked into no less than twenty-four different positions. Hofstee prepared to present his work. Jim Kahle and I walked in together, both dressed in sandals and shorts in celebration of the last days of summer. I lounged in the back of the room as usual and tilted my chair against the wall. Kahle moved to the front of the room and sat across the table from Akrout, who was already warming up the crowd. He was in prime form, chatting with each attendee as he or she entered the room, laughing with Kahle, greeting those who were attending by phone. About twelve other technical leads and a few managers sat at the table or on either side of the room against the walls. Jim Warnock, a newly appointed Distinguished Engineer who had recently joined Akrout's staff, flew down from IBM's Research Division in Yorktown just for this meeting. All the attendees were IBMers and all were male except for Mickie Phipps, Kathy Papermaster, and Linda Van Grinsven, three of the managers who were now responsible for the multicorporation design teams.

Akrout stood and put a hand on Hofstee's shoulder. "I asked Peter to research our competition, and he is ready to present his findings. This is my first time to see his data, too. What do we have to do to beat Intel? Where do we set the bar? Listen closely, for you are the ones," he paused to point around the room at us, "who will determine whether we succeed or fail at this endeavor." Through a wiring hub in the center of the conference table, Hofstee connected his laptop to the top-of-the-line projector suspended from the ceiling above the table. He looked more like a college student than the veteran engineer he was. Tall and lanky, perfectly straight sandy-red hair cut fashionably long, an open expressive face. He rubbed long-fingered hands together and clicked the button to pull up his introductory slide. Years of experience standing before engineering students gave him confidence and style. He carefully worked his way through a series of charts and graphs, clearly and methodically building the case to support his conclusions.

Akrout sat forward in his chair, intensely focused on the data Hofstee presented. Occasionally, he pointed to the screen and asked in his shortened version of English, "Why that?"

Questions were raised, interruptions were tolerated. Hofstee captured our complete attention. It was a topic of extreme importance to each one of us, as the conclusion of this meeting could very well dictate our workload for the next two to three years.

"When the STI project started in 2001," Hofstee said, "the best of breed in the industry was the Intel Pentium4 microprocessor. It topped out at about 1.5 gigahertz in a high-end PC. That design has eighteen FO4 gate delays in the basic pipeline. However, an inner integer core in the Pentium4 executes at nine FO4, or twice that speed!" He illustrated this point with a detailed diagram showing how Intel's design frequencies improved year to year. "Based on this data," Hofstee concluded, "Intel could very well produce a microprocessor in the 2005 timeframe that could achieve nine to ten FO4 and over four gigahertz, so to be competitive in this timeframe, we need to match that frequency in our seventy-five-watt power budget. We need a ten FO4, four gigahertz frequency!"

The room exploded. It seemed impossible!

I took Hofstee to task over a few of his basic assumptions, and he gave reasonable and believable explanations. Others argued back and forth about his predictions for Intel's ability to make such rapid improvements in the frequency of their chips.

There was much skepticism and vocal opposition from Warnock. "I am very certain four gigahertz will push the chip power well beyond the seventy-five-watt power target, but even so, I doubt we can ever come close to achieving the frequency goal anyway. You'll only demoralize the team if you present them with this unachievable goal."

Other naysayers joined in, voicing opinions that bespoke worry about the team, or about the accuracy of Hofstee's predictions, or the lunacy of reaching for the stars. The din in the conference room grew louder and louder.

Hofstee spoke clearly and loudly over the roar of discussion: "Guys, guys!" He held out his hands, patting them up and down like a priest bestowing blessings on his congregation. The roar dropped down a notch. "Intel already knows how to do this! They currently have a three-gigahertz fixed-point unit in their Pentium4. If they can do it, we can."

Kahle immediately agreed with Hofstee. "I've fought the 'dark side' before and lost," he said, referring to Intel, "and the last thing I want to do is to come up short again." He pounded his fist on the table to let us know his decision was final.

Kahle let us debate the point for a while, but we all knew it was pointless to argue. We settled on 10 FO4, four gigahertz at 75 watts as the mind-boggling goal for the STI chip. This meant a quantum leap in frequency with only a fraction of the power compared to the best-of-breed, Intel-based PCs. These were such far-reaching targets—like projecting into outer space—that we could only trust they would be enough to push us ahead of Intel. I sincerely hoped the chance to grapple with Goliath would motivate my team to overachieve and slay the giant.

It was 2001, and no one even knew if a four-gigahertz clock speed was physically possible. To start with, it required ultraefficient circuits with no excess fluff or nice-to-haves. We had to invent a new animal that ran like a cheetah, roared like a lion, and ate like a kitten.

We ended the meeting with concerns weighing heavily on our minds, but before we left, we all stood together and vowed to do whatever it took to achieve the goals. Akrout looked each one of us in the eye, shook our hands, and encouraged us: "Before Roger Bannister broke the four-minute mile barrier, nobody thought it was possible. We can do this." His bold vision for the team and his confidence in us won us over.

The bar was set, a multicore four-gigahertz microprocessor chip with a power budget under 75 watts! In comparison, the fastest Intel chip at the time was a single core Pentium4 microprocessor running at 1.5 gigahertz. The best IBM microprocessor in production was the Power4 microprocessor running at 1.1 gigahertz. It was an aggressive goal that would push us to innovate on all fronts and would require an extraordinary effort from each engineer. We would have to quadruple the speed in a single generation of microprocessor design and also meet a much lower power budget.

Our efforts to top the 1 gigahertz mark on the Power4 microprocessor had been a real struggle. We had spent nearly a year in high-level design defining the high-frequency microarchitecture. During the implementation phase, we tweaked timing paths until we were blue in the face. For that design, we didn't even consider a power budget. These new goals made my head hurt just thinking about them.

Now that we understood the competition, we were able to share Kutaragi's bold vision for the future of this little game machine.

CHAPTER 4

Do Your Homework

The only way to be prepared for the unique
challenges of the next-generation product is to
do the homework—study the past, analyze the
market, research the entire scope of the problem,
and learn from the mistakes of your predecessors.

THE ELECTRONIC GAMES INDUSTRY burst onto the
scene when I was a sports-fanatic teenager, when anything that didn't
involve physical activity, a ball, and a competitive challenge held no
interest for me. Shortly after that came college, then career building,
marriage, and parenthood, in rapid succession. Who had time for
video games?

Then in 2001, as a very experienced senior engineer, I plunged
headfirst into the PlayStation design and suddenly discovered I was lacking some vital skills. Shockingly, I couldn't converse in game-ese with
my still-wet-behind-the-ears coworkers, who grew up with a joystick in
their hands. It was a foreign language to me. I couldn't relate to their
animated conversations about the games that consumed their teenage
years. I felt like a dinosaur! This had to be rectified in a big hurry.

Though I didn't have a clue how the games industry got started, or who the heroes were, or which game piled up the most record-breaking sales because of its bad-ass villain, the thing I wasn't lacking was determination. I vowed to become the resident expert on those things. Just because I didn't live through the games phenomenon didn't mean I couldn't understand the drivers and the hype. I forced myself to do the research so that I wouldn't sound like an idiot in my new environment. In a nutshell, here's what I learned.

The first coin-operated pinball machines appeared in the 1930s, but it wasn't until the 1970s that these machines incorporated solid-state electronics for operation and scoring. With flashing lights and clanging bells, they drew youngesters with their pocketfuls of change to amusement park midways. Coin-operated computer games quickly followed and corner video game arcades sprang up in shopping malls, restaurants, bars, movie theaters, and gas stations all around the world. Games such as PONG, Space Invaders, Pac-Man, and Donkey Kong were very popular. Space Invaders's greatest legacy is that it introduced the world to the concept of "high score." The highest score stayed posted on the machine's scoreboard, motivating players to keep putting their quarters into the slot, playing again and again in hopes of beating the previous record. Atari's Asteroids game carried this one step further by allowing players to input their initials to identify who achieved the highest score. As the frenzy for this competitive game swept across the nation, arcade owners found themselves in the happy position of having to exchange the game machine's coin box for one that could hold more quarters.

The first game console ever made for home use, Magnavox's Odyssey, appeared on store shelves in 1972, but I mark Christmas 1975 as the real beginning of the world's love affair with home video games. That's the year when Atari's PONG game console was Sears's biggest selling item, with people camping outside the stores for hours, sometimes even days, to get one. In a very risky move that paid off hugely, Atari cofounder Nolan Bushnell tapped venture capitalists for over $10 million to help him put together the facilities to build 150,000 PONG machines to meet Sears's orders. As a result, PONG created the market for video gaming in the home, setting the stage for companies to produce complex systems with advanced graphics, fuller sound, and the possibility of an endless number of games.

As a kid, I had a real ping-pong table in the basement where I often spent an entire afternoon playing games with my father or with a friend. When there wasn't a playing partner, I turned on the Atari game machine and played PONG, mindlessly watching that little white light bounce back and forth across the screen. During my teenage years, the game machines in video arcades had a bigger impact on me. I liked pinball best, but on occasion I still played PONG.

The emergence of any hot new technology has the potential to spark other fires, and of course the game technologies were no exception. Here's an interesting piece of trivia I learned along the way that reinforced this theory: In 1972, after dropping out of Reed College in Oregon, Steve Jobs worked as a technician at Atari. After hours, he frequently let his good friend Steve Wozniak slip into the factory to play the arcade machines. Boss Nolan Bushnell offered Jobs a bonus to design a reduced-chip circuit board for another arcade variation on PONG where players would use the electronic paddle to propel the ball at a wall of bricks across the top of the screen. Jobs, who wasn't highly skilled in circuit board design, coerced Wozniak to do the design work for a split of the bonus. The game used only a black and white display, but Wozniak found that he could simulate color by using colored Mylar overlays on the screen. This inspired him to find an easier way to use color in the games, and eventually led to the introduction of color in personal computers using his methodology. In addition, Wozniak gained powerful skills when he found he could manipulate his computer version of the games through software. Soon after this experience with arcade games, Jobs and Wozniak left Atari to build a prototype computer under the auspices of their newly founded Apple computer company. Now I'd say that's a pretty big spark.

It was in 1976 that Fairchild introduced the Channel F, which was then totally eclipsed by Atari's Video Computer System (VCS) the following year. There were other contenders, but the market remained pretty thin for a few years with profits declining rapidly and developers struggling to find the right niche.

Then in 1980, Atari blew the lid off the games industry with the release of Space Invaders, the game that motivated people to rush out and buy the VCS system just to be able to play. There were over a hundred different variations on game scenarios available, including invisible aliens, moving bunkers, and simultaneous two-player action. The family entertainment room became a daily war zone, while neighborhood youngsters lined up to compete with each other and show their prowess at zapping the incoming alien invasion. Atari raked in over $100 million and virtually squashed whatever competition still existed.

The VCS also spawned a healthy sideline cottage industry for third-party developers of hardware, including prototype computer add-ons with keyboards and storage devices for the system. With games to fuel their imaginations, those prehistoric (in electronic terms) neighborhood kids of the 1970s and 1980s evolved into smart teenage techies. They tweaked their Space Invaders games and computer hardware, and exchanged lengthy notes about how to optimize performance and allow for more complexity in the battles. They figured out how to have multiplayer games before the concept was even a glimmer in the eye of a game developer. They unwittingly became the catalyst of change, with their unquenchable desire for more realism, interaction, and mobility.

Completely new industries were born to feed the voraciously hungry gamers. Game developers wrote and coded games, graphic designers created scenarios and characters, hardware designers designed faster processors with more memory, and mechanical engineers fashioned sleek packages to house these game systems. Atari and Sega became household words.

Throughout the 1970s and 1980s the PC industry skyrocketed, too, providing the perfect low-cost platform for game developers. They capitalized on each step up in the PC's speed or bandwidth, each increase in the size of its memory or access time, and every decrease in power consumption. Graphics engines (separate chips that could handle the graphics creation for the games) allowed the PC's microprocessor to focus on the calculations to create characters that move and behave more like real people and environments that are more intense. Sound cards provided more realism as players could hear the grunts and groans of their combatants, the bombs bursting, and the helpful background dialog and story narration. Later, DVD formats allowed developers to include deeper story lines and richer graphics, sound, and video.

The rise in the PC games market dealt a near death blow to the game console industry. By the early 1980s, even with new models still on the shelf, consumers were rapidly losing interest in the aging Atari game machine, and no heir-apparent was in sight. As the market softened, many small games publishers folded, leaving retailers little choice but to slash prices on unsold game cartridges instead of returning them for credit if they didn't sell.

This tipped the first domino, and tumbling, industrywide price cuts soon followed. Unsold merchandise piled up in vast warehouses. By the end of 1984, the implosion was complete. Abandoned retailers, ruined publishers, and disgruntled customers led many to believe that the video game fad was over. The perfect storm that wiped out the video game industry was so severe that it splashed over onto personal computers as well. No one wanted to have anything to do with games—not the financially ruined developers, not the frustrated public, not the weary media, and certainly not the disadvantaged retailers.

During these years of the rise and fall of game consoles, video game arcades also experienced significant change. As home consoles improved in quality and the games took on more depth, arcades found it harder and harder to compete with the big, expensive systems. Kids found better entertainment at home in their living rooms. Then, in much of the nation, the arcades gained reputations as being seedy, unsafe places where children could be exposed to the fringes of an unsavory adult world. Parental fears finally pushed the arcade business into near oblivion, where only nostalgia kept it alive.

It took nearly a decade, but the game console market suddenly bounced back from the dead with the launch of Sony's PlayStation in 1994, then the follow-on PlayStation 2 with its Emotion Engine in 2000, and then Microsoft's Xbox in 2001. Low-cost PCs continued to provide a ready platform for many gamers, but it was this new generation of game consoles, with their powerful application-specific microchips, that provided the most exciting jump in performance.

As I studied this fascinating history, I understood very well how these new machines recaptured the interest of America's youth. I loved my physics classes in college, and now here was a most unexpected place where the laws and rules of the universe came together. In these new games, physics described the smooth trajectory of the missile I fired from my F-15 Eagle, including the effects of fuel burn-off. It was the determining factor in the game of pool I won where the cue ball collided with the 8-ball, sending it into the corner pocket. Physics was the reason my Alfa Romeo hugged a tight curve without skidding. It was what sent my home run baseball flying after I slammed it with my trusty digital bat.

The shimmer and froth I saw on the water as my character paddled down a river, the dynamics of my kayak as it bounced and slammed through the rapids, the physical force required for my character to push the water with the oar—all required millions of complex computations calculated at a very high frequency. The game replicated the physics of reflection, refraction, acceleration, deceleration, friction, fluid dynamics, and more. Sticking to the actual physics made it believable; the speed and precision of the calculations made it real.

My father was a college professor who taught mechanical engineering, and I distinctly remember him passionately lecturing me on the forces of movement. It must have been in my genes, because I found that the physics in games was something I really wanted to understand better. So I immersed myself in the twenty-first century world of gamers; call it what you will—game studies, ludology, or research— I call it fun. I read about games and game technologies, dropped in on a few online gamers' chat rooms, bought a PlayStation 2, and played everything I could get my hands on. I told everyone that I was buying the PlayStation 2 for my kids. It was a good line.

Games come in all kinds of genres, just like books and movies: action, thriller, comedy, horror, science fiction, and the like. My favorite games were first-person shooters like Quake II, or the big-seller fast-action adventure games like Metal Gear Solid that featured bad-boy heroes like Snake or the obsessively technical series of high-speed racing games. My Gran Turismo game promised "precise calculated physics designed according to each car's real-life specifications" and "the drive of my life." My little boys got a real kick out of my new-found interest. In short order, I found that I was no different from half of all Americans who would rather play games than watch movies. That was an astonishing revelation. It was suddenly easy for me to understand why games sales topped over $7 billion (more than double what it was in 1996 according to the Entertainment Software

Association). Games do something that movies can't—they make you sweat. In real life, gamers, mainly guys between 18 and 40, are students, engineers, flight attendants, doctors, construction workers—but in the ever more popular role-playing games, we're all warriors. Ruthless, immortal, and totally in control. The games propel us into extreme danger in foreign countries, distant universes, and alternate realities. The rush is pure adrenaline as we eviscerate another beast or blast a demon back to hell.

The games I played most centered on overtly obvious male-dominated roles. To me, the whole industry seemed to be male oriented. Was that just perception or was it reality, I wondered? More research was required. One surprising piece of information I uncovered was that not only are most game players men, so are the game developers. Less than fifteen percent of all game developers are women. It must be difficult to draw women into this field where seventy percent of their target market is male, and where most of the female characters are brainless, barely-clothed, voluptuous babes, mere accessories to the gun-toting, sword-swinging, fast-driving macho male characters who are busy masterminding bloody shootouts. Many of the games are overtly hypersexualized, where the female characters have bedroom eyes and accentuated curves, and they wander across the screen from one sexually suggestive pose to another.

I did a little more reading and found that, at least in part because of the ongoing controversy over the amount of sex and violence in video games, there is an increase in the number of games being developed with a female audience in mind. The women's market was only in its infancy when I started work on the PlayStation 3 in 2001, but as of 2008, according to game publisher Entertainment Software Association (ESA), 38 percent of all game players are women. That represents real market power. The success of The Sims, a nonviolent role-playing game, is proof. The Sims is a strategic life-simulation computer game created by game designer Will Wright, published by Maxis. It is a simulation of the daily activities of one or more virtual persons ("Sims") in a suburban household near SimCity. As of 2008, Redwood City, California-based Electronic Arts Inc. has sold more than 85 million units of "The Sims." It's the best-selling PC game in the industry, is now available for play on several different consoles, and boasts that about 55 percent of its buyers are women. So maybe things are changing . . . slowly.

The games that attract female players are often those that feature a strong female lead character with believable motivations, superior intelligence, and other skills besides killing. Many still want the tension, excitement, and suspense of the shoot 'em up games, but women also want to be more than just a sexy sidekick following along behind the male lead. They want to be able to fight with equal attack power and use their brains to untangle complex webs of deceit. Women are just as likely as men to shout " 'Oo-rah!" when the interstellar marines, led by the strong female captain, annihilate the hordes of three-headed cannibalistic aliens.

Women tend to look for the emotional draw of a game, which depends on a good storyline, or a complex plot, or a deeper experience with the characters—things male gamers don't necessarily seem to need or want. Games that provide opportunities to connect to other players, that have a social component, or that foster cooperation among the characters or players—all reasons why women are so fond of massive multiplayer (MMP) games—are particularly appealing. Women are the MMP networkers, the glue that holds the social groups together, and the ones who run the fan sites. They're the last ones to desert the base.

As I continued my research, I began to understand the complexities behind game development. A developer had to not only understand all these nuances in order to get the twists and turns in the storyline tuned for the right market, but also had to have a firm grasp on the deepest nooks and crannies in the hardware—in the chips themselves.

The game developer industry intrigued me, and I often thought if I got bored with chip design I would branch out into that area. The cool artistry of today's games might satisfy my desire to develop the right side of my brain. A small handful of expert game developers have earned the title of "top guns," and they interested me most. They strive to squeeze every last ounce of performance out of the hardware by writing low-level, lean-and-mean cryptic machine code to run on the bare metal. It's the only way to achieve the best efficiency, the flat-out top speed. Though high-level design languages look more like

English and could simplify the job of writing code, the top developers refuse to accept the inherent overhead penalties that come with the use of such software development tools. I met two top-gun game developers early in the project, and we hit it off immediately. Their long hair and beards reminded me of the computer hackers from my college days. Armed with a formidable bank of knowledge about games and a wrist sore from jockeying the joystick around, I wasn't too far out of my league when I talked to them. I was amazed at their ability to talk "bits and bytes" with me about the hardware. They gave me several things to think about in terms of providing high-performance hardware for their precious games.

I knew microprocessors inside out, backwards and forwards, but I didn't know much about graphics chips, the other important piece of game console hardware. I sought out my old friend Charlie Johns to help me understand the entire hardware and software model. Charlie and I played soccer together and shared a fondness for brewing our own beer. With his extensive background in graphics chip development, he once served as the chief chip architect in the now defunct IBM Graphics Division. For twenty years, this specialized group developed high-performance graphics processors for top-end workstations; but even though their products were superior, they could never compete on cost with the smaller, more nimble niche-focused companies like NVidia. Sadly, IBM disbanded the division in 2001, and several of these highly skilled engineers landed in the STI Design Center. As one of the first STI employees, Charlie took on a key role in developing the architecture of the new PlayStation 3 chip, and when I returned to IBM, I was thrilled to learn that I would be working with him. It was an added bonus that he could also explain the strange new world of graphics hardware.

Charlie was patient as he translated strange words like rasterization, pixels, and polygons into a language I could understand. He described how a television or computer screen is made of thousands of tiny pixels that form the images on the screen. A unique string of 1s and 0s represents the color and characteristics of each pixel. The job of the graphics hardware is to calculate the fundamental primitives of the lines, characters, color, and shades to form each scene, store these scenes in sequence in a graphics memory called a frame buffer, and then display them on the screen. Charlie gave me a book by James Foley called *Computer Graphics Principles and Practice*, the bible for graphics hardware and software design. I lost all sense of time as I spent hours buried in this engrossing book. To me, it was more gripping than an exciting adventure novel.

Charlie also gave me a valuable education on the history of some of the recent important graphics chips. The demise of IBM's graphics group left only two major competitors on the field—ATI and NVidia. ATI got its start in the mid-1980s by developing graphics chips for the Commodore computer. NVidia burst onto the scene in the early 1990s with slick new graphics adapters for PCs. A few years later, Microsoft paired an NVidia graphics chip with an Intel microprocessor in the original Xbox console. Sony chose to tightly couple their graphics chip with the main processing chip, the Emotion Engine. Their simplified graphics chip was much easier to design and debug. At the start of the PlayStation 3 project, going this route again seemed like a reasonable plan of attack. Part of Charlie's job was to keep Sony honest about their ability to design a graphics chip that would be compatible with the Cell chip.

Charlie introduced me to Barry Minor, another transfer from IBM's Graphics Division. Barry was a graphics software guru, an understated genius. I always envied the guys who wrote the software that would power the PlayStation 3. Their job was to give the game developers the necessary foundation and tools to create cool action characters and high-definition, movie theater–like visual scenes more realistic than any ever produced on a game console before. The software team got closer to the games than the hardware guys did, and it was even more necessary for them to really understand what the game developers needed. No doubt, that was why they were all experts at games like Quake and Metal Gear Solid. It was job related research. They also needed an in-depth understanding of the hardware my team designed. These were very smart guys.

I contemplated asking a bunch of high-browed questions that wouldn't expose my ignorance in this area, but in the end I simply asked, "Barry, how does the graphics software work?"

Barry smiled, happy that someone was interested in his work. He was in a minority, being one of the very few software guys working in a hardware development organization. He said, "Let me show you with a simple software demo."

We turned to his computer and, in moments, the dark screen was blank except for a three-dimensional object, created with just a few sparse dots. Gradually, more and more detail appeared. With each stroke on his keyboard, Barry demonstrated how the 3D figure became more and more recognizable as he drew more dots. It soon took on color, texture, and shape until it was fully identifiable. To give a scene a realistic, full-bodied look, the objects needed lighting and shadows. He showed how the type and direction of light—uniform lighting, a spotlight off to the right, a bright sun with blocking clouds, back lighting, etc.—could dramatically change every scene. The mysterious graphics hardware and software puzzle pieces started falling into place for me.

But what kept the hardware and software moving in sync? How do they talk to each other? I met with Sony's chief architect, Takeshi Yamazaki, to learn about the Sony game console programming model. Since our first meeting, Yamazaki and I had found cryptic ways to communicate. With the help of a whiteboard, we conversed with short sentences, drawings, and hand gestures. If we got too frustrated, we brought in another Japanese engineer who possessed a better grasp of English to fill in the blanks of the conversation. Over time, we came to respect each other's engineering abilities. Yamazaki had a wealth of knowledge from his years on the first and second PlayStation consoles and really understood how the game chip hardware interacted with the software. He drew on the board descriptive block diagrams of the operating system's job, the game code's job, and the game chip's job. It was a symbiotic relationship; all three needed each other and each couldn't exist without the others.

I was finally getting the picture. Now I understood the central processing chip, the graphics chip, at least some of the software, and the Sony programming model. There was only one piece of the puzzle left—the operating system. To delve into that subject, I sat down with Mike Day, the software technical lead. Mike came to the STI Design Center from the group that developed AIX, IBM's version of the popular Unix operating system. Mike was a very sharp engineer with an even sharper tongue. He liked to argue, and made his voice heard at every meeting. Like Charlie Johns, he was one of the very first employees at the Design Center, and he too was instrumental in the overall architecture of the PlayStation 3. Mike explained how they planned to use Hypervisor technology to allow multiple operating systems to run on the game machine simultaneously. Under a Hypervisor scheme, a Unix operating system served as the master supervisor, and a game kernel operating system ran underneath it. The kernel is a piece of software, maybe several hundred thousand lines of code, which directs the operation of the game console. The top-level Unix code handled the normal system-level scheduling as well as managing interaction with the disk drive, keyboard, and display console—all the same functions an operating system handled on a traditional PC.

Mike was passionate about the Cell chip's software, which encompassed much more than just the PlayStation 3 operating system he'd just described for me. He needed additional funding to hire more people who could fully develop the operating system and tools. It was the only way to enable the use of the Cell chip in future products to realize each STI partner's grand vision. Yet he was constrained by a meager budget that only allowed his small team to design the bare bones for the first game application in the PlayStation 3 console. Day and Ted Maeurer, the software team manager, argued frequently with Chekib Akrout over the scope of their work. Mike's Coke-bottle thick glasses magnified his angry glare while he ranted and raved, and his belligerent words echoed through the Design Center. Maeurer, with his ready laugh and spiky Simpson haircut, diffused the situation. Akrout was more than supportive of their quest. He knew they were right, but he didn't have the authorization to approve the funding.

Day and Maeurer continued to pursue this grand passion, but the road they traveled was often a steep climb. They waged battle at the corporate level, external to the Design Center. The software team developed extraordinary demonstrations to showcase the Cell chip's capabilities to executives, reporters, and clients. They produced an incredibly lifelike flyover of a three-dimensional representation of Mt. St. Helens—an exact replica of the real mountain, with details of every cliff, ravine, pasture, and road. Reminiscent of those popular IMAX films of helicopter rides over the Grand Canyon, the view from the sky over the volcano was realistic enough to make those watching "feel" in their guts the sideways roll and rapid descent down the flank of the mountain, the gravitational pull during the next steep ascent. But these were just demos. The really sophisticated stuff would be in the compilers and the tools they yearned to develop.

The work the software team did for the PlayStation 3 was a remarkable achievement, but they could have done so much more. We all wondered what IBM's real goal for this chip was if they weren't willing to invest in the software.

My new knowledge about games, the business of games, graphics hardware and software, and operating systems influenced my design work, and Ken Kutaragi's dream for the PlayStation 3 found a place in my head. The dilemma, of course, was how to cram all of that functionality into a small, low-power chip. Kutaragi, with his Midas touch, created the multibillion dollar PlayStation business by following the model of using low-margin hardware to sell high-margin software. Released in 1994, the PlayStation represented one of Sony's most successful ventures ever, and Kutaragi's insistence on backward compatibility in the follow-on PlayStation 2 (launched in 2000) led to another phenomenal success in the marketplace. Backward compatibility meant that customers who purchased games for their PlayStation could still play those games when they upgraded their system. Nothing became obsolete. This brilliant marketing strategy pushed Sony far into the lead in the game console market, as the library of PlayStation games was enormous. The PlayStation 2 took the market by storm in 2000 and was still on the 2001 Christmas wish list of every kid in America and Japan.

Kutaragi wanted the PlayStation 3 to offer an amazing contrast to predecessor game machines. While characters in the original game machines were very cartoonlike, he expected new characters to take on realistic human features like wrinkles, lines, and freckles. Things in motion, like a warrior's magic sword swooping through the air, Dale Earnhardt, Jr.'s #88 Chevy careening around the last corner of a racetrack, or Kelly Slater's surfboard slipping into the tube of a curling wave, were somewhat jerky in the old machines but would have magnificent fluid movement in the PlayStation 3. He demanded dramatic improvements in even the finest details. Instead of a green-colored flat carpet of grass in the next Tiger Woods golf game, Kutaragi expected to see each blade of grass individually animated, moving naturally as the wind blew or as the golf ball rolled across it. Trees that used to be green blobs would exhibit realistic features resulting from detailed modeling of each leaf, twig, and shadow.

With the preponderance of evidence from the original PlayStation and PlayStation 2, I had every reason to trust that Kutaragi knew his business. I embraced his vision for the PlayStation 3 and continued to feed my voracious hunger for all things related to games. Justifiable research, I thought, as I plunked down in my old beanbag chair and powered up my PlayStation 2 again.

CHAPTER 5

Inspire Innovation

*Nothing we have done in the past is sufficient
for what we need now to fulfill the grand vision.
Innovation is and always will be the magic
bullet that insures our success.*

JIM KAHLE WAS A MASTER at fostering innovation through team effort. Starting in the summer of 2001, he held grueling daily meetings to define the PlayStation 3 central processing chip's architecture, which is similar to defining the architecture of a house. Kahle's architects were responsible for drawing the blueprint to show how to build the chip. This task required an understanding of all of the functional interactions as well as an ability to think in three dimensions. The chip's bricks and mortar are millions of tiny transistors and wires, intricately laid out in artistic three-dimensional drawings. His daily meeting was an effective tool for pushing steady progress. We held our meetings in the "War Room," a large rectangle of space with whiteboards covering nearly every inch of three walls. Kahle effectively organized each meeting by writing on the board the objectives for the day and week. We then used the remaining board space to brainstorm. Every idea was valuable, and the entire team evaluated each one. By pulling in the top talent from each engineering discipline, we could scrutinize every idea from every angle.

Kahle expected all of the key leaders on the project to participate, as many as fifteen to twenty at a time, including the designated architects from Sony and Toshiba. Kahle knew that twenty smart brains were better than one. He just needed to harness those brains in a productive manner to innovate the best solution.

I was busy hammering out the blueprint for the PowerPC core, interviewing engineers to fill out my team, and mentoring the junior engineers to turn them into hotshot designers, but Kahle also expected me to help develop the architecture for the overall Cell chip. I welcomed the challenge and liked being in the thick of things, but I soon felt the pinch of being spread too thin.

Kahle came into the War Room promptly at 9:00, as he did every morning, grumpy as usual. He scanned the room, took a quick headcount, and growled, "Where's Keaty? We need him here." Kahle insisted on noninterrupted mandatory attendance, but we didn't always obey. John Keaty, the lead integrator for the PlayStation 3 chip, was responsible for the overall physical design, and his presence was crucial.

"I haven't seen him this morning," Keryn Mills said, rising to her feet and scrambling to gather her stacks of blue papers. "I'll go see if I can find him."

"No, stay." Kahle vented a frustrated sigh and with a flip of his hand dispatched Peter Hofstee to find the truant Keaty. Hofstee raised his eyebrows at this, but since he just wanted to keep the peace, he agreed to be Kahle's enforcer.

We went through a similar scene every time a key member of the team was late or absent. Open laptops suddenly consumed the space on the massive tabletop as most attendees quietly and quickly caught up on e-mail while waiting for the bad boys to return. Kahle, who never carried his laptop around, brooded in silence and studied the previous day's work, still displayed on the whiteboard.

Kahle's leadership style was a little too dictatorial for me, but I tried to keep quiet about it. I was only somewhat successful at this since subtlety was not exactly my forte. Silence didn't keep him from knowing how I felt anyway; we'd known each other long enough that he could read the frustration on my face. This waiting around was simply a frigging waste of time, and my patience wore very thin. Some days, if Kahle happened to be in a reasonable mood, he and I could carry on a side conversation while we waited for the meeting to start. It didn't appear to be one of those days, so like everyone else I decided to get a little work done. I opened my laptop.

The primary goal of Kahle's daily sessions was to define a PlayStation 3 Cell architecture that could execute computations on an order of magnitude faster than any previous design. This would require innovation and risk taking on all fronts—physical, logical, and architectural. Kahle used these sessions to discover the key to high performance gaming architecture. Although it may seem like magic to most people, game code is really quite simple. It can fundamentally be broken down into three major operations. First, it requires incoming streams of large amounts of data generated from a peripheral such as a joystick, controller, or keyboard. This is called "read streaming." Second, that incoming data stream has to be processed by one or more numeric engines. Finally, the data processed in the numeric engines has to be streamed back out to the video display to create the colorful graphics. This is called "write streaming."

Most chips grind to a screeching halt when confronted with the mathematically intense operations used in high-speed graphics. To pour on the speed, we needed to break up the data into bite-sized chunks and work on it in parallel (a technique known as multiprocessing), and we needed to move large blocks of information into, out of, and across the chip very quickly to perform the read streaming and write streaming operations.

Multiprocessing wasn't exactly a new concept. Many microprocessors and computer systems, including flagship IBM servers, incorporated this technique to handle different threads of computation in parallel. A separate multipurpose microprocessor chip was responsible for each single thread, so each server might house many of these chips. However, the PlayStation 3 had no space or budget for multiple chips. We needed a single chip that could execute multiprocessing capabilities. A simultaneous physical/functional design solution was required in order to achieve the most efficient movement of data, which was why Kahle needed both John Keaty (to talk about the physical layout of the design in silicon) and me (responsible for the design itself) in the room at the same time.

Finally, a sullen Keaty, bearing the latest hot-off-the-presses chip layout rolled up under his arm, and the ever-pleasant Hofstee slipped quietly into the room. Without a word, Keaty claimed his royal rights to a place at the table, and everyone shuffled around to make room. Laptops clicked shut. Conversations ended midsentence. We all knew the routine. Kahle immediately turned his attention to the day's agenda, and he expected our undivided and immediate attention. I sank into my seat, happy to end the needless waiting and start the real work.

Day after day, month after month, Kahle's team of high-powered architects gathered in the War Room to chip away at the PlayStation 3 design, painstakingly sculpting a high-performance multicore processor that we hoped would turn the electronics industry upside down. We were all eager to finish this concept work and move on to the next stage of the design.

Kahle knew we would have to create something new. A traditional multiprocessor would require too much real estate and power. He envisioned massive parallelism through multiple, simple cores that would provide the necessary horsepower within our given area and power budgets. This heterogeneous chip would be a new breed. It would be like having two different motors under the hood.

During these interminable meetings, we created a highly efficient workhorse or "muscle" for our chip concept and dubbed it the Synergistic core. The Synergistic core provided the numeric engine component of the game processing puzzle. We used six of them on the Cell chip, operating them in concert to calculate millions of floating-point computations to generate extremely realistic graphics in real time. Kahle recruited Sang Dhong, a brilliant circuit designer, to lead the Synergistic core team. Though he lacked experience in putting a product out the door, Dhong brought a wealth of microprocessor expertise to the STI Design Center. He was among the first to transfer in from IBM's research group, where he had gained worldwide fame—along with Peter Hofstee—by designing a test chip demonstrating the first one-gigahertz capability in the entire industry.

The more traditional PowerPC core that my team was designing served as the "brains" of the chip, running the game platform's operating system and dispatching number-crunching duties to the Synergistic cores. It functioned like a traffic cop directing the flow of information throughout the entire game console. The PowerPC core was perfectly suited for control intensive tasks, and in addition to running the operating system, it also ran the top-level control thread of a game application such as scene traversal. The scene traversal code was structured like the branches of a tree, where each branch indicated a decision point, a choice to be made. The PowerPC core was much better at handling these types of decisions than was the Synergistic core.

While microprocessor speeds have increased dramatically over the last twenty years, memory technology has not kept up. So we paired a memory subsystem, called the Memory Flow Control, with the PowerPC core to provide close-proximity, high-speed memory services. This subsystem included a 512-kilobyte Level Two (L2) cache, similar to that found in traditional PCs. The PowerPC already had a dedicated Level One (L1) cache that, when coupled with the memory subsystem's L2 cache, provided fast access and helped minimize the time required to fetch instructions and data from memory. The use of caches placed the game code and streaming data close to the processing elements, virtually eliminating the huge time penalty associated with retrieving data from the more distant main storage. The small size of the caches also helped to provide faster access.

We knew that this type of traditional memory subsystem could have an adverse impact on real-time applications. The caches are fast but can be unpredictable. Because they can only hold a small subset of the data found in main storage, they dynamically cast out old data to make room for new data. This unpredictability can be detrimental to game code. Picture this: you're playing an online game, a gun battle ensues, and you're splattering the enemy when your machine gun suddenly freezes because the underlying hardware is fetching data from main memory instead of the local cache. When the action resumes, it's too late. You blinked, you're dead.

To eliminate this memory access problem in the Cell architecture, we invented a new heterogeneous architecture which could efficiently fetch instructions and data from memory and keep them in the Synergistic cores until they were needed. In addition, software explicitly controlled this exchange so hardware could not inadvertently cast out some valuable instruction or data. To get instructions and data loaded as quickly as possible, we devised a three-tier organization of storage: register file, local store, and main storage. New asynchronous Direct Memory Access (DMA) operations transferred data between local store and main storage, allowing execution of game code to proceed in parallel while data and instructions were fetched from the slower main storage. The resulting hardware allowed each Synergistic core to have many concurrent memory accesses in flight, and each core stayed busy because it was not waiting on the slower main storage.

We spent one entire morning poring over Keaty's Cell chip layout, tweaking the positions and sizes of the components to achieve the shortest routes for data to travel. The PowerPC core, its memory subsystem, and the six Synergistic cores were the three primary real estate–consuming components on the chip, though there were many other smaller subcomponents still to finalize.

"If you don't give me that extra space at the top of the PowerPC, I won't have any buffer for corrections on a second spin of the chip," I argued. I pointed to another spot on the layout. "And look at how tight it is here. This is a very high-risk part of the design, lots of potential for error. Can't you give us a little more room?"

"I can't give you space in both of those areas or we'll push outside of the manufacturable vertical height for the chip. Pick one or the other," Keaty said firmly. "I can give you a couple of tracks along the side, if that helps. Sang doesn't need all of that for the Synergistic cores."

Sang was quick to fight back.

We each had our own territory to defend, and boundary disputes ebbed and waned as the morning progressed. Congested spaces on the chip could overload our timesaving design tools and make the work considerably more labor intensive and difficult for my engineers. So I fought hard to keep some slack in both width and height allocations for my PowerPC core and memory subsystem. We needed room to grow and to maneuver as we launched into our detailed design. Chip design was an art form. To design a super-high-performance microprocessor, we first had to define the physical aspects of the chip.

It was nearly noon when our group of mentally exhausted architects came full circle and began to rehash space arguments settled just that morning. Kahle called a timeout, the fingertips of his left hand punching into the palm of his right hand to form a T. "We're done," he announced. "I'm calling the concept for the Cell chip complete. Good job, guys! Congratulations!"

About time, I thought.

No one cheered. No one shook hands or felt obliged to smile. We silently packed up our stuff, and in less than a minute, Kahle sat alone in the big conference room, brooding, clearly disappointed in the glum reaction to his pronouncement. I glanced at him as I walked past the glass wall that bordered his War Room, but I simply wasn't motivated to try to cheer him up. In my opinion, Kahle allowed this concept definition process to drag on far too long, and I bit my tongue to keep from telling him so. Finally, we could move on to the more rigorous task of flushing out the details, determining how to interconnect all these high-powered engines, and figuring out how to interface them to the rest of the PlayStation 3 system outside of the Cell chip.

Kahle continued to hold his daily meetings, but they evolved into a less intense forum aimed at improving technical coordination and communication. That, I could live with.

A subset of Kahle's group broke away to work on a new data highway. If one were to look through a microscope at a computer chip, one would see what looks like a tightly packed urban city with many little suburbs and multilayer complex highways and road systems. The city planner (chip architect) wants traffic (information) to move along quickly and efficiently with no logjams or, God forbid, standstills, even at peak hours. Cars waiting at entrance ramps need ample opportunities to enter the traffic flow. Ideally, good utilization of the road systems means that even bumper-to-bumper traffic will not cause a problem. Maybe most importantly, the city planner doesn't want the citizens to have to go outside of town (off-chip) to get necessary services, because that just means the cars will be on the roads longer, coming and going, and there will be inevitable bottlenecks at the entrance and exit points.

Programmers want hardware that will allow them to write software to run on the chip without time-consuming excursions to store or retrieve data from off-chip memory devices. It was common in the past to use off-chip staging points to shelve data temporarily while the processor was busy on another piece of data; that was the limitation of technology then. With the Cell chip, things changed. To move data around, Kahle and his team invented a clever ring structure to loop through the chip like a big four-lane highway. There are entrance ramps where any one of the processors can launch data onto the highway and exit ramps where the processor at the intended destination can extract the data. Each of the four lanes (buses) is 16-bytes wide and can support up to three simultaneous data transfers. A special traffic cop (arbiter logic) decides whose turn it is to jump on the highway. Kahle's highway engineers and city planners redefined the state of the art in data transfer. It was team-inspired innovation. They called it the "Element Interconnect Bus" or EIB.

This is the real art of computer architecture—moving information in the most efficient way. Each night, when I inserted a game disk into my new PlayStation 2, I experienced firsthand that the time it took to load a scene and start the action was dependent on how fast massive amounts of data moved in and out and around the chip.

Time marched on, but I applied precious little of it to the design work Kahle hired me to do. His directive was clear: design the world's fastest PowerPC core in the smallest possible area while keeping power usage to an absolute minimum. Under no circumstances could my PowerPC core slow down the Synergistic cores that were the workhorses of the game chip. I was anxious to devote myself to that delightful and challenging task, but administrative tasks, Kahle's mandatory daily sessions, and other assorted useless status meetings consumed my days.

"There's no time for the technical work!" I complained.

I finally rebelled, ignored all other demands no matter how urgent, and disappeared into my cubicle for a week, where I constructed the fundamental pipeline of the PowerPC core. This was where my passion lay, inventing new architectures. Here I could apply my microprocessor design experience as well as the knowledge gained during my undergraduate studies at the University of Kentucky and my graduate studies st Syracuse University. One of my graduate school instructors once said, "Computer architecture is good to learn, but keep in mind, only a handful of engineers in the world get to actually create a new architecture and define new pipelines." I was glad I was one of the lucky ones.

A processor pipeline is like an automobile manufacturing assembly line. In an assembly line, no matter how fast each individual worker completes his or her assigned task, the slowest person on the line ultimately determines the speed at which the line moves. Similarly, as data moves from point to point on the chip, the slowest stage sets the chip's frequency.

While I was defining the basic pipeline, I also laid down the fundamental floorplan of the core. The floorplan defines the relative location of each of the functions in the core with respect to each other. The pipeline, in conjunction with the floorplan, formed the start of the PowerPC core blueprint, similar to the blueprint to build a house. Later, a much larger team could fill in the details. Creating the architecture of a new design was quite complex, as I balanced performance, area, and power, all before a single transistor was laid down. They didn't teach that when I went through school! Most of my engineering design work tends to be logical, sequential, left-brained activity involving lots of complex mathematics, rules, and deductive reasoning. However, long ago I found that I'm most effective when I can also use the right side of my brain to visualize my designs spatially. I imagined the flow of instructions moving through my PowerPC core like a magnificent fluid piece of art, flowing in such a way that they met the least amount of resistance. This is what I drew on my whiteboard. I spent hours studying the drawing, compulsively balancing and rebalancing the stages. Each time I encountered a slow spot, I broke the design into smaller pieces to push the frequency higher. I also imagined with my right brain how all of the pieces would fit together in the floorplan.

One of my favorite movies during my college years was *Tron.* In this electronic-age version of *Alice in Wonderland*, a video arcade machine magically zapped a sharp game developer and pulled him into the guts of the machine. Finding himself in an alien world of flowing electrons and dangerous power grids, the developer experienced the adventure of a lifetime as he battled other characters traveling through the guts of the computer game chip. That movie helped me visualize the flow of information in my chip. What if I immersed a miniature version of myself into this complex pipeline? How would I most efficiently travel through the stages of the pipeline? What obstacles would I encounter to slow my progress?

One of the tricks to microprocessor design is to specify the exact number of stages that will maximize the performance of the design. Too few or too many stages will slow the chip down. Back to the assembly line analogy: there is a point where adding more people to the line (breaking the work into even smaller tasks) is no longer helpful. Each additional person carries a certain amount of overhead, time required to retrieve the result from the last person and hand it off to the next one downstream. So exceeding that optimum number of workers may still increase the frequency of the product moving through the line, but it will actually take longer to complete the assembly of a whole car. There is a delicate balance between improving the chip's performance from higher frequency versus improving performance from higher efficiency at each stage.

In recent years, IBM's rival, Intel, journeyed down both paths. The initial number of pipeline stages for their highly successful Pentium3 was fairly modest, and the clock frequency was also fairly low. Their next-generation Pentium4 pushed the leading edge in frequency (> 1 gigahertz) by using a very deep pipeline, but they gave up on throughput. There were some embarrassing moments for Intel when they introduced the Pentium4, with some of the older software running faster on a Pentium3 than it did on the newer Pentium4. They exceeded that subtle point of diminishing returns when it came to a deep pipeline, high-frequency design. The chips IBM provided for Apple's desktops could actually beat Intel's chip in performance, but not in frequency.

I continued to balance my pipeline stages, keeping in mind that Kahle demanded a very high-frequency PowerPC core that didn't come at the expense of higher power. That presented yet another dilemma. I could get higher frequency by giving it a deeper pipeline, but that just resulted in higher power because each additional pipeline stage included a certain number of storage elements (latches) to save the intermediate results. The latches and the circuitry to clock the latches are very expensive in terms of power.

I realized that now, rather than later, was the time to deal with the power consumption issue. We needed to consider the use of clock gating. This technique turns off clocks to latches when they are not being used, thus reducing the power. I utilized a new form of clock gating called power tokens. As an analogy, think of walking through rooms in a dark house and turning on the light of a room when you enter, then turning off the light when you exit. The idea behind the power tokens was to have the clocks for latches turned off as a default, and then only turn them on when required. The power tokens trickled down through the pipeline whenever valid instructions were fetched from storage; then they passed from pipeline stage to pipeline stage turning clocks on and off as instructions flowed through the design. This allowed latches to be shut down when pipeline stages were not busy.

I kept working at it, simplifying the design so that I could achieve a very high frequency with a modest pipeline depth and minimal power. Finally, I was satisfied that my design would work. It was time to bring in the critics.

I took every opportunity to show off my prized pipeline, proudly treating it like a classic piece of artwork or a trophy. I showed it to every engineer who entered my cubicle. I used it as a tool to show new team members how each piece of the design related to the whole. I solicited advice and input from veteran designers. Lengthy technical discussions and whiteboard explanations allowed some fine-tuning of the basic pipeline, but my past microprocessor design experience and a strong gut feeling told me that this design would stand the test of time. Now I could really get my team focused on a coherent plan of attack.

After a week of pipelining, I returned to Kahle's meeting to find the War Room's huge wall-to-wall whiteboards covered with a maze of task lists, logical flow diagrams, snippets of circuits, and block diagrams with lots of arrows running in every direction to indicate changes, highlight problems, or show ownership. There was a big red handwritten sign at the top of the center board that said "Do Not Erase." I walked around the room and scanned the boards to catch up on the latest progress. I was impressed. They had been busy while I was off working on my PowerPC pipeline.

For once, I was the first to enter the room, but Sony's chief architect, Takeshi Yamazaki, soon joined me. He never missed a meeting, and I had to give him credit for his diligence. As I mentioned earlier he struggled greatly with conversational English, so these meetings, where so much vital information was verbal, had to be boring for him. Both Sony and Toshiba sent their most talented architects to Kahle's meetings.

Most of these Japanese engineers could read and write English quite well, but there were many, like Yamazaki, who could not understand the spoken word. Some could understand it, but had difficulty speaking it. Only a very small handful could do both. None of the IBMers could speak or write Japanese, so the language barrier was quite problematic. Sony quickly found a work-around solution and drafted an English-speaking Japanese engineer to translate for Yamazaki. Additionally, Sony and Toshiba hired an English teacher to visit the Design Center two evenings a week to teach conversational English to the Japanese engineers, but it was a painfully slow process.

Due to the limitations of some of these engineers we all tried to be more conscientious about writing the salient parts of ongoing conversations on the whiteboards to insure that our Japanese partners followed and understood the issues at hand. We IBMers worked harder to understand the Japanese culture and to bring some of it into the work environment, and these efforts helped the Japanese partners feel more comfortable. Where they were once silent and restrained, many finally voiced their questions more freely when they did not understand something. They began to contribute in a real way.

Kahle possessed in his team all the ingredients for a unique system of checks and balances if only he could combine the enthusiasm and risk-taking nature of the Americans with the meticulous eye toward detail of the Japanese. Easier said than done. These two cultures didn't always mesh well, so Kahle was often forced to arbitrate and make a command decision, inevitably upsetting one group or another. Kahle was certainly not one to avoid confrontation—and even instigated it when in a bad mood—but his nature was to seek consensus. He took pains to avoid stepping on the toes of his Japanese engineers, who preferred careful planning, a thorough understanding of the minutiae, and frequent approvals from Kutaragi or his minions. This slowed the

progress considerably and the IBM team of computer hardware designers, software architects, and circuit and physical designers grew
impatient.

We trudged forward, digging deeper into the design that grew
from our concept, and our frustration with Kahle's torture sessions
paled in comparison to the pain of what came next.

As Jim Warnock predicted in our earlier goal-setting meeting with
Chekib Akrout, we truly did face enormous challenges in our efforts to
achieve our four-gigahertz goal with such a small power budget, leading us to redefine the way we designed microprocessors. Traditionally,
we accomplished microprocessor design in six phases, correlating
loosely to concept development, high-level design, initial design, detailed design, final design, and completion of the physical wiring layout to hand to manufacturing. This was how we all grew up, how we
sharpened our saws and developed our muscles. We knew this
process well.

However, the constraints on frequency, area, and power forced us
to begin with the end in mind. This included considering not just the
inner workings of the chip, the microarchitecture, but also the physical
aspects of the design—the fundamental floorplan layout and the
power consumption. We suddenly moved out of our comfort zone,
and everyone got a little more edgy, a little more protective of "the
way we used to do things." This new way of thinking really stretched
us. No surprise to me, I thrive on taking risks and getting out of my
comfort zone. To achieve the high performance, high frequency, and
minimal power required for the project, we went "back to the future"
and applied some old tricks from previous designs.

CHAPTER 6

Work Hard, Play Hard!

Working hard enough to win, playing hard enough
to stay sane. No one understands better than
coworkers the extraordinary effort it takes to
persevere day after day. Who better to share in
the release after having been in the trenches
together?

BRINGING LIFE TO A NEW MICROPROCESSOR re-
quires innovation as well as hard work and long hours. I learned early
in the project that we needed to take some time to have fun during
our long stretches of intense engineering effort. Without this, our team
would self-destruct before we got to the finish line. The time we took
off to play together also helped us get to know each other and bond as
a team. We were becoming an engineering family, and every member
of the family mattered. My team adopted the motto, "Work hard, play
hard."

In his book, *The Soul of a New Machine*, Tracy Kidder described
a practice known as "the mushroom theory of management," which
was: "Put 'em in the dark, feed 'em shit, and watch 'em grow." I
wanted to spice things up for my team of mushrooms.

Now that I had the basic pipeline of the PowerPC core and a first-pass floorplan in hand, it was time for my team of engineers to fill in the details of the blueprint and complete the high-level design activities. During the second half of 2001, I held daily design meetings, similar to the torturous ones Kahle was conducting for the overall central processing chip architecture, but hopefully ones that were far more fun. My measure of fun was how much laughter there was in the room.

I relied on my team leads Dave Ray, Jim Van Norstrand, and Tony Truong to help define the finer details of the blueprint. We carved up the design into fundamental building blocks and then estimated each block's size and power. We created timing budgets for each block to allow us to estimate how close we were to achieving the final timing target. Then we pinned each block to a specific location on the PowerPC core real estate and created signal-interconnect definitions to allow us to visualize how all of the pieces of the puzzle connected together.

The next step was to determine the performance of the design as measured in instructions per second. Computer instructions form the low-level language that talks to the hardware and dictates the flow of information. I had to convince myself that our design allowed instructions to flow through the pipeline with minimal resistance.

To simulate the instruction behavior, I needed to create a performance model of the PowerPC core, a C++ software representation. I was willing to do most of this work myself because there simply was no one else on the team that had the depth of knowledge of the whole design—except perhaps Kurt Feiste. Kurt was a shy, soft-spoken engineer who was quite brilliant, but who sometimes needed a little cattle prodding to get moving. He was one of the few folks on the team who had both the software skills and the architecture background to help me. We'd worked side by side on the groundbreaking IBM Power4 microprocessor design, so I was well aware of his remarkable skills as well as the maze of idiosyncrasies I was going to have to navigate in order to work with him.

It was already late evening as I walked toward Feiste's cubicle, and only a handful of people were still at work. When I turned the corner, I was not surprised to see him still at work, even though it had been dark outside for hours. Feiste was a night owl. He didn't come into work until 11:00 A.M. most days, so typically he was one of the last to leave in the evening. He was single, so I hoped he would be willing to put in a burst of extreme overtime to help me code up the model.

I handed him a bag of hot popcorn as a bribe (Kurt was a fiend for popcorn), and said, "Hey, I know you're chomping at the bit to get into the detailed design work, but since we're not ready for that just yet, I thought I might convince you to help me on something else. I have some really cool short-term work to be done on a performance model. I could use your help writing the code to simulate the core's behavior. You're one of the few engineers on this project with the depth of knowledge in architecture and the software skills to pull this off, and I've always been able to rely on you in the past."

Feiste crunched on a handful of popcorn and pulled his pale-blond eyebrows into a frown. He was a veteran chip designer, and he quickly figured out that what I neglected to mention was that the due date was yesterday. I wasn't sure if he was buying my flattery either. I could see that I was going to have to throw in more enticement.

"You know, when stock options and award time comes around, they'll look first at those folks that put in the extra effort." I was in no position to make such promises, but I knew how to push Feiste's buttons.

He squinted his eyes at me, but didn't answer. I reached out to snag a handful of popcorn, but he pulled the bag away from me. "I'll do it," he sighed, "but starting tomorrow." He turned his chair and faced his computer again, effectively ending the conversation. That was good enough for me.

For me, writing software was therapeutic, a short escape from the high-pressure responsibility of being a team leader. For a few weeks, I simply dug deep into the design and enjoyed the creative process. I wrote complex mathematical equations to mimic the logic of the microprocessor, and I visualized the flow of instructions through the design, removing the areas of the pipeline causing the most resistance to the natural flow. With the C++ code Feiste and I wrote, I finally observed the dynamic behavior of the instructions flowing through the pipeline and measured the performance of the design. The complex puzzle took on a life form.

We used this C++ model to gain insight into the expected performance of the customers' specific application code, too, so it was important to maintain and update the model to keep up with the ongoing design changes occurring on the other side of the shop. I found that there was little time during the day to do that work, so Feiste and I spent many nights and weekends on this activity . . . as well as many shared bags of popcorn—well, maybe "shared" is the wrong word.

The enjoyment I gained from this work reminded me of all the reasons I got into electrical engineering in the first place. When I was just a kid, my dad gave me a simple electrical kit, which allowed me to wire up all kinds of neat switches, lights, buzzers, etc. Then in high school, I learned about computers and took an electronics class. It all seemed like cool stuff, so I decided to give engineering a try.

I went on to the University of Kentucky, where my father taught engineering. The first couple of years were fun but painful. In high school, I was able to make good grades without really trying, but in college, especially in engineering, I soon found I had to work very hard to make good grades. I remember being in a freshman engineering class when the instructor said, "Look around at your fellow classmates in this room. Two thirds of these people will not be with you when you graduate." Sure enough, most of them bailed out after a couple of grueling engineering classes and went into other fields.

I partied way too much during my freshman year and got the first (and last) C of my life. It was a valuable wake-up call. I wanted to make the good grades that would land me a top-notch engineering job and allow me to make my mark on the computer industry. For that to happen, things needed to change. I limited my partying to weekends and concentrated on my electrical engineering curriculum instead. I took my first computer class and my first digital design class, where I learned a completely new language, binary mathematics. Suddenly, I was ignited with a newfound passion. It all made so much sense to me. Manipulating those 1s and 0s with logical gates was absolutely magical for me. I hadn't been this excited since I hit a grand-slam homer in Little League. For the rest of my days at the university, I was a regular on the dean's list, and I graduated with honors.

Having experienced a reigniting of my passion for engineering as I worked on the PowerPC's performance model, I understood why spirits soared as my team of bricklayers finally got their hands on the initial blueprint for the PowerPC core and its memory subsystem. They were chomping at the bit to dive into the detailed implementation, but we still had a mountain of high-level design activities to complete before I could allow that. I had a devil of a time holding them back, forcing them to slow down and *think* before they started writing willy-nilly code that would only have to be ripped up later. Jittery logic designers bobbed their heads up and down in unison when I explained that they first needed to develop a deep understanding of the function of each assigned block of logic. I watched their eyes glaze over when I suggested that they develop plans for their logic and make sure their counterpart circuit designers and verification engineers were on the same page. Logic design was hard work filled with complex problems to solve—exactly what these talented engineers wanted.

After working through a particularly difficult issue, one of the quirky new college graduates happily sighed, "Complexity is the oxygen of the soul." It was a little too poetic for me, but I completely understood the sentiment. I was thoroughly enjoying working with the junior engineers, explaining the architecture, walking through their logic with them, and helping them find and understand the bugs in the design. The executives were happy with the progress, so it was a fairly upbeat and positive time.

Quite often, an engineer came to me with a sticky problem, threw up his/her hands, and claimed there was no solution. My first response was always, "Come to me with solutions, not problems." It wasn't that I didn't want to help them. What I wanted was for them to start brainstorming and problem solving before they even approached me. I also wanted them to have a positive can-do attitude that was open to all possibilities. Finally, I wanted them to focus on the end result and not get caught up in all of the obstacles in the way.

Meeting all of the PlayStation 3's "must have" requirements for this PowerPC core was daunting enough, but the requirement to include additional features to support Chekib Akrout's vision for future IBM products became a monumental task. The complexity of this design called for intense concentration. My head hurt from trying to consider every possible scenario where my design could break.

The extended PowerPC core and Memory Flow Control design teams worked through the rigors of high-level design, which included the creation of more detailed circuit schematics and timing analyses to prove out the designs. I relied heavily on Tony Truong to keep things going in the right direction on the Memory Flow Control design activities while I was off attending customer reviews or otherwise distracted from the day-to-day business of the design work. He provided strong leadership during this phase.

By the end of 2001, we were ready to exit the high-level design phase. Before declaring victory, I was blindsided by a phone call from the performance lead, Hal Kossman. Hal was a thirty-plus-year veteran from Rochester, Minnesota, who laid his claim to fame at IBM when he put multithreading on the first Rochester-based AS/400 server chips.

Hal cleared his throat and then said in a rush, "Dave, my performance team has done some studies that show you can get as much as twenty to thirty percent improvement in performance if you add multithreading to your core. In addition, we're seeing that dual-issue is only worth a five to ten percent performance gain. Maybe you should throw out dual-issue in favor of multithreading."

"We've already thought about that, Hal," I responded cautiously, my suspicious nature clicking into high gear. "It's not obvious the Sony programming model could take advantage of multithreading. Besides, it's too late in the game to tackle it."

"I know, I know. I was just thinking you might want to reconsider."

After we hung up, I leaned back in my chair, rested my head, and closed my eyes, trying to divine the underlying meaning behind Hal's words. Something was fishy. I slowly rolled my chair back and forth. His pronouncement wasn't news to me. I had seen the studies. However, right before exiting the high-level design phase was no time to make such a major change. Hardware multithreading was a technique that gave the illusion to a programmer that there were actually two PowerPC cores instead of just one. Dual-issue allowed two instructions to be issued and executed in parallel. Both were excellent ways to bump up the performance of a microprocessor, but our design was already locked down.

My eyes snapped open as the revelation hit me. Hal Kossman, ever the political animal, had probably met secretly with Kahle and Akrout to convince them to make the change. Even though I had no proof of this, I was already furious. This was nothing more than Hal wanting to put his stamp on the project.

Sure enough, the next day Kahle called me to his office and asked me to consider swapping dual-issue for multithreading. My throat tightened. "Jim, no matter what Hal says, this is no time to make this change. Besides, I'm quite certain you will regret not having dual-issue for some future applications."

Despite strong arguments from both Jim Van Norstrand and me, Kahle made the decision to extend our high-level design schedule by two months to give us time to incorporate multithreading. I made one last plea to Kahle, "Jim, let's have our cake and eat it, too. We have time to implement both dual instruction issue and multithreading."

However, Kahle had made up his mind. He could be so bull-headed sometimes. He said, "Nope, I've made my decision, dual-issue is out, multithreading is in."

One very quiet afternoon in early '02, I tucked my team in at their desks, where they focused on their assigned design tasks. The only sound was that of keys clicking, clicking, clicking as they typed. In the librarylike silence, even the sporadic soft wheezing of the stairwell door opening and closing was a distraction. Suddenly, a loud growl followed by a series of bangs and crashes shattered the peace. I jumped up from my chair and looked over the cubicle walls to see what was going on, but other than the surprised faces of my fellow rubberneckers, all I could see was the fuzzy top of Jim Van Norstrand's head as he moved quickly toward the center of an aisle several rows away. I jogged over to make sure no one was hurt, but I couldn't have been more surprised at what I found when I rounded the corner.

I stopped abruptly to avoid stepping on the shards of plastic and loose keys that lay scattered across the floor. I looked up from the mess and locked eyes with Brian Crockett, one of our best and brightest engineers. He sat there in his vintage rock-and-roll T-shirt, comfortably reclined in his chair with his hands locked behind his head, looking every bit as if nothing had happened.

Jim stepped closer to me and said quietly, "Brian got frustrated when he couldn't find the solution to a logic problem as quickly as he thought he should have."

I turned away so that Brian couldn't see that I was having difficulty smothering a laugh. "So he killed his keyboard? What's up with that?"

Jim shrugged. "Looks like he feels better now."

Brian, a quiet, shy, midlevel engineer, worked for days on a particularly ugly design problem. We always gave the hardest stuff to him. As was often the case, just when he thought he found the solution, another bug popped up. Bugs were design flaws, and just as nasty as finding a cockroach in your house. That was how it went for all of us. Debugging was a messy, iterative process.

"Have you got a handle on this?" I asked Jim.

He nodded and waved me off. I shooed away all the onlookers as I made my way back to my desk, leaving Jim to restore order. That was the first time Brian destroyed a keyboard, but certainly not the last. After that, few of us bothered to get up out of our chairs when we heard him slamming his keyboard on his desk.

Brian wasn't the only one living with high-levels of stress. In one way or another, each one of us was in a dangerous state of mind. Sliding along the bleeding knife-edge of technology meant that we were constantly discovering new problems that forced us back to the drawing board. Forward progress was frustratingly slow.

While most of us didn't resort to destroying our keyboards, we did find other ways to battle the debilitating effects of stress and fatigue. I found the most relief in exercise. My regular routine consisted of a strenuous workout at a nearby 24-hour fitness club, usually at lunchtime. The facility had an indoor track, and I found running to be the best calorie-burn-per-second workout option. Several times a week, I rushed over there, got my three-mile run in, showered, and returned to work after a quick stop at Taco Cabana for fast-food Mexican, which I ate in the car. Life was fast and furious in those days. Taking time to burn off some stress from the day was a requirement for my sanity.

After flushing out the details of multithreading, we declared victory on the high-level design. It was time to move into the low-level implementation phase, in which we carefully layered the bricks and mortar (millions of silicon transistors and wires) in a very specific order to build the house we called the "PU," short for PowerPC Processing Unit. The transistors computed the solutions to complex mathematical equations that for the game application of this chip determined the physics of the scenes and characters.

I called for a high-level design completion celebration with an invitation to my team to join me at Building W, our nickname for the nearby Waterloo Icehouse, a restaurant and bar. I don't know how many pitchers of cheap beer and heaping platters of greasy chicken wings Mickie and I bought, but it was a lot. Empty glasses, orange-stained napkins, and stacks of plates and chicken bones filled every table in our noisy little corner of the restaurant's outdoor patio. Not surprisingly, our wearisome communication problems disappeared when the engineers of all three companies turned to the universal language of beer to help bond us together. Japanese and American traditions may have collided at work, but here they fell on common ground. We spent many evenings at Building W, where my rowdy multicultural team was well known. Over the course of the project, I became particularly fond of the lead engineer from Toshiba, Hiroo-san, and the lead engineer from Sony, Masa-san. Building W became a nice place to get to know them. They were two of the best engineers I have ever worked with, bar none, and I relied on them heavily.

I leaned across the sticky table and spoke loudly over the din, "Hiroo, how do you and your family like living in Austin?"

Hiroo smiled broadly, bobbed his head, and said, "It is very nice and very big."

I waited for more, but he seemed to have said it all. I kept probing. "Have you done much sight-seeing?"

Hiroo nodded again. "We have visited the Alamo in San Antonio. And we have been to Houston and watched the Rockets."

"How about that Yao Ming?" I knew he was a big fan of the Houston Rockets star, Ming.

After a second round of beer, I took another shot at a conversation. "So Hiroo, what do you like to do when you're not at work?"

Hiroo replied enthusiastically, "I like to watch movies and TV."

"How does this compare with what you see in Japan?" I asked.

Hiroo laughed. "Here, they say the F-word a lot, and include lots more violence and sex."

Others joined in the conversation, commenting on their favorite thriller movies and the highly popular TV series, *24*, starring Kiefer Sutherland. This moderately violent series told the story of a single, absurdly action-packed day in the life of a counterterrorist FBI agent, exploiting our fear of additional terrorist attacks, our eroding faith in our political leaders, and our desire to fight back. We loved the action. Someone mentioned that a PlayStation 2 game based on *24* was under development. That was going to be a must-have for this crowd.

I was feeling pretty loose, so I pulled out my cell phone and called my buddy, Chekib Akrout. Following a lot of shouted encouragement from my half-drunk compadres, Akrout agreed to join us for a drink.

Now, it's not often that a vice president of any big corporation will join the workers for beer, but Akrout did it quite often. He was one of us. When he showed up, he winked and asked, "So Dave, you got that design done yet?"

I smiled and shook his hand. "Sure Chekib, we're all done. We're taking the rest of the year off."

As Akrout glided from table to table with his easy smile, greeting everyone by name, shaking hands, clinking beer mugs, I could tell the team was very pleased to have him join in. They laughed and joked with him about all kinds of things, trusting that tomorrow he would kindly forget any indiscretions. His presence changed the moment, and made each one of us glad we were there. Later that night, emboldened by the beer, we hooked him into a serious discussion (which we had no business doing in that state!) about why we were faced with such schedule pressure. We pushed the tables aside and sat in a rough circle around Akrout.

"Christmas '05," he said. "Sony's business is hanging on that date." The Japanese partners in our group nodded in agreement. I understood deadlines, but I also knew from experience that the world didn't fall apart when one was missed. The year '05 seemed like a long way off.

I topped off Akrout's beer and drained the pitcher into my own mug.

"Let's backtrack from there," Akrout patiently continued. "We need to get the prototypes to the game developers eighteen months in advance of launch, so that's June '04. That means we need to deliver the design to the manufacturing team by November '03. Back up four months from there to the day we have to lock down and hand the design to our physical design team, and you're at July '03. So you've got about a year and a half to finish the design of the world's fastest, most complicated processor and then debug and verify it. Does that sound like a lot of time to you?"

He looked around at us to gauge the impact of his words. Typically, a high-level design for a start-from-scratch microprocessor required six to twelve months, during which time we designed and analyzed small pieces of the chip to ensure that we were capable of meeting the chip area, timing, power, performance, and schedule goals of the project. The designers estimated where the worst timing paths would be. The circuit designers created schematics to depict these small critical paths, and then they used a timing tool to measure the time it took to transmit a signal from one side of the path to the other. In addition, we refined the floorplan and made estimates of the total size of the blocks in the core. We were in the middle of that work now. But we also had to complete what we typically called initial design, detailed design, and final design. A year and a half suddenly didn't seem nearly long enough.

I let the front legs of my chair hit the floor with a bang as I straightened up. "Okay, boys. Back to work!" I said. Some laughed, some groaned. I was only half joking. What Akrout said had a sobering effect. We were going to be running full blast for the next couple of years, and I could only pray that my team was in it for the long haul. This was going to be a marathon, not a sprint.

Back at the Design Center, we started the detailed design phase of the project. It was a good thing, too, because the logic designers and circuit designers were antsy to start implementing the actual design. This work would include a parallel effort of writing a logical representation of the design in a Very High-level Design Language (VHDL) as well as designing low-level transistor schematics to match the logic.

Not long into the low-level implementation phase, we discovered a new frustration—the fundamental laws of physics.

For the past four decades, the silicon chip technology had advanced at such a steady pace that the number of transistors per square inch on a chip had doubled every two years. Gordon Moore, co-founder of Intel, first made this observation of doubling data density in 1965; hence, it was dubbed Moore's Law. Later, people stretched the definition of Moore's Law to predict that microprocessor performance would double every two years.

Shrinking a microchip's feature size (the width of the smallest device a certain lithography technology can produce on a silicon chip) results in smaller chips, and smaller chips mean that the manufacturer can pack more chips on a single silicon wafer and produce more chips during a single run through the fabrication process. Smaller feature sizes also allows the chip's basic building block, the transistor, to operate at higher frequencies, performing more computations per second. Sounds good, right? But serious engineering challenges go hand in hand with shrinking chip sizes, and the impact of these difficulties is enormous and extends far beyond the delicate manufacturing process. The design process itself now demands sophisticated tools and very high levels of design automation, both of which are extremely costly. The investment that chip design companies must make in the development of custom tools is staggering, so it is no wonder that these become the family jewels, so to speak.

Using these sophisticated tools, our analysis revealed that the time it took electrons to travel the length of the wires across and around the chip (known in the business as wire delays) was consuming a major portion of each clock cycle, leaving little time for the actual number crunching. With the nanoscale silicon technology we planned to use, transistors were so small that the speed of the transistor was no longer the dominant factor in our ability to achieve our frequency goals. This phenomenon, known as an "interconnect bottleneck," was a major problem in our high-performance design.

Obviously, we needed to carefully craft the length of the wires to minimize these delays. During high-level design, I had created a piece of artwork, an optimal, short-wire microarchitecture, to show where we should locate each function in the core so that the flow of information traveled the shortest distance possible. During the detailed design phase, this artwork became a complex three-dimensional jigsaw puzzle where optimizing one function often came at the expense of another.

In my previous microprocessor design projects, life had been much simpler. The bulk of the work was coding up the design and debugging it. In this new world of bleeding-edge frequency at low power, life was much different. The early design phases became a jumble of wire delays, area constraints, power consumption, critical timing, and complicated logic. Talk about out-of-order processing! We were living it! We coined a term, "triple constraints," to describe the measurement of the frequency, power, and area of a given function.

Monitoring power consumption, especially this early in the project, was also a new concept for us. In my previous designs for the server chips, power was the last thing considered. Jim Kahle created a new position in the Design Center called the "power czar" to police the power budget. Dan Stasiak landed the role, but the bold position title was disarmingly incongruent with Dan's quiet, mild-mannered personality. Dan taught yoga classes in his spare time and probably would have been a far better mediator than an enforcer. Yet his job required him to carry a big stick to beat down the chip's massive power consumption to fit into the budget constraints. I thought Dan was technically capable for the job but probably not aggressive enough to push back against the resistance from an overworked, oversensitive crew. As the job title suggested, the czar needed to be all powerful.

To make matters even more stressful, the project managers tracked us on a weekly basis for our progress on the triple constraints: area, frequency, and power. Keryn Mills was a fiend for tracking every detail. Every week, she posted the progress of each team's triple constraints. If any team did not show progress in one area, Keryn resorted to daily updates in order to apply the most pain. When this happened to my team, I refused to give in to the peer pressure, and Keryn and I stayed at odds with each other over this.

Not everyone in the Design Center liked Keryn. No one likes to be pushed, and Keryn didn't know any other way to get things done than to pound the halls in constant search of progress. She shoved those deadlines down our throats, and sometimes we hated her for it. Of course, the executives loved her and trusted her completely.

I first encountered Keryn several years before on another project.

With a reputation like hers, it usually preceded her, so I conjured up my own image of this fearsome project manager. I expected a savvy, polished manager who dressed in fashionable power suits and never had a hair out of place. When I entered the conference room, I noticed a short middle-aged woman with shoulder-length, frizzy, black hair sitting at the end of the table nearest the overhead projector. She wore a form-fitting striped T-shirt, faded jeans, and well-worn platform tennis shoes. While the room filled with engineers and managers, the woman concentrated on a stack of dog-eared papers in front of her. I kept waiting for this famous Keryn Mills to enter.

Then the woman spoke, immediately taking command of the room, and I realized with a jolt that this was she—the woman that engineers feared more than anyone else. Could it be? She looked more like a biker babe than an IBM project manager.

As I quickly learned, Keryn's domineering style got results, even though she gained very few friends. She was thick skinned, loud, demanding, technically astute, and possessed the memory of an elephant. It was nearly impossible to bluff her, to make her think you were making progress when in fact you were stalled, or goofing off, or trying to recover from missteps in the design process.

Keryn came to every one of Jim Kahle's brainstorming meetings, which evolved into a place to bring back results and kick off new ideas or problems to study. She tracked everything, and I did my best to avoid her. I don't know when she slept, but she seemed to be at the office 24/7.

Out of necessity, we all became masters at juggling many activities at once during the project. In addition to leading the PowerPC design and helping with the overall PlayStation 3 architecture, Kahle asked me to be a part of the STI Design Center's patent evaluation committee. Since the PlayStation 3 was a new start-from-scratch design, it was ripe with opportunity for invention. Kahle encouraged the team to document their innovative ideas in patent applications to add to IBM's heavy-weight patent portfolio. He assigned to the committee the task of determining whether each idea was unique enough to warrant the pursuit of a patent. IBM prides itself in having the largest patent portfolio in the industry, and they even pay small bonuses to engineers for every patent filed.

I enjoyed the patent committee meetings very much, although it was hard to find time to read through the ten to twenty patents up for evaluation each month. The meetings were lively and filled with much stimulating debate. Quite often, we pulled in engineers from the Design Center to justify their patent proposals.

"So can you explain why this idea is unique?" I'd ask.

The engineers were clearly intimidated as they stood before a panel of microprocessor design experts. More than one left the room with his tail between his legs. We didn't go easy on them, but I don't regret that. The process shouldn't be so harrowing that engineers refrained from submitting their ideas; but on the other hand, we wanted to weed out any weak, poorly thought-out ideas. We expected the submitters to be tough enough to be able to discuss the technical details with us. So after the presentations (or the grilling, according to one engineer's interpretation), the committee voted. Normally, we reached consensus. When there was dissension, there were often comments like, "Come on, this is trivial. A five-year-old could have come up with this idea." However, sometimes it was the simplest ideas that were the most innovative.

I encouraged my PowerPC team to submit patents. "This is an excellent way to get recognized and get a little extra money, so put your inventions in writing," I said.

"But what constitutes a patentable idea?" one of my junior logic designers asked.

I smiled. I could talk about inventions all day long. Throughout my career, many mentors, including Jim Kahle, had encouraged me to patent my ideas. "First of all, the invention needs to provide some intrinsic value, like making the chip run faster or improving the performance of a function. The gamers can see that improvement as the commands from their joysticks are translated into action on the video display. They might experience a faster response time from movement of the joystick to scene translation, or they might find themselves immersed in a more realistic game environment. Other patentable ideas might emerge as we design a function that uses less power or takes up a smaller silicon footprint. For the companies that manufacture this chip, those improvements translate to reduced cost."

Now I was on a roll, so I described my first patent at IBM. "Your first patent will be an exciting experience. I wrote my first one two years after joining IBM. I collaborated with another engineer to define a new algorithm for bus arbitration. A bus arbiter is like a traffic cop who directs traffic through a busy intersection. We researched prior patents on the subject of bus algorithms. I talked to other senior engineers at IBM who were experts in the field and asked them about the best-of-breed bus arbiters. My partner and I came up with a new scheme that was more efficient and provided higher performance than any prior algorithm."

The junior engineer's face lit up with enthusiasm. "How did you know what to do next to get your idea patented?" he asked.

"I had help, and you will, too. The whole process was exciting. We met with a patent attorney and described the idea. He searched all of the proper databases for prior art and gave us a stack of patents to review and compare to ours. I had already done a lot of this work in my own research, so I was confident there was nothing out there like our design. The patent attorney then translated it into legal jargon. When it finally got filed with the U.S. patent office, I got a plaque from IBM indicating the name of the patent. You'll get one, too, for your first filing.

"After that, I was hooked. If my fingerprints were going to be on a design, then I wanted to provide unique value. People have often asked me how innovation occurs. I tell them to identify the parts of the design with a problem to be solved. Then just keep chugging away at it in your mind. Sometimes my best ideas come in the middle of the night. I'll run to my desk and scribble down some notes. Sometimes they come when I'm in the shower, or when I'm driving in traffic. I never know when I'll get that spark. It's a combination of identifying the problem to solve, then keeping it in the forefront of your mind. Eventually the answer will come. You have to be persistent. Also, the IBM patent award system provides a nice bonus. I recently earned the Master Inventor Award, which is given to the top inventors at IBM. Stick with it and you can get that kind of recognition some day."

I think I fired that young engineer up that day. He went on to write several patents in the coming months.

During the project, I practiced what I preached by authoring or coauthoring over twenty-five unique patents, covering everything from new high-performance techniques to advanced low-power ideas. I admit that when my PowerPC design team submitted patent ideas to the committee, it was hard for me to be objective. My sales hat sat squarely on my head as I described why each PowerPC invention was the greatest thing since sliced bread.

There was much parallel activity going on at this point outside of those meetings. Within my PowerPC and Memory Flow Control teams, we continued to reshape and move blocks of logic within our little piece of confined real estate, trying to find a way to make it all fit.

"Can't be done!" Jim Van Norstrand declared, and Tony Truong nodded in agreement. Though I was the overall technical lead for both of these units, these two shared the responsibility for the daily one-on-one technical guidance delivered to the team.

Carrying the nickname "Big Kahuna" from his days on the PowerPC 630 Server Group project, Jim was a big, beer-bellied guy who ruled with a big stick. Literally. Everyone knew he was seriously displeased when he walked down the hall with his sawed-off wooden baseball bat, tapping it in his hand as if he was on the verge of taking a swing at someone. People filtered out of their cubicles and quietly followed him down the hall, hanging back a little, glad that he passed by them. Like rubberneckers on a highway who see a cop giving out a speeding ticket, they just wanted to see the poor guy who was in trouble. The bat was only symbolic, but it saved Jim from having to explain his feelings when he marched into the cubicle of an engineer who had screwed up. There was no question the engineer was in trouble. By that point, Jim had already done his homework on the problem at hand and was pretty sure the engineer did something incredibly stupid. He knew how to get your attention.

I liked Jim Van Norstrand. In fact, all the engineers on the team respected and liked him. They went to Longhorn football games together, played poker, knew their way around Vegas. They teased him endlessly and played practical jokes in the office. There was generally a lot of laughter when Jim was around. He did have a darker side though. If he and I had a disagreement, if he got too much flak from Keryn Mills, or if he was so overloaded that he wasn't seeing enough of his family, he would sink into a sullen, moody slump. Fortunately, that wasn't often.

Tony Truong was more aloof from his Memory Flow Control team; however, he managed to endear himself to them anyway. He considered himself a comedian, and he loved to stand in front of an audience (any audience would do) and tell jokes. They were always long, corny, stupid jokes, and everyone groaned dramatically when he launched into one. Mickie organized a team event at a nearby park, where I noticed a small group of people circled around Tony. I could hear the raucous laughter from a couple hundred feet away, so I walked over to join in the fun.

"Please don't tell the one about the plumber again!" the group of engineers shouted at Tony, laughing. They rolled their eyes and shook their heads in mock disgust. The response from the audience was truly funnier than the jokes!

"Okay, okay!" he replied, holding up his hands in mock surrender. He told the one about the plumber anyway.

I heard Tony tell the same corny joke at a retirement luncheon where he served as emcee and at a going-away luncheon and at a staff meeting. As I said, any audience would do, and he always made us laugh.

"Can't be done!" Jim Van Norstrand repeated, as he, Tony, and I studied our bursting-at-the-seams floorplan. When Jim, Tony, and I agreed on something, it was powerful. With the confidence that comes from knowing we were right, we marched into Jim Kahle's meeting one morning to demand an increase in our chip real estate.

We stuck a huge to-scale block diagram of the chip on one wall of the War Room, and I used a red marker to indicate the places where the PowerPC core and the Memory Flow Control unit bulged outside our given boundaries. I formally requested additional space.

John Keaty was the guy responsible for stitching together all the cores and other miscellaneous components into a full chip design, laying down all the complex layers of wiring tracks to connect them, and working with the fab to translate the paper design into a silicon chip. He was the appointed gatekeeper that made sure the chip didn't grow in size. Keaty and Kahle grilled Jim Van Norstrand, Tony, and me to make sure we considered every alternative. Fortunately, we had, and Keaty finally agreed to release some of the space he was holding as a buffer for just such occurrences as this. Keryn, of course, wrote all this down on one of her blue pieces of paper, and we all knew it might as well have been a contract. I had no idea at the time how important— or maybe how *un*important—that contract would become.

Meanwhile, while my team was busy grinding out the detailed PowerPC low-level design, Chekib Akrout and Jim Kahle fielded numerous reporters' requests for interviews. They turned these over to IBM's public relations department, which always politely declined. Guided by Sony's well-defined disclosure rules, all three STI partners agreed to keep secret all STI and PlayStation 3 plans and activities. But word started to leak to the press that something big was going on behind our tightly-closed doors, and it began to feel like we were missing out on some great publicity opportunities. Then one day in the spring of 2002, an industrious reporter from one of the leading trade journals got through to Akrout. He and Jim Kahle skipped over the public relations department and agreed to give an interview. It was an exciting opportunity, and they were naturally flattered by the attention. It's not every day that engineers get to see their names and quotes in a major magazine. Mickie, who was assisting Akrout at the time, quietly escorted the reporter into his executive conference room in the Design Center. The reporter, a woman who looked to be in her early to mid-thirties, came well armed with information gleaned from other sources.

Prior to the meeting, Kahle and Akrout agreed to the type of information they could safely cover without violating Sony's rules (well, at least not by much). However, they hadn't counted on this reporter being so good. She asked very good probing questions and deftly cornered Kahle into unforeseen traps. There was some stumbling and bumbling, but all in all, Kahle and Akrout managed to steer the reporter away from the most sensitive areas. Halfway through the meeting, Mickie suddenly realized that STI confidential information filled the whiteboards that surrounded the walls of the conference room, information that Kahle and Akrout had agreed not to share. Information that the reporter was discreetly copying into her notebook. Mickie nudged Kahle and got him to look up at the whiteboards. His eyes got big for a second, and then he quickly curtailed the meeting.

It's highly likely that Sony and Toshiba were also quietly meeting with customers and reporters around this same time, because the trade journals began publishing more and more information about the Cell chip, much more than could be attributed to what that reporter had gleaned from our one interview. We never experienced any backlash from Sony for this interview, so it's possible they never found out. Or it could be that they were secretly pleased with the press.

October 2002 found us working like fiends under skyrocketing schedule pressure, when we'd all much rather have been out enjoying the deliciously cool weather. Texas summers, which last from May through September, are miserably hot with numerous days of triple-digit temperatures. We have one really great month in the spring, April, when the bluebonnets are all blooming, and another one in the fall, when the weather is comfortable and the lake water is still warm. Then there's a brief winter, where we may or may not see a frost. If you can stand the hot summers, Central Texas is a great place to live, and October is the best time of all.

The managers decided to provide a bit of a relief valve by hosting a Halloween party. In our clumsy attempts at team building, we sought to incorporate pieces of the Japanese culture into the workplace and to introduce our foreign visitors to a little bit of American tradition at the same time. We had tea celebrations as well as barbecues. We made a point to celebrate both Japanese and American holidays, including Chinese New Year, the Cherry Blossom Festival, Fourth of July Thanksgiving, and, of course, Christmas. Surprisingly, Halloween turned out to be a favorite of our Japanese partners. The whole STI team went all out on the costumes—smiling Krispy Kreme donut attendants, spinning ballerinas, grunting cavemen, guitar-playing Mariachi bands, and sword-waving Samurai warriors spent the morning working at their computers.

Even as pressured as we were, we couldn't resist the temptation to take an afternoon off to play every now and again. All morning, I'd heard the laughter and music coming from the nearby break room as volunteers decorated it for the big Halloween celebration. They hung black paper bats from the ceiling, draped fake spider webs across the windows, and twirled black and orange crepe paper streamers around the tables and chairs. When the appointed hour finally arrived, I huddled in the back of the noisy room eating store-bought cake with Jim Van Norstrand while costumed engineers pushed into the room until we all bumped up shoulder to shoulder.

Then Chekib Akrout entered the melee. His huge boyish laugh revved up the crowd as he commented (in Chekib-speak) on each outrageous outfit. He called for a show of hands for votes and handed out awards for the best costumes. Since Akrout insisted that each participant in the contest move to the center of the floor and act out the character they were portraying, it took the better part of the afternoon to get around to the finalists. The crowd roared when Masubuchi, the director from Toshiba—sporting psychedelic shirt, sunglasses, and huge frizzed-out wig—won for his excellent portrayal of Jimi Hendrix. It was totally out of character for this stoic, serious man, but that was the appeal. We all hung around talking and laughing for a few hours, and even though I was trapped in the back of the room, I wouldn't have left even if I could. Our Japanese friends really loved Halloween, and the spirit even rubbed off on us jaded Americans.

Meanwhile, Akrout was busily drumming up additional business for the PowerPC core. The response from potential clients to the high-frequency aspect of the core was very favorable. Akrout asked me, "How fast can we get this core to run? Can you get it to six gigahertz?"

The six-gigahertz target seemed to be the magic mark, but, using IBM's 90 nanometer silicon technology, we were currently designing for four gigahertz. After silicon wafers come off the manufacturing line, the next step is to dice them into individual chips. It was safe to assume that if we sorted those chips according to their achievable frequencies and then plotted that data, the data would define a bell-curve distribution with the peak of the curve (where the majority of the chips fell) centered on four gigahertz. Because of variations in wafer manufacturing, in any given lot some chips ran faster and some ran slower. Without measured data, we couldn't know for certain how far out the tails of the bell curve went, but it was possible that we were going to find some chips that could run at six gigahertz.

I asked a few of my smartest engineers what it would take to increase the number of production-level parts running at six gigahertz. With slightly tighter timing constraints (more design work), a slightly higher operating voltage (more heat to deal with), and cherry picking the fastest parts from the manufacturing line, we were within spitting distance of a low-volume six-gigahertz product. I gave the news to Akrout, and it was like giving a kid a new toy. He was ecstatic.

However, I became concerned that Akrout was trying to take on too much new business too fast. I confronted him about it. "Chekib, while it is possible we can re-target the timing to get to six gigahertz, this will be a significant new effort for our team, and could jeopardize the current PlayStation 3 schedule. I think we should be cautious about taking on any new customers. You're starting down a slippery slope if you want one microprocessor core to serve more than one master." I was already overloaded, and the thought of additional work was not appealing.

Akrout fired back in true cheerleader form, "Dave, you and your team are the best on the planet. Let's shoot for the moon!"

I rolled my eyes and walked away grumbling, "The moon, the moon, the moon . . ."

With this promising outlook on frequency, Akrout secured two additional customers for the PowerPC core besides Sony. The two new customers were Apple Computer and the IBM Server Group. The news traveled fast, and we soon faced a storm of interest from other potential customers. Akrout was one of Big Blue's greatest evangelists, and he loved to spread the word. But was he being too greedy?

I went with him to several meetings with potential customers where I had the opportunity to see this fascinating man in action. He was dynamic, motivating, captivating, and his audience was riveted by the hot new microprocessor he was promoting. It was selling like hotcakes! I could hardly afford the time away from design work to participate in these meetings, but the positive feedback we received from the customers was both gratifying and energizing. I had trouble saying no. Always the optimist, Akrout saw no conflict in pursuing multiple customers, as long as they were willing to accept the PowerPC core "as is" and on the current schedule. Only that's not how it worked in the real world. As I discovered (the hard way), it was tough to design a single product that met the requirements for three different high-profile customers. This was not some general-purpose microprocessor! It wasn't just the technical challenge that was the problem, but also the overhead: three different sets of customer reviews, three different and often conflicting sources of design change requests. It was mind-boggling and exhilarating to be in such high demand. Most of the time, I didn't know whether to laugh or to cry over my sudden popularity.

To add to the misery, my team was working around the clock and starting to complain about the new demands placed on their shoulders. News leaked out to them that Akrout had committed to a 2006 product roadmap that included a PowerPC core capable of operating at six gigahertz. "Six gigahertz! What was he thinking?" they screamed. At that time, Intel was just beginning to offer products exceeding 1.5 gigahertz, and we were already having doubts about our ability to reach four gigahertz for the Sony chip. At six gigahertz, we would not just leapfrog Intel but pole-vault over them.

While the six-gigahertz target caught Apple's interest, they wanted even more. Akrout agreed that if they would put the current PowerPC core into an Apple product "as is" (in other words, exactly as we were designing it for the PlayStation 3 chip), he would start a parallel effort to enhance the current design and meet Apple's future needs. It was a deal.

Akrout asked me to kick off this new effort in my "spare time."

My breath caught in my throat, but I finally managed to stammer, "Chekib, I don't have any spare time left. Do you want me to work twenty-four/seven?"

He patted me on the back and said, "Do the best you can."

So, in addition to my day job of PowerPC technical lead, I began architecting a high-frequency core to meet all of Apple's needs. The task wasn't too time consuming at first. I decided the design needed a simple form of out-of-order processing. I could keep the basic pipeline, which we tuned for high frequency, and add out-of-order mechanisms. This technique allowed faster, shorter instructions to move around slower instructions in the pipeline. It was like standing in line at the bank. With a single line and a single teller, everyone has to wait when one person makes a long transaction. However, if there are two bank tellers, then multiple customers with shorter transactions can move around the slower customer to complete their transactions.

I first designed out-of-order mechanisms on IBM's PowerPC G3 microprocessor. Out-of-order processing requires queues or holding stations to hold instructions while they wait for data to arrive. While these instructions wait their turn, if the next available instruction is ready to go, it can move around the earlier instruction and execute. The trick is to minimize the number of these complex mechanisms in the design, because they have the potential of increasing the risk that the fundamental pipeline will slow down. I applied mechanisms similar to those applied to the G3, providing a nice combination of high frequency and simple out-of-order techniques. My only other experience with out-of-order processing was on the more complex Power4 server class design, an inappropriate style for the land of ultra-high frequency.

It took me a couple of weeks to draw up a rough draft, and then I handed it over to our performance modeling team. Their job was to help refine the details. The pace picked up when Akrout started "inviting" me to meetings with Apple, and I quickly discovered that Apple would require a lot of my time.

Meanwhile, the bricklaying of the PowerPC core continued to proceed nicely. I had completed my job of drawing up the blueprint of the design, and now it was up to a large engineering team to grind out the design through lots of blood, sweat, and tears. During the implementation phase, my role shifted to that of firefighter, enforcer, and cheerleader. I participated in numerous (more than I'd like to count) status meetings. They were painful but useful, as they helped me anticipate the problems and keep an eye on where the project was heading. There were days when I put on my policeman's hat and got the team back in line when they strayed off course. Then there were days when I put on my fire fighter hat and listened to the latest engineering problem needing immediate attention. Most engineering problems have more than one solution, and the trick is to sort through the alternatives and make decisions that factor in schedule, risk, and quality.

In early 2003, one of my IBM engineers burst through the narrow opening to my corner cubicle and whispered urgently, "Have you seen the Sony patents on the Web? Sony claimed they invented the Cell architecture all by themselves! We slaved through Kahle's high-level design meetings together, but they took all of the credit!"

"That is not happening!" I said. In shock and disbelief, I spun toward my computer and jabbed a few keys, quickly pulling up the patents on the Web. Sure enough, there they were. The blueprint for the PlayStation 3 described in all its glorious detail. That was my baby! The *San Jose Mercury News* featured the Sony Cell architecture patents on the front page. Sony filed several patents, claiming they were the sole inventors.

I ran across the building to Kahle's office. "Jim, how can this be? Sony's trying to take all the credit for our hard work."

"I know, and I agree it's a low blow," Jim said, fuming. "I just found out about it myself. It's really disappointing. I have a meeting scheduled with Suzuoki this afternoon to discuss it, so stay tuned. Don't worry. I won't let this one go down without a fight."

Suzuoki was the Director from Sony and surely had to have known what was happening. The Sony engineers seemed embarrassed by the subterfuge, and I got the impression that someone from the higher echelons in Sony had dictated the move. Kahle hit them hard with threats of lawsuits. I wish I could have been a fly on the wall of Suzuoki's office during that conversation. Sony agreed to alter the patents and add some of the IBM and Toshiba engineers involved.

Toward the middle of 2003, as we approached the final stages of the design work, I was blindsided with my biggest problem to date. The Rochester, Minnesota, design team uncovered a major timing problem in the PowerPC memory components. Small memory elements in the core, called caches, store data and instructions close to the executing engines. We had very sophisticated design tools that could predict the final electrical characteristics of these caches, allowing us to make timing estimations before any of the transistors were laid down in silicon. In other words, with a very high degree of accuracy, we could determine in advance if our design was likely to meet our frequency goals. The tools were based on a complex set of rules that calculated the resistance and capacitance of the design. Unfortunately, the Rochester team did a sloppy job on their earlier electrical estimations and did not update those estimations as the design evolved. Data from the final design revealed that the memory elements would limit the achievable frequency of the whole PowerPC design to the 2 to 2.5 gigahertz range, a far cry from the four-gigahertz we promised our customers.

After a sleepless night, I hopped on the first flight I could find and flew to Rochester. How could this team of expert array designers fail like this? The consequences were deadly, for it was far too late in the design cycle to fix the problem. The error was totally unexpected because this team was one of IBM's most experienced in this very specialized type of design work. Trust, but verify. That's what Chekib Akrout cautioned all of us. I was kicking myself for placing too much trust in the team's vast experience and too little focus on verifying that nothing fell through the cracks.

When I arrived in Rochester, I headed straight for the first-line manager in charge of the memory design. I barged in, slammed his office door and shouted, "How in the hell did you let this happen? What kind of engineering shop do you run around here?"

The manager looked as surprised as a deer caught in the headlights. He was just a youngster, a first-time manager. He put both hands up with his palms toward me. "Dave, calm down, we're working on the problem." But I could tell he was scared.

I could feel my heart pounding. I thought of all the times I'd sat in on those status meetings and heard this man give a good report. Too late, I realized that he was just the mouthpiece for his technical team; he was in way over his head. He wasn't experienced enough to spot the problems. I sighed and rubbed a spot near my temple that threatened to explode. "You better be. I want a full review of the design first thing tomorrow morning. Put everything on the table." I pointed my finger at him. "It's time for full disclosure."

I went to my hotel room and called Mickie. Word leaked about the Rochester troubles, she said, and Akrout and Kahle were on a rampage. Together, she and I tried to piece together what had happened. How had we missed this? There were no easy answers. While I was on the plane traveling to Rochester, she had called our IBM team in Germany. Like the Rochester team, they were famous for their expertise in array design. At her request, Juergen Pille, one of IBM's most experienced circuit designers, was already on a plane to the States to help us sort out the issues. A highly respected engineer, Juergen could provide an independent assessment of our options going forward.

A glum Rochester team was waiting for me when I arrived at the plant early the next morning. Lucky for them, I had calmed down some by then. I made them crawl through their design one transistor at a time (or close to it). There was no obvious solution in sight that didn't require a complete restart. It would take months. The rest of the chip team was waiting on us to deliver our final drop of the PowerPC design, so we had no time in the schedule to fix the problem. I made the decision to lock down the design, knowing we would have to fix the problem in a subsequent revision of the chip. Luckily there was a full second-pass chip revision planned in the schedule. It was a long, lonely flight back to Austin that night. I dreaded the inevitable meeting with Akrout and Kahle.

There was an "invitation" from Akrout waiting for me on my desk when I got to work the next morning. Mickie received the same message, and we trudged down the hall together in silence. What could we say? There was no silver lining here, no fallback position, no recovery plan. When we got to Akrout's office, Jim Kahle was already there.

For the first time on the project, Akrout lashed out at me, "Dave, how could you let this happen? You are in charge of the core and everything that goes into it. I am very disappointed in you. I am holding you personally responsible for this." He turned to Mickie. "And you. Why are we just now finding out about this? Weren't you tracking their progress, or did you just stop asking questions?"

Kahle had similar flaming words.

I thought about arguing, but knew it would be pointless. My own first reaction to this turn of events was just as fiery, my own angry words to the Rochester team just as blaming. Instead of explaining what happened, which we knew would only sound like lame excuses for this million-dollar mistake, Mickie and I did our best to explain what we believed was our only course of action for the future. And it was ugly.

With a catch in my throat, I said, "We recommend that you move forward with the design 'as is' for this first spin of the chip. The whole chip team will benefit from having a real chip in hand to test. It'll give them an opportunity to work through most of their issues and clear up any outstanding bugs. We just won't be able to run the chip at full speed. Meanwhile, we'll start working on the fix—the redesign."

Mickie explained the personnel side of things. "Juergen and I have discussed what it will take to fix this, and he's recommending that we beef up the array team with a lot more people. We can pull in more from Germany, a few more from here in Austin, and, of course, the Rochester team. Juergen will be here tonight to help us plan the new work, and I can give you both an update tomorrow on a schedule," she promised. "At first glance, I think we can fix the design and be ready to drop it into the second revision of the chip on schedule."

Kahle folded his arms and gave a little snort, a familiar nonverbal response that let us both know he was not willing to extend us any measure of trust just yet. "Without full four gigahertz capability, we won't be able to test a huge portion of the Synergistic core's operation," he said. "Remember at the beginning of this project when I said that I didn't want the PowerPC to limit the Synergistic core? Do you remember that, Dave?"

I nodded. How could I forget?

Akrout gave us a penetrating stare without even a faint glimmer of his characteristic smile. Neither of them believed anything we said about plans or commitments for the next drop. Who could blame them, under the circumstances?

I mumbled, "I'm sorry I let you down. It will get fixed, I promise." I crawled out of the office, leaving my bruised ego in the dust. Up to this point, I had been Akrout's golden child. It hurt me to know I had let him down.

Mickie followed me out the door. I didn't look at her, but I know she was holding back tears.

It worked out pretty much as we'd said. Juergen helped us ask the right questions, analyze the performance of the existing arrays, and plan the new design work. His assistance was invaluable. The rest of the PowerPC core was completed in time to meet the top-level schedule of the overall chip. It was bittersweet when we released the final version of the design to John Keaty to integrate into the chip, and it was painful to think of the amount of work still ahead of us to fix the timing problem for the next spin of the chip.

CHAPTER 7

Enable Engineering Risk-Taking

Risk-taking forces us to focus on the future,
to take that next big step. It jump-starts
the creative process.

THE SYNERGISTIC CORE WAS THE MUSCLE for the Cell processor. The work that went into this core embodied the notion of engineering risk-taking. It required not only a new instruction set architecture, but also a new paradigm of heterogeneous multiprocessing. In addition to this incredibly inventive, challenging design work, the team signed on to produce a prototype silicon test chip in less than a year. I figured they were either very brave or just totally demented. During the second half of 2001, the Synergistic core team launched into high-level design, running parallel to my design team's effort on the PowerPC core.

The Synergistic core processors made the PlayStation 3 architecture unique. They provided the heavy engineering lifting and gave the design the amazing supercomputer-on-a-chip performance. Sony's Ken Kutaragi wanted to pack as many of these babies on the chip as possible. The initial specification called for six of them on the chip, but that was not the end of the story.

"Eight is beautiful." Jim Kahle dropped this bombshell, and we just blinked at him, stunned, blindsided! Five of us, hastily summoned from various locations throughout the building, dutifully crowded into the tiny office behind Kahle and Chekib Akrout. It was close enough quarters that we could smell each other's sweat, but I swear you could've heard a pin drop. I don't even think anyone was breathing.

"What?" I finally gasped, unable to phrase a more meaningful question.

Kahle leaned on Akrout's desk, supporting himself on the tips of his fingers while he hung his head. He repeated Kutaragi's succinct justification for an absurd demand to increase the number of Synergistic cores on the Cell chip from six to eight. "Eight is beautiful." Kahle was just one heartbeat away from a full-blown rage. I couldn't bear to look at him with all that raw emotion clearly visible on his face. If he exploded, I knew the rest of us would, too. We were hanging on by a thread. I glanced out the partially frosted glass wall just as two engineers slowly passed down the aisle outside, craning their necks to blatantly ogle our high-powered huddle. They probably got a good enough view to feed a dozen or more rumors, all of which would be flying from floor to floor before we left this office. Over the past year, I heard rumors on everything from in-shop romances to impending layoffs, but as they say, truth is stranger than fiction. Kutaragi's demand certainly took the cake. I turned my back to the glass wall.

Kahle and Akrout had stepped out of a private meeting with Ken Kutaragi to strategize with us before responding to this new demand. They quickly replayed the whole discussion, and I could easily visualize the conference room scenario as they spoke. Everything would have been very proper and polite, very structured, as it always was when high-ranking Japanese VIPs came to see us. No doubt the room was sparkling clean and carefully arranged to look spacious and elegant. A spread of delicate pastries and flavored coffees, served on IBM's best china, probably sat virtually untouched on a side cart. Akrout said Kutaragi didn't waste any time getting straight to the point, obviously deeming further justification or discussion unnecessary. He simply waited silently for his IBM partners to succumb to his request.

Kahle barked out orders, but we all knew what to do. It was obvious. "Keaty, put together a plan for a new physical chip implementation," he said.

"You do realize that adding two more cores will require a totally new physical floorplan and only makes our chip's manufacturability that much more difficult. This was already a huge chip, and we're pushing the physical limits," John Keaty was quick to point out.

"Goes without saying," Kahle responded gruffly, obviously not in the mood to debate the issues. "Just do it."

As usual, Keryn Mills, our cast-iron unflappable project manager, grabbed her ever-present stack of dog-eared blue papers. "I need to talk to the chip verification team and to those responsible for the I/O, the ring bus, and the clock grid in order to address the impacts to the overall schedule."

"I want all input by the end of the day," Akrout croaked, as Keryn, her curly hair flying out behind her, darted out the door.

At first glance, this change didn't seem to affect the PowerPC core, the memory subsystem, or my team unless the changes to the chip's physical layout were going to result in changed real estate allocations for us. I wanted to help, but there wasn't much I could do except brainstorm with the others.

Sang Dhong and Peter Hofstee would address impacts (if any) to the Synergistic core team. Akrout patted Dhong on the back, then he and Kahle, looking a little like the wind got knocked out of their sails, headed back to the conference room.

The rest of us stayed in the semiprivacy of Akrout's office to talk through the possible impacts. We were incredulous. After all the daily aggravation we had taken from Kutaragi about the size of the Cell chip creeping ever upward, how could he suddenly decide to grow the chip by a gigantic 20 percent? Where was the sense in that? I suppose it might have been easier to swallow if Kutaragi claimed he needed the powerful computational capabilities of eight Synergistic cores to achieve his grand vision for the broadband market or to make a bigger step up in performance from the PlayStation 2. But "eight is beautiful"? I guess to Kutaragi's way of thinking, eight had a certain aesthetic balance. Or perhaps he simply wanted to push the design as far as possible. But this decision would be very costly both in terms of a larger silicon chip and in terms of schedule. It was a major change, one that we could not absorb without re-baselining the schedule.

By design, the chip was modular so that we would have the flexibility of adding or subtracting Synergistic cores to fit future applications, but none of us dreamed it would happen *now*. Months ago when we exited the concept phase, we agreed to six Synergistic cores for the PlayStation 3. We were deep into the high-level design activities now, and Kutaragi's request would set us back months in some areas.

John Keaty unrolled his well-worn picture that showed the details of the existing chip floorplan and quickly pointed out the most significant problems facing us if we agreed to make this change: "Our only option is to add the two new cores on the right side of the chip, here, but I'm certain the chip's height will also grow when we make necessary changes to the ring bus looping through the center of the chip."

Hofstee jumped in. "There will be significant logic changes to our bus rings and the bus arbiter to accommodate eight requesters instead of six."

In other words, there would be road construction to add new highways, and the traffic cop would have a lot more balls up in the air to juggle. We were already bumping into the maximum manufacturable size, so we were severely limited in vertical growth options. It was possible to go wider, but, of course, that would most certainly decrease IBM's profits. That was the rub. Larger chips meant that fewer could be packed onto a single silicon wafer; therefore, a single run through the manufacturing process would produce fewer chips. It would cost more money to produce the required volumes for the PlayStation 3 launch. Now I understood Akrout's dejected look. Kutaragi's request changed the entire profit outlook for IBM, the primary manufacturer of these chips. While the STI Design Center itself remained a financial boon for IBM, the outlook for the huge profits from the silicon foundry was not so rosy anymore.

Keryn Mills burst back in with the schedule impacts, and they were significant. "I still think we can meet our end date," she said, "but this will eat any buffer we have for the remainder of the project. We can't afford even one more hiccup."

"It's an insane thing to do for this kind of high-risk inventive work," John Keaty growled.

"It doesn't sound like Kutaragi gave us any choice but to concede to his demands," I added. My confidence in our ability to succeed was tumbling.

After Jim Kahle and Chekib Akrout rejoined our group later in the afternoon, they confirmed what we all suspected. Kutaragi got exactly what he wanted. IBM and Toshiba accepted the inevitable schedule hits and the growth of the chip area and the increase in overall power.

Six or eight, it really didn't matter to the Synergistic core team. They were still just concerned with designing one Synergistic core, and they didn't particularly care how many times it was replicated on the chip. I think some of the team secretly liked the fact that more copies of their design would be on the chip. It was like a popularity contest.

So in parallel with the PowerPC core high-level design activites that my team and I were pursuing, the Synergistic core team moved forward on their own design. Experience from the Somerset Design Center days convinced all of us that if IBM went head to head with Intel by building big uniprocessor cores, we would lose again. Kahle wanted a new form of a small, simple accelerator core that would allow him to attack Intel with parallel processing. Small and simple. Small and simple. That's the message he repeatedly hammered into the Synergistic core team.

As Kahle's handpicked technical lead for that team, Sang Dhong ruled with an iron fist, and he took Kahle's direction very seriously. Though he was quite brilliant, Dhong could be difficult to deal with at times. Like all of us, he had very strong opinions when it came to computer design. Only Kahle, when he chose to, could get him to conform. All of Kahle's technical leads (including me) were bullheaded control freaks, but I think Dhong found it most difficult to connect with his team on anything other than a technical level. His adversarial, dictatorial leadership style was effective, but eventually led to some discontent on his team.

I had gotten to know Dhong well during the early days of the STI Design Center in 2001, when we were interviewing job candidates like crazy. We were woefully understaffed and working hard to build a team from scratch. At the end of each harrowing day of interviewing, the IBMers met in a big glass-walled conference room to discuss the potential candidates. Dhong was typically most interested in candidates who graduated from prestigious engineering schools with advanced degrees. He paid little attention to the candidate's personality.

I came from the opposite camp. Partly being serious, partly just to irritate Dhong, I said, "If the guy's got a Ph.D. he's probably got an attitude. So if he's not going to be fun to work with, I vote that we write him off."

Dhong threw up his hands in frustration and rolled his chair back from the table, turning his back to me and mumbling words no one could understand. I loved working with Dhong, and highly respected his technical capability. He was the first person I went to when I had circuit design questions. However, I couldn't help pulling his chain every once in a while. Chekib Akrout, ever the peacemaker, mediated, drawing Dhong back to the table while he warned me to tone it down a notch. Interviewing was such a tedious process; I was just spicing things up a bit.

Dhong was an expert in circuit design techniques used in high-performance microprocessor development, but he knew he needed a strong architect to drive the internal microarchitecture of the Synergistic core. He called up Brian Flachs, a brilliant former colleague from his days at the Austin Research Lab. Flachs graduated from Stanford University with a Ph.D. in electrical engineering, and he lived and breathed computers, and loved to talk shop.

Dhong also brought along some of the best and brightest circuit designers from the Austin Research Lab, Osamu Takahashi and Hwa-Joon Oh. These two rounded out Dhong's leadership team. They, along with Flachs and Dhong, set the personality for the Synergistic core design effort. They were all serious, hard-core computer engineers who seemed to gain a lot of their pleasure in life from designing computers. At happy hours, at parties, at lunch, in the hallway—no matter where they were, if two or more of them were together, they were always discussing some technical design problem. As the project evolved, we saw a marked contrast between the "serious" Synergistic core team and the "fun-loving" PowerPC team. The PowerPC team took on more of my personality and that of Jim Van Norstrand—both of us were known to work hard, but also play hard. Thus began a rivalry between the two core teams that would last throughout the life of the project.

Peter Hofstee was a nice counterbalance to Dhong's heavy-handed rule. He was optimistic, pleasant, and generally got along with everyone. Hofstee was Akrout's personal firefighter, and he went wherever he was needed most. He linked himself to the Synergistic core team early on, unofficially becoming one of their technical leads. As a former university professor, he had the patience and the skills to become the in-resident tutor. He spent many tireless hours explaining new concepts to the less experienced engineers on the team. Hofstee somehow managed to fall into the role of a "high plains drifter," never really owning any one part of the design, but contributing to many different areas. I think I would have liked Hofstee's job on this project. Having no ownership certainly worked to his advantage, and it would have saved me many sleepless nights.

In addition to bringing in Dhong and Hofstee, Kahle called on his old friends from Yorktown, New York, to help define a new instruction set architecture for the Synergistic core. (The instruction set describes the aspects of the design visible to a programmer, including instructions, registers, addressing modes, memory architecture, interrupt and exception handling, and external I/O.) Faced with the ongoing need to have old versions of software run on new processors, the computer industry settled on a mere handful of standard instruction set architectures, like Intel's X86, so defining a new instruction set architecture was a rare and cherished event. Fun work to an engineer.

I guess there is one argument that says Kahle should have opted to use a standard instruction set architecture if he wanted to propel the Cell microprocessor into the mainstream PC world. But one tailor-made for our hardware would really make those Synergistic cores scream, resulting in much higher performance for the games. Adopting a new instruction set architecture was a risky undertaking—it could be a quick death for the Cell chip if those who develop the applications for it find it to be too much trouble to learn a new set of instructions or too complex to program. The boost in performance has to be high enough to make it worth their while. When it came to revolutionizing the game machine, Kahle and Kutaragi were both fearless.

With Yorktown's Marty Hopkins—the famous and well-respected father of the instruction set architecture used in IBM's RISC-based servers since the 1980s—on board, the STI project took on a new level of prestige. STI was the place to be, no matter how intense or complicated the work.

Kahle's goal was to provide game and media applications with improved power efficiency over traditional processors. Exotic heat dissipation techniques were taking a huge bite out of Sony's current profits as the PlayStation 2 developers added costly heat sinks and fans to keep the Emotion Engine cool. For the game machine of the future, the Synergistic core needed to operate at a high frequency while keeping the power low. With a simplified instruction set and a simplified microarchitecture, Kahle felt he had a chance to run the Synergistic core at increasingly higher clock frequencies and still pack more function in the same area.

Simplification was a concept that Kahle was very familiar with from his earliest days at IBM when Marty Hopkins was his mentor. Back in the 1970s, Hopkins capitalized on the notion that most software used only a small subset of the overall instruction set over and over. He eliminated the less frequently used and the more complex instructions. This was the RISC approach, discussed earlier, which allowed IBM to move from their complicated mainframe processors to today's streamlined microprocessors.

In the mid-1990s, Kahle and I sweated together over the Power4 microprocessor design, which was considered a RISC architecture. We brutally whacked out the most complex RISC instructions from a library of over 300, optimizing the design around the smallest, most important subset. As a result, the Power4 achieved the highest frequency of any 64-bit microprocessor in the industry at the time.

One drawback was that we moved a significant amount of complexity back into the hardware to compensate for simplification of the instruction set and to continue to provide higher overall performance. IBM wasn't the only company doing this. Dave Ditzel, a veteran engineer from Sun, noticed this trend toward hardware complexity in RISC microprocessors and attempted to rectify it. He believed complex control functions consumed too much computer real estate and not enough attention was being applied to the real execution engines that produced the results of computations. His idea was to simplify microprocessor architecture by moving much of the complexity to the software instead. He set out on a bold new venture and formed a new company, Transmeta, to build on these concepts. Unfortunately, he attempted to move too much functionality into software and never delivered on his performance claims. His head-to-head battle with Intel over the low end of the PC business ended in dismal failure. But the lessons learned stuck in Kahle's mind as he attempted to find the right balance between simplicity and complexity.

Unlike my PowerPC core, which was constrained by the requirement to be fully compatible with the industry-established PowerPC architecture, Kahle and his architects could afford to take a fresh new approach with the Synergistic core. Marty Hopkins believed that he could remove even more instructions from a RISC architecture set to simplify the design specifically for compute-intensive applications. Because the Synergistic core relies on a traditional PowerPC host processor to handle memory management, interrupts, and caches, Hopkins eliminated these complex and costly functions from the design. The Synergistic core itself evolved into a simple, in-order, two-instruction issue design which runs at a very high frequency.

The magical performance boost comes from the fact that there are so many of them on a single chip.

With Hofstee and the Yorktown folks working on the instruction set architecture, Flachs working on the internal microarchitecture, and Takahashi and Oh working on the physical implementation (circuit design), the design of the Synergistic core quickly took form. Because of the simplification in the architecture, the team could spend most of their time figuring out how to run at a frequency never before accomplished in the industry.

In parallel, development began on a prototype chip or, as we called it, a test chip. The manufacturing process was a weird blend of science and magic, and at these very high chip frequencies, it was not always easy or even possible to predict exactly how a chip would behave once the design was actually cast in silicon at the foundry. Long before the design process would start, the manufacturing facility would hand down design rules to the STI team to make sure that we put together something that was actually achievable in a given silicon technology (90 nanometers, 65 nanometers, etc.). Even so, too often it seemed what worked on the whiteboard didn't come together in silicon. The earlier we could get some or all of the design off the drawing board and into a real live physical silicon chip, the more time we would have to correct any errors in the real product.

The successful design, test, and manufacture of this test chip would also prove that we knew what we were doing, that we had the right tools to do the job, and that we could work together in this novel multinational organization. Of extreme interest to our Japanese partners, it would demonstrate that IBM's latest silicon manufacturing technology was mature enough to manufacture the Cell chip in very high volumes. Because the Cell chip was going to be one of the first to run through the new 300 millimeter fabrication facility in Fishkill, New York, there was a high probability that we would encounter problems along the way. We needed to get some learning under our belts before we put the full chip through that process, so it made perfect sense to siphon off some of the team to work on this test chip.

IBM often used test chips to flush out tricky circuits that could only be fully characterized once they were implemented in silicon. However, Chekib Akrout and Ken Kutaragi, both optimists and overachievers, demanded that we put the entire Synergistic core on a test chip. No one had ever done this before! No one had ever put an entire core design on a test chip because it would be such a huge drain on the team. Not to mention that this request seemed utterly impossible to accomplish on the current schedule.

Though Dhong and Hofstee each put on a brave face, I heard from others on the Synergistic core team that they believed they were being set up for failure. No matter how many hours a day they worked, even if they pretty much lived in the Design Center for the next four months, they still would not be able to do what Akrout was asking. They feared the end result would bring irreparable damage to their reputations. In the meantime, who would be working on the real product? The integration team was only one-deep (no duplication, no backup) in most of the critical skills, and they were the ones who would be in high demand—on both the test chip and the real product—to lay out the clock grid, to stitch together the designs from all the engineers, and to lay down the metal tracks between components.

Nevertheless, the test chip plans rolled on like a freight train, unstoppable. Kahle made sure it was the first area staffed, leaving the rest of us to meet our deliverables with limited resources and creating much interdepartmental tension.

The risks quickly piled up. For Dhong, Hofstee, and most of the Synergistic core leadership team, this was their first taste of putting together the design of a microprocessor that would actually become a product. In their previous experience in a research lab, they could cut many corners and leave parts of the design at lower quality, since their test chip would never become a real product. When they applied these same shoot-from-the-hip design practices on our test chip, they found themselves butting heads with some of STI's chip-level integration folks who came from the more conservative Server Group processor design team. Server chips had to be perfect; no corner cutting was ever allowed. The Cell chip's lead integrator, John Keaty, was very upset with Dhong's loosy-goosy design practices, and tempers flared. The shouting matches completely stalled the design process as Keaty fought to bring the Synergistic core design practices in line with those dictated for the whole STI Design Center.

For the most part, I was not involved in the test chip work, but I witnessed plenty of fireworks. In one encounter, the normally soft-spoken Keaty shouted at Dhong and the Synergistic core integration team: "I will not allow you to jeopardize this project with any sloppy work! No one gave you permission to deviate from the design rules, so you better clean up your act immediately."

Dhong yelled right back, "We made the only design choices we could under this ridiculous schedule."

Hofstee backed up Dhong's claims. "Kahle told us time and again that schedule is our highest priority for this test chip."

I'm sure Dhong felt pressured to make many design decisions based on expediency and not necessarily on the best long-term solution. He ignored design guidelines, those rules thoughtfully and painstakingly defined for the entire chip by the convergence team, a group of handpicked Distinguished Engineers and senior technical staff members. Instead, in his characteristic bullheaded way, Dhong used trusted tools he was familiar with. But Keaty was the man in charge. Red-faced and breathing hard, he wouldn't back down. He demanded compliance, and Dhong flat-out refused.

Akrout attempted to be the peacekeeper and to arbitrate a truce, but his attempts were ineffective. He was unwilling to dictate a solution, so the problems just festered. Then the fearsome Keryn Mills took control and made the hard calls. She forced Keaty to accept some of the practices that Dhong's team used, because it was too late to start over. She forced Dhong to conform to as many of the established design guidelines as possible, and she put a halt to his renegade design practices.

Though I didn't always agree with her tactics, I had the utmost respect for Keryn. She was a forceful and decisive project manager who carried around a million dates and design specifics in her head. Her knack for being able to sort the key tasks from the trivial stuff—not always easy since everyone thinks their own job is so important—was phenomenal. And you better have your facts straight when you talk to her, because they would come back to haunt you if you were wrong. She would remember! We bowed to her demands and did our best to meet her rigid schedules, because we feared the consequences of not doing so. The executives were huge fans, because they could count on Keryn to pull, push, prod, or bully a team to on-time delivery. But she was also known to leave dead bodies in her wake. She was either loved or hated. I don't think it was possible to be lukewarm about Keryn.

Once the test chip team was over the hurdle of adhering to the design guidelines, another challenge appeared. Akrout pushed them to achieve full frequency and full function. They worked night and day, tweaking the design to get record-breaking timing, working diligently through every bug, no matter how severe. Work on the test chip consumed them, yet they needed to move on to the real product. Eventually, reality set in and even Akrout realized that putting such a high-quality Synergistic core on the test chip was actually adding significant risk to the final PlayStation 3 product deliverable. He backed off, and Hofstee and Dhong sent the test chip off to the fabrication facility with a lower frequency than the final product and at lower quality.

In the background, there were many "I told you so" comments directed at Akrout. The experience damaged the morale of the Synergistic core team and left many feeling like failures. This insane request put the first chink in Akrout's armor, and for the first time the team questioned Akrout's leadership. My view from a distance was that the test chip was a success. They had pulled the design together and finished the test chip in record time. More importantly, the test chip had served as a pipe cleaner for many of the Design Center's tools and methodologies. I had nothing but admiration for Dhong and his team.

CHAPTER 8

Enable Corporate Risk-Taking

Everything's a risk. Sometimes you have to gamble
big to take the whole poker pot of money.

THE PLAYSTATION 3 was a monumental design effort, full
of complexity and challenge, but overall proceeding as well as any difficult project could be expected to. Then in late 2002, the shit hit
the fan. That's when Microsoft came knocking on IBM's door about
an Xbox follow-on project. It was a risky proposition. Sony had a two-
and-a-half-year head start, so Microsoft knew they were late to the
game again. However, they were willing to take huge corporate risks
to get back in the game and beat Sony to market.

If I happened to be the richest man in the world and my software
dominated the personal computer market, what would I do for an en-
core? I can say with certainty that the thought would never have entered my head to engage mega-giant Sony in a war over who was
going to rule the game machine market! But then, I'm not Bill Gates.

As I discovered later, Microsoft's bid for world domination via the
living room actually began back on Valentine's Day in 2000, when
J. Allard, a restless young corporate vice president, met with executives Bill Gates, Steve Ballmer, and Robbie Bach to convince them to

make the $2 billion commitment to build a video game console. He sketched out an ambitious multiyear roadmap that showed how Microsoft could get to a product that would eventually trounce Sony, the powerhouse in the game industry. Gates was intrigued; he believed Allard's plan was the key that would open the door to the home by turning the living room into a digital, wireless, networked computing and gaming nerve center. It was finally feasible now that all media could be digital, including: movies, music, games, cameras, phones, and TVs. Bach liked the idea and wanted to develop the Xbox without using Windows, Microsoft's goldmine operating system for the past twenty-five years. That was a stretch for Gates, and the proposal made him pause. Ballmer, on the other hand, thought both Bach and Allard were crazy and pushed back hard. Sony was so far ahead with the PlayStation, he reasoned, and it would be impossible to have a product ready for a head-to-head confrontation at the Christmas 2000 launch of the PlayStation 2. Nonetheless, Allard convinced both Gates and Ballmer to take the leap even though the first few years would be tough and probably not profitable.

Looking back at these events as an outside observer of history, I am amazed that Gates decided to buck the odds. Time to market is everything, and there are countless examples where the better product failed to excel or even survive in the marketplace simply because it was not introduced first. Remember Betamax versus VHS? The latecomer is almost always at a disadvantage and faces many significant barriers to entry, including the necessity to overcome the consumers' natural resistance to change. As Ballmer predicted, Microsoft was unable to put together a product in time to compete with the Christmas 2000 launch of the PlayStation 2, which was the hottest-selling item that year. Sony cleaned house. When the Xbox game console arrived on the shelves more than a year later, Microsoft faced a steep uphill struggle in the market.

Most financial analysts agreed that latecomer Microsoft suffered a major setback and lost forever the opportunity to capture a more significant portion of market share. By the time the Xbox launched, hundreds of thousands of gamers worldwide had already made their product choice and had tied the knot by heavily investing in their own personal libraries of PlayStation and PlayStation 2 games. But Gates entered the race with his long-term strategy firmly in mind. The goal, not to be forgotten in the hoopla of the PlayStation 2/Xbox competition, was to get to the point where he could launch the follow-on Xbox 2 (later named the Xbox 360), the initial product that would allow Microsoft to expand from the PC into the living room. The original Xbox was a necessary stepping stone.

To achieve Allard's roadmap, Microsoft was necessarily under severe schedule constraints during the design of the original Xbox. In an attempt to reduce the design-cycle time, they adopted Intel's off-the-shelf Pentium III microprocessor and force-fitted it into the Xbox. In a remarkably successful rush job, Microsoft sold over 1.5 million Xbox consoles in North America between the mid-November launch and the end of calendar year 2001. The Xbox was suddenly the biggest threat to Sony's domination of the game console space. Game development for the Xbox proceeded at lightning speed on its Intel X86 microprocessor. This was the same X86 architecture used in practically every PC on the planet, so all software developers were intimately familiar with the design. There was no learning curve. And though Sony was on its way to selling 250 million PlayStation games a year, Microsoft made powerful inroads as gamers bought more than three Xbox games with every system, the highest-ever "attach rate" for a video game console launch. They may have been late to the ball, but Microsoft was still able to produce the fastest game console available and the first one to include a hard disk space comparable to that of a PC.

Making a profit, on the other hand, was more difficult for Microsoft to achieve with Xbox. Instead of developing core components in-house, Microsoft outsourced the expensive parts to Intel for the central processing chip and to NVidia for the graphics chip. They were painfully aware that custom hardware would have allowed them to better control costs and achieve the best price-performance ratio, but Allard's production timeline simply wouldn't allow it.

Since Sony's parts were custom-made, they were able to reduce the cost of their hardware by combining the central processing chip and the graphics chip into a single unit for the PlayStation 2. Consequently, the price of the PlayStation 2 dropped from $299 to $149. Sony even made a small profit on the game console. Microsoft, however, could not motivate Intel or NVidia to reduce the cost of the Xbox chips, nor did they have the opportunity to combine the two chips into one, as Sony had done, because they were dealing with two different vendors.

About the same time that Microsoft launched the original Xbox in late 2001, I was barely getting my feet wet in the PlayStation 3 project. The ink was still wet on the contract that bound Sony, Toshiba, and IBM into the STI partnership to start development of the Cell microprocessor. At that point, the Xbox was an interesting phenomenon, but only so much as it represented Sony's hottest competition.

Still breathing hard from the Xbox race, the Microsoft team quietly regrouped. It was important to get the follow-on design right, so they carefully analyzed the competition, listened to their customers and their game developers, and learned. They embraced Gates's bold vision for a digital entertainment system that included the ability to play and record CDs, play DVDs, plug in a digital camera, plug in an iPod and listen to music, play online games with a global team, and hold live chats with other gamers. Those were the functions near and dear to the hearts of the generation whose lifestyles revolved around being connected.

With the passion of an unlikely underdog, Microsoft began a relentless pursuit of the means to beat Sony with their Xbox follow-on. Billions of dollars were at stake as the two competitors raced to be the first to market with the next generation consoles, and they were gearing up for a new world war. Microsoft went to Intel, AMD, and others, but found nothing off the shelf that met their requirements, and those companies were unwilling to design a custom solution. If Microsoft had any hope of competing and profiting in a next-generation console market, they needed a customized processor to provide a quantum leap in game experiences. So it was at the very end of 2002, just as the STI Cell chip was undergoing final wiring in preparation for fabrication of its first prototypes, when Bill Gates approached Sam Palmisano, CEO of IBM, about teaming up to design the microprocessor for the Xbox follow-on game and entertainment system.

An IBM/Microsoft pairing was surprising to say the least, as they had a long, well-known history as bitter rivals dating back to the 1980s when they collaborated to deliver a revolutionary new PC. At that time, IBM hired Microsoft to develop an operating system for the PC. Unbeknownst to IBM, Microsoft reportedly bought QDOS (Quick and Dirty Operating System), from Seattle Computer Products, for a mere $50,000 and then modified it for the IBM PC. Gates talked IBM into letting Microsoft retain the rights to market this operating system, MS-DOS, separate from the IBM PC project. Despite schedule problems, contrasting views of the product security requirements, and a clash of corporate cultures, IBM introduced the new PC in 1981. Developing the operating system had been a true labor of love for Microsoft, but to IBM, the PC was just another product. And Microsoft, just another vendor to IBM, was not even invited to the product launch ceremonies.

By allowing Microsoft to sell MS-DOS for use on non-IBM platforms, IBM unknowingly opened the floodgates for PC clones. The supersonic rise of the clone business took the entire industry by surprise. Compaq beat IBM to market with a portable PC clone in 1986, capturing a sizeable chunk of the market right out from under the sleeping giant. Failing to realize the ultimate significance of compatibility across platforms, many computer manufacturers (IBM included) developed personal computer models that were not 100 percent compatible with the IBM PC, making expensive software packages obsolete with every change in hardware. IBM made other major blunders by introducing proprietary technologies that only intensified the incompatibility issues.

Over the years, Microsoft and IBM continued to argue over operating systems, with Microsoft trying to convince IBM to go with Windows. IBM chose instead to develop a proprietary operating system, OS/2, and enlisted Microsoft's help in writing it. This created years of controversy as the two companies argued over where each product fit into the marketplace. The relationship between IBM and Microsoft finally exploded and evaporated, with IBM taking over the job of trying to write OS/2, and with Microsoft going full speed ahead with a plan for Windows to dominate the world. Though IBM compatibles still owned the home and business computer market, by the early 1990s IBM's influence over the PC architecture dwindled to irrelevance, yielding instead to the powerful combination of Microsoft's Windows operating systems and Intel's microprocessor architecture.

In reality, IBM practically gave away the PC business. The suspicions, rumors, and corporate jealousies between Microsoft and IBM have continued to thrive over the years, even to this day.

So it's significant that these two rivals would once again seriously consider a joint venture, but it's even more astonishing that the product that finally drew them together was a game machine. That's certainly evidence that these corporate visionaries recognized the enormous potential of the game industry and, putting aside their differences, opted for a piece of the pie. When Microsoft came knocking, IBM tentatively opened the door.

Gates hoped to pool his team's software and games expertise with IBM's computer design and semiconductor foundry experience. With that powerful partnership, they could deliver unprecedented entertainment experiences with the Xbox follow-on while simultaneously creating new business opportunities in the technology and entertainment industries.

At the time that Gates and Palmisano met, IBM had just formed a new division whose mission was to provide engineering and technical services to other companies; hired guns, so to speak. "Services" was the new buzzword at IBM, after all. This organization (E&TS) was eager to prove itself and viewed the Microsoft deal as a mouth-watering opportunity to show their ability to capture big contracts. Initially E&TS offered various previously designed products, known as embedded cores or virtual components. These cores have already been through rigorous functional verification, and customers often integrate them with other peripheral or application-specific devices to help speed up the design process for system-on-a-chip solutions. IBM has a whole product line of these embedded cores, such as the PowerPC 440, that they presented to Microsoft. None of these options appealed to Microsoft—which was also Sony's response when they saw these same offerings a couple of years before. Time continued to march on.

In spring of 2003, Adam Bennett, an IBM Distinguished Engineer in Rochester, Minnesota, presented Microsoft with high-level information about a novel high-frequency microprocessor core still under development within IBM. The core he described had an operating power of less than 10 watts when it was running at four gigahertz. In comparison, the personal computer microprocessor cores from Intel and AMD at the time were in the range of 50 to 75 watts at 1.5 gigahertz!

Finally, IBM was showing an option that caught Microsoft's attention! Nobody in the industry had anything like that in the works or even on the drawing board. Intel and AMD remained focused on their bread and butter traditional PC chips and were unwilling to invest in such a custom paradigm-shifting design. Besides, Microsoft had already been down the road with Intel and was looking for a way out.

The PowerPC microprocessor core Bennett disclosed to Microsoft was close to what they wanted for their next-generation Xbox, but Microsoft wanted some additional features including a wider instruction issue design and a more powerful vector-processing unit. The wider instruction issue would allow more game code instructions to be fed to the execution units that performed the computations. A more powerful vector-processing unit allowed faster execution of the game code instructions, and faster is the key to creating the impression of realism in the games.

Unknown to Microsoft (or Sony or Toshiba or me), the design Bennett proposed was in fact my PowerPC core, the one designed for the PlayStation 3. Bennett worked side by side with Kahle and me in the very early stages of the definition of the Cell chip prior to his transfer to E&TS, and his idea was to extract the PowerPC core and beef it up to meet Microsoft's needs. With these enhancements on top of the already high-frequency, low-power PowerPC core, Microsoft was ready to jump on board.

Chekib Akrout began to hear tidbits about the presentations to Microsoft at executive-level meetings with his boss, John Kelly, IBM's senior vice president in charge of the Microelectronics Division. But so far, no one asked for Akrout's opinion or his participation. He discussed the Microsoft deal with Jim Kahle, and both men were alarmed by the potential impacts. Adam Bennett had not consulted with them prior to his presentations, and the idea of using a component from the STI chip was disconcerting. Though all three STI partners previously agreed to the use of parts of the Cell chip in future derivative parts, and it was certainly within IBM's rights to do so, it never occurred to anyone that this would happen before the Cell chip was completed and the PlayStation 3 launched. So it wasn't illegal, but it reeked of unsportsmanlike conduct.

Oblivious to the storm brewing back at IBM, Microsoft was eager to move ahead, and the next step was to write a contract agreeable to both companies. This was no simple task under the best of circumstances, but with IBM and Microsoft's history of contentious software wars and costly litigation, expecting either side to trust the other was not realistic. Inevitably, the entire contract process got bogged down with the corporate attorneys.

As word reached Akrout that the Microsoft deal was indeed going through, he found he had very mixed feelings. Though Akrout had not been involved in the romancing of Microsoft up to this point, John Kelly now wanted him to take the lead. Of course, he was honored by the high level of trust Kelly placed in him but, on the other hand, he was extremely uncomfortable with this new responsibility simply because Microsoft was Sony's closest competitor. His position as leader of the STI Design Center and of chip development efforts for Apple and Nintendo was consuming, and he had poured himself into developing strong personal relationships with his Sony and Toshiba counterparts, as had his team. His own internal conflict was exhausting, and he knew the situation would be extremely difficult for the team to understand.

It was the summer of 2003, and I had been working tirelessly at IBM for two and a half years, breathing life into the Sony PlayStation 3 microprocessor chip. We ordered our lives around the idea of beating Microsoft to market. Slotted for a Christmas 2005 launch, our chip was going to power the PlayStation 3 to new heights of computing power and market share. Gamers worldwide would flock to the platform to blow away ghouls, race speedboats, and seduce bikini-clad vampiresses.

Now Akrout was telling me we had a new customer for our baby. It was Microsoft. We were about to be competing against ourselves.

I was numb when I left Akrout's office. My first instinct was to turn to Jim Kahle, who was still my mentor and one of my closest friends (in spite of all the work-related stress and strain). Kahle was one of the best and brightest IBM ever produced. I needed someone who would let me vent. No one would understand me like he would.

"Jim, did you know about this Microsoft deal?"

Kahle came around his desk and quietly closed the door of his office before answering. He turned to face me. "Yes, but I only heard about it just recently." A flash of fury blazed in his eyes.

"You mean they didn't consult you before they presented our design to Microsoft?" I was incredulous. I sensed part of his anger stemmed from the fact that this news took him by surprise. I could relate to that. He was a recently promoted IBM Fellow, the highest rank on the company's technical career ladder, and the overall chief engineer for the STI project. He should have been told about corporate's little dance with the devil.

"Disclosing the technical details of the processor unit to Microsoft was reckless. This could potentially blow the entire alliance," he said, speaking of the partnership between Sony, Toshiba, and IBM, which he helped to forge.

Many times over the years, he had spoken of a grand and glorious future in which chips from the STI alliance not only took over the game market but the entire home computing environment, replacing every household's PC and powering broadband home servers, high-definition televisions, and handheld devices. There were even plans for high-end IBM supercomputers. It was a "palmtops to teraflops" vision. In this vision, scalable versions of Cell processors would power everything from low-end devices like mobile phones all the way up to massively parallel supercomputers, which would compute floating-point operations on an order of magnitude greater than any existing computers. The Microsoft project threatened that vision. Kahle believed that his crackerjack processor design team would be stretched too thin, and he would get less mindshare for his world-conquering vision. He worried that the engineers would become so consumed with the Microsoft project that they would not be available to create innovative solutions for the STI project. He saw STI as IBM's next big growth opportunity, one of those twenty-year pivot points similar to IBM's s/360 mainframes from the 1960s. He liked the idea of his name being attached to it. He worried that IBM, with this flirtation with Gates, was trying too hard to please too many customers.

"They just need to learn to say no," Kahle said.

Though Akrout wanted the potential Microsoft deal kept under very tight wraps, that afternoon he gathered a handful of his most trusted technical leaders and managers to review Microsoft's requirements. We met in the conference room adjacent to his sixth floor office. The air conditioner struggled under the load from a sweltering summer day, so we were all hot and sticky. Akrout was uncharacteristically agitated, unable to sit still for more than a few moments at a time.

"I need your best assessment here," he said, pacing back and forth across the conference room floor. "Are these requirements achievable? What are the pitfalls?"

I quickly pointed out my biggest concern. "Even though the two PowerPC cores will be similar in many respects and can share many of the same subcomponents, there will be significant differences, too, driving the requirement for more design and vertification resources and more testing."

Mickie feared our team was already spread too thin, even with twenty additional Sony and Toshiba engineers. She reinforced my point. "Only IBMers could make the new enhancements to the core for Microsoft. Where would these extra people come from?"

"Unfortunately, there will also be more chance for error as the team struggles to keep the two designs straight in their minds. As much as I hate it," I said, "if IBM decides to go forward with this Microsoft deal, we need to keep the Sony and the Microsoft PowerPC cores as similar as possible . . . but separate."

"What about the technical requirements?" Akrout reiterated. "Can we meet them?"

"Absolutely," I said.

"Probably," Peter Hofstee replied, nodding his head.

"Given enough time and people," Mickie added.

"But *should* we? That's the question I want answered," Kahle challenged. "Just because we can meet their requirements does not mean that we should. We are jeopardizing our relationships with Sony and Toshiba, who are very high-value customers as well as our partners. We're risking hundreds of millions of dollars here. Doesn't that make you pause?"

"I understand your concern. We all feel the same way," Akrout said. "Sony and Microsoft are competitors. But they can both be our customers. I think the train has left the station on that one, Jim.

Microsoft wants us to deliver an enhanced PowerPC core in time for a Christmas '05 launch, and I need to know if we can do that. That's all."

During the ensuing months of legal maneuvering, Jim Van Norstrand and I commiserated on our impossible task. "We have to continue to keep Microsoft's desired changes in mind as we make day-to-day technical decisions. Once this contract gets nailed down—and it will—we don't want to have to backtrack and rip up stuff to add back in the features they asked for," I said.

Jim shook his head. "I know, I know. I'm trying to keep the design flexible and easy to modify, but in reality, as this legal finagling stretches out, the design work is going right ahead as planned without any of the changes that Microsoft wanted."

Jim spoke the truth, and I knew it. We couldn't proceed on faith in a contract that may or may not materialize.

Of course, the Sony and Toshiba partners could know nothing of these discussions, so more and more often, there were closed-door IBM sessions where they were not invited. Rumors were flying. The stress between the STI partners began to percolate, especially at the engineer level where strong friendships and collaborative working relationships thrived.

The IBM/Microsoft contract went through revision after revision over the summer of 2003. Jim Kahle was adamantly opposed to anything that could potentially impact the STI project, including the signing of a contract with Microsoft. Because of his hard stance and because of his position as the technical director for the PlayStation 3 chip, Kahle was (rightly so) not allowed to participate in the contract work or negotiations with Microsoft. Under duress and sworn to secrecy, I was drafted to help write the technical details of the contract while the attorneys attempted to capture all the right legal jargon. Meanwhile, my lengthy absence from the technical leadership of the ongoing PowerPC and memory subsystem work was creating a problem, though Jim Van Norstrand and Tony Truong did their best to keep things going in the right direction. Jim and I constantly stepped on each other's toes as we both attempted to assert consistent leadership over the team, and he began to resent my sporadic reappearances. I had no choice but to continue working on the contract, but I kept a tenacious grip on my leadership role, too. It's where my heart was.

The first pass of the contract was a frustrating disaster, and it appeared the IBM/Microsoft relationship was never going to get off the ground. Microsoft included numerous penalty clauses for missing key chip metrics such as chip area and performance and for missing dates for key design deliverables. In total, the penalty clauses amounted to hundreds of millions of dollars of risk to IBM, and IBM had no choice but to walk away from the deal. This time, Jim and I stopped thinking about Microsoft's desired design changes altogether, and with considerable relief, pushed full-steam ahead with the original Cell chip design. It was a load off my shoulders.

In Oregon and California, Microsoft was in turmoil. They knew they needed this technology and could not afford to wait for another company to develop it from scratch. Bill Gates met privately with John Kelly, without the lawyers. The two executives quickly reached a handshake agreement, and then called the lawyers in and bluntly told them to make it happen. It took several costly months, but they came back with a contract without penalty clauses. The second time around, the contract closure went much faster, and in September 2003, the unlikely partnership was formed.

Shortly after the contract signing, I flew to Rochester, Minnesota, to meet all of the new Microsoft players in an Xbox 360 kickoff meeting. (Microsoft actually coined the name "Xbox 360" much later, but for clarity, I'll continue to call it that here.) For obvious reasons, "Xbox 2" sounded like it was a generation behind the new PlayStation 3, so the Microsoft team came up with the more competitive "360" to imply that the gamer is at the center of the experience. The kickoff meeting, held offsite at IBM's Customer Briefing Center, bubbled with a level of excitement not usually found in an engineering environment. First, I met Todd Holmdahl, the Microsoft vice president in charge of hardware development. I was surprised at how young he was. I also met Bill Adamec and Dan Cooper, who would serve as project managers. Larry Yang was the executive in charge of the game chips. Finally, I met Nick Baker and Jeff Andrews. Nick was in charge of the overall game hardware and Jeff was responsible for the central processing chip architecture. I found out I would be working closely with Jeff on the architecture of the central processing chip.

Holmdahl kicked off the meeting. His laid-back nature and casual dress (he was in blue jeans) set the tone. The overall mission of the project, as he described it, was to deliver an unparalleled new game console for a worldwide Christmas '05 launch. I was amused as each new speaker got up on stage and highlighted the importance of achieving that Christmas '05 launch. The messages all sounded the same: "Blah, Blah, Blah, Christmas '05 launch!" Partway through the meeting, with the lights turned down low, they gave us an early peek at a yet unreleased version of *Halo*, the premier game which would run on the Xbox 360 someday. The demo was flashy and loud and sure caught everyone's attention. I thought, Wow, Sony never put on a show like this at the start of the PlayStation 3 project. I liked Microsoft's enthusiasm.

My first encounter with Robbie Bach, Microsoft's president of Entertainment and Devices, in charge of the Xbox development, was at a round table discussion he held with the IBM leadership team. He was only in his early forties then, but it was easy to see why Microsoft had promoted him to this high a level at such a young age. At six-foot-three-inches tall, he had a commanding physical presence, but when he strolled into the room, it was his confidence that I noticed first. As soon as he spoke, I liked him. He let us know in no uncertain terms that Microsoft would achieve a Christmas '05 product launch. He was self-assured and smooth and said all the right things. By the end of the meeting, he had me convinced that we would actually pull it off. Bach and the entire Microsoft team were laser focused on the end result—a Christmas '05 product launch—and what that would mean for the fortunes of their company. Christmas '05 was soon stamped on all our foreheads.

Bach, the son of a former Schlitz Brewing executive, received a degree in economics from the University of North Carolina and an M.B.A. from Stanford. He joined Microsoft upon his graduation from Stanford in 1988, and he has been moving up at an accelerated pace ever since. Bach may not have the Midas touch, but I'd say it's pretty close. In the early 1990's, he was the executive in charge of the marketing team that rocketed Microsoft Office into the number one position, where it is now Microsoft's second most profitable product suite, claiming billions in revenue. He wields a lot of power, able to tap into his company's massive treasure troves to go after new opportunities.

Microsoft knew going in to the Xbox project that they weren't likely to make a profit for quite a few years and, sure enough, they burned through plenty on the original game machine project. That level of expenditure clearly sent the message that the company stood behind Bach and his vision. As top dog in the Xbox team, Bach was the never-give-up warrior that led the charge to make online gaming a key feature of the Xbox. And it was under his leadership that Xbox overtook Nintendo's Gamecube to stake a claim on the number two spot in game consoles.

Bach had an interesting view of the entire project. It really wasn't just about making some fast computer chips. It was about the entire product, hardware and software. It was about lining up cool game titles like *Halo 3* at stores like Circuit City and Best Buy, and building up the hype. He was responsible not just for the development effort, but also for the relationships with retailers and partners who would get the product into the customers' hands. He had a good grasp of all aspects of the business. He knew when to be an aggressive risk taker and when to reduce risk with defensive measures to ensure he met the end goal.

The executives, managers, and engineers under Bach—like Larry Yang, Jeff Andrews, Greg Gibson, Bill Adamec, and Todd Holmdahl—were just as driven and talented. Each of them seemed to have real independence and weren't afraid to make decisions to move the project forward. They were empowered, thanks to Bach's confidence in them.

Chekib Akrout was initially reluctant to take on Microsoft, but that didn't last long. He was an ambitious, upward bound executive, and it was his nature to expand his domain. Once he met with these Microsoft executives, their mission became his. He was in full support of their project, which in his mind, didn't negate his allegiance to the STI project. Kahle, on the other hand, was ultraprotective of the STI project. He resented Microsoft's intrusion into his nice little pre-planned community. He became grumpy and difficult, especially when he had to work with me or anyone else remotely associated with the Microsoft project.

As for me, the longer I worked with the Microsoft engineers, the more I liked them and identified with them, and the more I wanted to see them succeed. Though I could still sympathize with my coworkers who detested this new mission, somehow, my own internal conflict grew quiet.

Sony's Ken Kutaragi, a senior vice president and father of the PlayStation, exuded charisma and power, like Robbie Bach. However, the cultural differences in the two companies showed up in neon colors at lower levels of executives and managers. Where Bach left the day-to-day operations in the capable hands of the people who worked for him, Kutaragi had to be involved in every decision, it seemed. Strange, for a culture that thrived on consensus, that he should be such a dictator. The team of Sony engineers and managers that drove the everyday operation of the project was conservative, calculating, and slower to act or react. This is not to say that they weren't very smart guys, because they were. Brilliant even, some of them. But they came from a different culture, where the company hierarchy played a much stronger role. They suppressed their own opinions and favored those of their superiors. Getting information up the ladder and decisions back down was sometimes a very slow and tedious process. But I guess a positive benefit is that it saved on time spent in arguments. All of this isn't to say that they weren't decisive, either, because once a decision was made, it was easier to climb Mt. Everest than to change their minds.

The management styles in both of these companies clearly started with the dynamic personalities at the executive level. My own personal style resonated more with the Microsoft team, but I can also see benefits in Sony's strict hierarchy. Bach and Kutaragi, both of them decision makers, risk takers, and visionary leaders, were taking us along on an adventure into the unknown, charting a course for Christmas 2005.

Everything is a risk.

CHAPTER 9

Stay Positive, Even in the Swirl of Controversy

Discontent can spread like a disease and
destroy a team's will to persevere. Mistakes
occur in the natural course of the creative
process, and disagreements arise. The leader's
job is to take the nuggets revealed
through that controversy and piece them
together into a realistic positive outcome.

THE SIGNING OF THE MICROSOFT CONTRACT, a
controversial and unpopular business decision, had a significant impact on my team. Many IBMers felt as Jim Kahle did: that the deal
forced them to betray their Sony and Toshiba partners, people who la-
bored side by side with them, coworkers who had become friends in
spite of the language barriers and cultural differences.

Before the Microsoft deal, we barthopped, boated, and snow
skied together. There were frequent parties, sometimes based on creative themes designed to add some fun to the Japanese-American cultural exchange. Brian Hanley, an outgoing fun engineer on the team

who often took the role of social host, was famous for his theme-based parties. At one event, they took turns in rough and tumble sumo wrestling matches wearing oversized, puffy bodysuits. In another, Brian rented a mechanical bull, and they all played like reckless cowboys. After a weekend hair-dyeing party in Brian's garage, a half-dozen or more young engineers showed up on Monday morning with bleached blond hair. (The Japanese among them were coiffed in Texas Longhorn orange.) This camaraderie was something we celebrated and encouraged. Making this multicultural connection grew into a passion in and of itself, perhaps even to the point where it bumped into our technical and business goals. The whole STI team, from executives all the way down to the newest employee, worked hard to create a fun, fair, and respectful give and take, a win-win experience that crossed global and corporate boundaries. We all drank the Kool-Aid. Caught in our isolated bubble of a happy, idealistic partnership, we forgot for a while that we were competitors, corporate rivals with different maps for the future clutched in our hands. It shouldn't have surprised me when Kahle and many others on my own team came to resent the role I played in the Microsoft negotiations. After all, I helped pop the bubble. Still, it was a very sad day for me when I realized that some of the team thought of me as a traitor.

With the Microsoft deal locked in place, Chekib Akrout suddenly faced a huge dilemma. It had been a very difficult uphill struggle to staff a design team for Sony's PlayStation 3 chip as well as one for Apple's PC chip. The delayed staffing created heavy burdens for the sparsely populated teams to carry as they struggled to keep on schedule. We were all stretched to the limit. Everyone was tired. Now Akrout needed yet another team, all IBMers, to design the modified core for Microsoft. To top it off, IBM was now in a virtual hiring freeze, and John Kelly required written justification on every new hire.

In October 2003, Akrout called his managers and key technical leaders to an emergency meeting in Raleigh, North Carolina, to solve this resource problem. We flew in late the night before the meeting, and Kahle, a few others, and I stayed at the hotel bar with Akrout until well past midnight. The stress was taking a serious toll on our relationships, but the situation always improved, even if only temporarily, after a few shared drinks and some laughter. I needed all the respite I could get. Dave Appenzeller, a third-line manager in Burlington, Vermont, and another of Akrout's protégés, also joined us. Appenzeller was responsible for the Apple PowerPC business. I quickly gained tremendous respect for this insightful, fun-loving, honest man. He and Mickie already shared a close bond, having served as peer managers for some time, and now I had a chance to get to know him, too.

The weather turned nasty in Raleigh overnight, and a cold wind drove the rain ahead of it, whipping splashes of water under our fluttering umbrellas and into our faces as we trudged across the enormous IBM parking lot the next morning. The windowless, overheated conference room was already jammed with Raleigh managers and senior engineers when I arrived with the weary Austin contingent.

We shuffled around, unpacked laptops, removed coats, stowed our wet umbrellas, and then introduced ourselves to Akrout's Raleigh team. Akrout, of course, already knew them. As I shook hands with these guys, I sensed their hostility, but I pretended not to notice. They had experienced significant turmoil in the past couple of months, and many of them blamed Akrout. I guess they thought anyone who came from Austin was part of the problem.

I purposely took a seat on the sidelines, right between two glowering Raleigh teammates. Call me brave. Mike, the antsy one sporting a graying, neatly trimmed beard, seemed to be overly anxious for us to get the meeting started. Anger was spilling off him like water over Niagara Falls. The other, Pete, looked like he was fresh out of college, and I wondered what he was doing in this meeting, but then I overheard him talking about his son who would soon start college. Something about encouraging him to go into any field other than engineering. His words were tinged with bitter disillusionment. Mike and Pete were both first-line managers.

I knew the Raleigh story. Over a period of maybe a dozen years, the team there established themselves as IBM's experts in embedded microprocessor design. They designed a family of embedded cores like the PowerPC 440 that both Sony and Microsoft had rejected for the game consoles. A steady customer base supported these products, designed for integration into low-cost products such as network switching components, set-top boxes, printers, and communication systems. This was the bread and butter mission for the team in Raleigh, and they believed in it, put their hearts and souls into it. I heard rumors that they were in financial trouble. The profits simply were not there anymore, so with direction from John Kelly, Akrout had cut almost the entire mission a month before, stopping nearly all embedded projects.

Naturally, this drastic action angered many in Raleigh, those who built their careers around the embedded technologies, customer base, and family of engineers. It was very personal for them, and they blamed Akrout. I could see it in their faces, hear it in their voices. For some, it was simply too difficult to let go of the dream, to say goodbye to well-known customers that counted on the next product, and to watch all the results of a decade of hard work simply disappear. Those in the conference room with us wore the beleaguered and shocked look of victims.

In a sense, it was understandable, for they just lost a lot of friends. In a mass exodus, fully one third of the 100-person design team—among them a powerful vice president, two of his most loyal senior managers, and several popular technical leaders from the embedded project—chose to leave IBM and join a newly formed high-tech company, Qualcomm, which recently settled in North Carolina's Research Triangle Park area. I figured the two men on either side of me probably still felt extremely loyal to the management team that had left IBM, and they felt mistreated. Who wouldn't feel that way under the circumstances? I'd been in their shoes before myself. Akrout was trying really hard to show them a promising future, to make them feel valued and respected. I heard rumors from my sources in Austin that he gave significant retention bonuses to the remaining team in Raleigh just to keep them on board.

Apparently, that hadn't been enough to smooth their ruffled feathers. Akrout attempted to open the meeting with a pep talk about all the exciting work that lay ahead of us, but the Raleigh guys just wouldn't let him finish talking. Mike, Pete, and the others had some things to get off their chests first, and there was no stopping them. Here we were, they said accusingly, trying to put together a credible resource plan to cover all the gaps, and yet it had only been a month since Akrout drove out a few dozen of IBM's best. They just couldn't see the sense in this, and loudly voiced their doubts about his ability to lead a team out of a wet paper bag!

To his credit, Akrout was very patient and diplomatic and allowed them to interrupt. He didn't even ask them to lower their voices. Nor did he attempt to justify or explain his previous actions. When he didn't rise to the bait, the angry spate of words eventually played out, and we were able to get back to the agenda. Akrout would be fighting an uphill battle if he planned to refocus the remaining Raleigh engineers onto the STI, Apple, or Microsoft projects. Gaining their cooperation and full commitment was unlikely, but how were we ever going to solve our problem without them? I guess that's why Akrout called this particular meeting in Raleigh, on their turf. He needed the Austin team to make the first move, to reach out to this wounded and bitter group.

Mickie Phipps arrived midmorning on a red-eye flight from California after presenting the project status to Microsoft executives. She worked most of the night on the plane to fine-tune spreadsheets showing how many people she still needed to fill out the PowerPC core design teams for the Sony and Microsoft products. Apple and the Server Group, our other two PowerPC core customers, were somewhat willing to accept the Sony design and the current schedule, so we were conveniently ignoring any hints that they might want something different. Akrout's job, of course, did not end with staffing the two game console projects; he was also still responsible for development of the PowerPC chips for Apple, the chips for Nintendo, and the remaining embedded microprocessor projects.

In exhausting brainstorming sessions that extended well past midnight, we examined and debated countless schemes for mixing and matching projects and people, looking for the right combination that would free up enough engineers from the existing IBM talent pool to fulfill the needs of all the design teams across Akrout's realm. We created, manipulated, and crossreferenced mind-boggling spreadsheets that compared the resource demand for all of IBM's commitments to the available pool in Austin, Raleigh, Rochester, and Burlington. It was extremely difficult to get our arms around this complex problem. IBM leadership at the highest levels gave top priority to the existing STI project and the new deal with Microsoft, considering all other projects and missions as possibilities for the chopping block in order to free up resources. Tempers flared as managers held stubbornly to their teams and to the projects that inspired and united them.

With our resource demand for nearly four hundred engineers, the PowerPC cores for the PlayStation 3 and the Xbox 360 were a huge focus. If we'd had a more relaxed design schedule, we could have completed the job with far fewer people. Mickie and I divided the design tasks, carving out a big piece for the Raleigh team to own. For many reasons, it was a risky approach. For one, it was going to require them to climb a very steep learning curve very quickly. Second, they were accustomed to working on projects where the entire team was under the same roof, like a very close-knit family. Here they were being thrust into a new dynamic, where the project's technical and managerial leadership teams were in Austin, while the rest of the team was spread all over the world. Their piece of the pie no longer seemed as significant and their in-house leaders were now "taking orders from Austin" (from Mickie and me). I wanted to tell them to suck it up, but Mickie convinced me that would be a little harsh. Third, the pull from Qualcomm was still very strong, with mouth-watering offers of stock options, the opportunity to get in on the ground floor on a new product line, and the promise of a more rewarding work environment (the grass is always greener . . .). Working-level engineers who had resigned from IBM and followed their beloved leadership team to Qualcomm were actively recruiting their buddies who remained behind at IBM, telling them of the sweet deal where everything was familiar, comfortable, predictable. So even though it was risky, I recognized the need to give Raleigh a significant and meaningful piece of the mission—and to be patient.

Day after day, night after night, we continued this painful process in the same stuffy conference room that now smelled strongly of leftover pizza, donuts, and scorched coffee. We were exhausted and cranky. Dave Appenzeller and Mickie took over the whiteboard and led the discussion, struggling to find the right mix of task assignments and people to give us a shot at success for both STI and Microsoft. Mickie refused to budge on the high resource requirement for the PowerPC core, even though she suffered a lot of badgering from the other managers.

"We've been running too lean for the past year," she said, "and we can't afford to keep going that way. Look at what happened with the timing problem on the arrays. That's what we get when we overload the team. Those mistakes were very costly, and we don't want a repeat."

Eventually, we were all convinced that no matter how we juggled, staged, augmented, stretched, or double-booked our resources, there was still a gap of about a hundred people from achieving full staffing, even with the addition of the Raleigh team. In the shaky economic environment of late 2003, hiring a hundred additional engineers was completely out of the question, especially in light of the fact that the staffing need was relatively short term. Would IBM have enough projects lined up for them next year or would a layoff be required to rebalance the workforce? A complete unknown, and an unacceptable risk. As the managers in the room knew well, the hiring process itself, not to mention the training of new hires, would create a huge burden for them and for the technical leads on the project, soaking up time and energy none of them had to spare. Hiring contractors was not a feasible solution either. Even if we could find enough qualified contract engineers to fill the gap, we couldn't do it fast enough to save the project.

It finally boiled down to two choices for Akrout:

(1) Bite the bullet and hire the additional engineers required to complete both PowerPC core designs, keeping the Microsoft and STI projects separate.

(2) Convince Sony and Toshiba that they should accept the new modified core, thus allowing both game chips' requirements to be satisfied by a common core design (and a common design team).

If Sony could be convinced to pick up the new design, the staffing problem would be at least partially solved and the two chips would share a common core, greatly simplifying bring-up and long-term support of the two products. Though the potential savings was enormous, this plan was not without major risks. For one, it required us to design a new microprocessor in just eleven months—a feat never accomplished at IBM or anywhere else. Many people thought it was sheer madness to attempt to do so. But I guess we were committed to doing that for Microsoft, no matter what we decided here about the staffing or the STI project. Moving to a common design added great risk to the

PlayStation 3 chip since it meant this new untested core would replace the PowerPC core which was practically finished. Sony's planned 2005 product launch schedule would be stressed to the limit. IBM would have less time to build the necessary volumes of chips for Sony's launch, and the games developers would have less hands-on time with the hardware to code new games to package with the consoles at launch.

I both feared and relished the idea of the common core. I'd already seen how complicated things could get with more than one customer, but it was very hard to resist the allure of the spotlight, too. When Akrout asked us if we could deliver a common core in time to make both Sony and Microsoft successful, Mickie and I said yes. We believed it, too, in spite of the challenges.

The final missing piece to the staffing puzzle was all of the miscellaneous chip-level logic required for testing and debugging the chip. Akrout awarded this design work to a team in Austin led by the second line manager Steve Curtis. His small design team was available because their work supporting the PowerPC 440 embedded cores had been scrapped along with so much of the Raleigh work.

Akrout finally adjourned the torturous Raleigh meetings, and he and Jim Kahle flew to IBM's headquarters in New York to confer with John Kelly. Once there, they weighed the pros and cons of both options. Akrout relayed the passionate pleas of proponents on both sides as well as the opposition from overloaded engineers and stressed-out managers. Kahle voiced his adamant opposition to any action that would add risk to the STI project, but he was overruled. Akrout and Kelly decided the common core was the only acceptable choice.

In retrospect, I can't help but think their decision was strongly influenced by the fact that Sony had only recently altered the entire IBM profit outlook by adding the two additional Synergistic cores to the PlayStation 3 chip. So even though Sony was considered one of IBM's most valuable long-term strategic partners and Microsoft was not, the Microsoft relationship and the revenue it could generate suddenly grew in importance.

With this controversial decision made, Akrout found himself utterly alone and in a very dark place. He had a tricky situation on his hands. First, he had to convince his own skeptical team that this common-core decision made sense, something he assured Kelly he could and would do. The problem with that promise was that Jim Kahle still ruled the team, and he was far from "bought-in." Kahle was a true-blue IBMer who would toe the line, but Akrout knew that most people on the team would be able to see through his fake veneer of support. He really needed Kahle to do more than just say the right words; he needed a show of force and enthusiasm. Second, Akrout had to convince the Sony and Toshiba partners to accept the new modified microprocessor core. He had to provide them with assurance that the benefits of the new design outweighed the additional risks. For that, he needed Kahle's full endorsement.

I wish I could have been a fly on the wall for the private discussion between those two willful, powerful, yet adamantly opposed men as they came to terms with the new reality. I'm quite certain it would have been entertaining at the very least.

Initially, convincing the onsite STI directors, Masakazu Suzuoki from Sony and Yoshio Masubuchi from Toshiba, to switch to the new PowerPC core was not that difficult. Akrout previously conceded to several major design changes at Sony's request (including Kutaragi's "eight is beautiful" demands) and could reasonably expect some amount of fair play. It also helped that Akrout and Kahle were well respected and trusted by these Sony and Toshiba partners. All three companies were committed to helping each other achieve success, and Suzuoki-san and Masubuchi-san believed that Akrout would not knowingly do something to jeopardize that partnership or their mutually assured success. Akrout pointed out the virtues of the new core, touting its higher performance with the wider instruction issue and a more powerful vector unit. Kahle indicated that IBM planned to build this core for another (unnamed) customer anyway, and that it was in STI's best interest to pick up the new design in order to avoid the higher risk of splitting the team. He hinted at the possibility of using the new PowerPC core in IBM's low-end servers, which was a true statement but not the whole story. There were now plans to use the core in Apple products as well as in Sony's archrival Microsoft's game machine. As they said in an old Monty Python episode, "Nudge, nudge, wink, wink. Say no more." IBM was going to have to pull people from my team, Kahle explained, in order to meet this "other" commitment.

Akrout, Kahle, Suzuoki-san, and Masubuchi-san flew to Japan to present this new proposal to the Sony and Toshiba executives. With considerable reservations, they agreed to bow to IBM's wishes on this point. However, to reduce risk, Sony opted to stick with the vector unit defined on the original PowerPC core. They didn't see a need to take advantage of the more powerful vector unit planned for the "other" project since the Sony programming model called for most of the game code vector computations to be done by the Synergistic cores. I didn't like that stipulation at all, because it meant that my team had to design a PowerPC core that could interface to either the old or the new vector unit. It was like having a powerful, monster truck with two detachable, interchangeable transmissions. Who would ever do that on purpose? It was feasible, but it was just one more complexity to add to our already convoluted workload. It also meant that we needed more people on the Raleigh team to support two different physical implementations of the vector units. Additionally, our Rochester team, who designed the original vector unit, would have to continue to support the old design, so they wouldn't be free to move on to other assignments. Our "common" core was suddenly diverging again and bumping up against our fragile resource solution.

With that potential crisis hovering on the horizon, I tackled restructuring the work assignments (again). The presence of the Sony and Toshiba engineers in Austin complicated my decisions. I wanted to minimize their involvement in any design work directly related to the major new features for the Xbox 360. In addition, I was really tired and struggling against a tidal wave of uncertainty. Was I fooling myself, caught up in Akrout's enthusiasm and optimism? Or could we really pull this off? The consequences of failure were too scary to contemplate. I supposed I could put my badge on the table and walk, or just refuse to take on the Microsoft chip. The thought occurred to me. Life might be easier if I just said no.

These thoughts ran through my head as I gazed out the floor-to-ceiling windows that covered two walls of my corner cubicle. It was a cloudy, blustery day, and the tall, skinny cedar trees that uniformly lined the front lawn bent back and forth in unison, like a synchronized dance troupe.

I pushed my useless regrets aside and called on Jim Van Norstrand to brainstorm some ideas with me. We commandeered a conference room, and I went directly to the whiteboard and started listing Microsoft's new requirements. The diagram I drew showed the partitioning of the current core with its major functional units. The instruction unit (IU) handled fetching and dispatching instructions. The execution-unit (XU) handled all the execution of normal fixed point and load/store instructions. The vector unit (VSU) handled all of the vector and floating-point operations. Finally, there was the Memory Flow Control unit which we expected would have a lot of similarities to the one being designed for the Sony chip, except that it would be designed to handle three PowerPC cores instead of just one.

We were living on the edge, talking about the competition in an STI conference room, where one interior wall was a partially frosted glass window. It would not be all that difficult for a Sony or Toshiba engineer to walk around the corner and see our diagram and notes if they happened to be at the right angle. I constantly checked over my shoulder for hallway intruders. It would be a disaster if one of the Sony or Toshiba partners gained access to this list of Microsoft's design requirements. It was an eerie feeling, like being in the middle of some complex corporate caper.

Just as I did on the original design with the Rochester and Yorktown teams, I wanted to give the new Raleigh team some meaty and self-contained units. As we looked at the headcount and the skills, the only thing that made sense was to give them the new vector unit and the new Memory Flow Control unit for the Xbox 360. Raleigh had some really green engineers, so I knew I would be making a lot of trips out there.

Next, we drew a functional diagram to help us better understand how we could partition the instruction unit and the execution unit among the current Austin design team. We wrote names by each function to show which designer owned it. We subdivided some blocks and added a few new names, not wanting to reassign anyone unless it was absolutely necessary, because the learning curve was so steep and time consuming. It was unfortunate, but a couple of the most vital pieces of logic were owned by some of our more junior engineers. We wondered if they were ready for this. They were smart people, no doubt about it, but this was tough stuff. I thought about "Hubcap" (so nicknamed because he liked to hang around the directors, executives, and other big wheels). We put his name next to one of the most complex pieces of the design. He was aggressive and smart, but green. Would he be up for the challenge? What I really wanted to do was to give this logic design assignment to Masa, an extremely bright Sony engineer. But of course I couldn't, because it would give him too much inside knowledge about Microsoft's new vector unit.

Jim Van Norstrand and I leaned back in our chairs and continued to study the diagram. Neither of us spoke for a long time.

Finally, he looked at me, and I looked at him. He nodded. We knew what had to be done.

"If we give these assignments to these guys," I said, "you know we're going to have to stay on top of them. It could get tricky in a hurry."

Jim seemed resigned to fate. He rolled his eyes and said, "All we can do is try. They'd be very pissed off if we didn't give it to them, you know. There'd be a mutiny. Besides, what options do we have? This team is already spread so thin."

We shrugged our shoulders and decided to go for it (as if we had a choice). Before we left the room, we meticulously copied our diagram onto paper, and then thoroughly erased the board.

Needing to reassure myself that Jim and I had made the right task assignments, I went to see Hubcap. He was an energetic superhot Purdue graduate, hungry for the recognition he would gain from solving big problems. The fact that he was already generating patents confirmed (at least in his mind) that he was on a fast track to an executive position. Maybe he was. He was definitely bright enough, but I thought he needed a little more experience down in the trenches with the troops before taking over the CEO's position. I hired him fresh out of college for this project, so I found it amusing that he held such grand visions for his future with IBM. He was still so young, one of the so-called Millennials, the new me-generation.

It was already late evening as I walked toward Hubcap's cubicle on the other side of the building. I thought about the day in early 2001 when I first interviewed him. I instructed him to meet me at the security station in the pink building next door to the one that housed the STI Design Center. After signing in there (where his briefcase was inspected), following me through a maze of magnetic card readers at the doors and on the elevators, signing in once again as he actually entered the Design Center, and then finally signing a strict nondisclosure agreement, the wide-eyed young Hubcap questioned, "What exactly did you say you were designing here?" It did have the feel of a top-secret military facility, but I assured him that the high level of attention to security was necessary only in order to protect the three companies' proprietary data and market advantage.

The Sony and Toshiba employees were restricted to the two floors that housed the STI offices, and even IBMers were restricted from freely roaming in and out of the Design Center floors—only those IBM employees who were a part of the STI design team had access. We considered all others as guests and escorted them at all times. STI confidential information was strictly limited to those with a "need-to-know," which was a little too military for many of the veteran IBMers, who were used to being able to talk freely within the walls of IBM.

During the interview, I gave Hubcap a sheet of paper and asked him to design some moderate engineering widgets. He flubbed it. Later he said, "Wow, I can't believe you guys hired me after I screwed up your questions."

I told him, "Having the right answer was not as important as approaching the problem in the right way. Besides, you seemed like you would be a fun guy to party with."

And I was right on both counts. Hubcap was fun to party with, and he had strong engineering skills and an even stronger work ethic.

When I turned the corner near his cubicle, I was not surprised to see him still at work, even though most people had departed hours earlier. He was peering through his thick glasses at his monitor, tugging on his unruly hair, twisting it into comical tufts all over his head. I startled him out of his concentration when I said his name, and he jumped. He looked a little wild with his blue eyes magnified behind his glasses and his hair poking up in every direction. I was proud of my protégé, but I couldn't help but laugh at him, too.

Hubcap was excited by the very important and very complex

work I was assigning to him, instantly promising to tuck the extra work into his "spare" time. He was a newlywed, and I knew that he wasn't seeing much of his young wife lately, but I didn't feel too badly about loading him up with more work. If he wanted a fast track to the executive world, he was going to have to earn it by demonstrating that he was better than all the other hotshot engineers on the team. As I walked away, I felt slightly more comfortable, but I knew we were going to have to keep an eye on all of our junior engineers. They were eager to please, but hadn't made enough mistakes yet to fear their own inexperience.

Soon there was a dramatic increase in the number of IBM-only meetings, both one-on-ones and group gatherings, and the tension in the Design Center was thick enough to cut. Behind closed doors, my team argued that working for Microsoft was a conflict of interest for them and for their Sony and Toshiba friends, who were unknowingly designing and verifying logic that would be going into their competitor's product.

"Do you think Intel worries about delivering the same chip to Dell and to Gateway?" I said. "It's up to those companies to provide product differentiation. We just have to change the way we've been thinking about our core and, to be frank, we've been living a fairy tale. It was nice while it lasted, but now it's time to get real. IBM is entirely within their rights to market the PowerPC core to multiple customers. You've been at all-hands meetings where Akrout and Kahle showed a number of products, besides the PlayStation 3, that will carry this chip in the future. Well, the future is here, and its name is Microsoft. So get with the program."

It was a hard line to pull, but I knew that I had to get the team past the emotional upheaval. I was already tired of coddling them. We were wasting time with all this yakking about something we couldn't change. It was time to move on, to get back to work.

One young, idealistic engineer came to me with tears brimming in his eyes, completely stressed out by the Microsoft deal, an unwilling participant in what he considered unethical shenanigans. He was one of our very brightest engineers, and the last thing I wanted was for him to become so disillusioned that he left the company. I moved him to an area where he would only be dealing with STI work. That seemed to work for him, but he continued to be a vocal (almost belligerent) opponent of our work on the Xbox chip. He reveled in bringing up touchy topics in mixed company—in other words, in front of our Sony and Toshiba partners—just to watch us squirm as we tried to keep the lid on Pandora's box. Mickie and I frequently had to rein him in before he pulled others down that rabbit hole yet again. Jim Kahle could have taken lessons from this outspoken young radical!

Things really got exciting when Microsoft launched a travelling roadshow to kick off the Xbox 360 project at the various design sites. I dreaded the day they came to Austin, because we couldn't exactly invite the whole core design team to the meeting. It would really liven things up to invite the Sony and Toshiba partners to the Xbox kickoff meeting, wouldn't it? These were strange times at IBM. Akrout agreed to allow Steve Curtis's team to go to the meeting along with a handful of my core IBM designers. We hoped it would be enough critical mass to convince Microsoft that we really had a dedicated design team. They, of course, still had no idea that the PlayStation 3 team was developing their core. It still seemed deceptive, not being able to invite the entire core team to the meeting. Here I was again, caught in a strange, international spy drama.

The roadshow invitation arrived via e-mail, vaguely indicating 10:00 A.M., 1st floor, Building 908, which was a neutral building in the same complex as the STI Design Center. Realizing I still needed to find the specific meeting room, I took the short hike over from my office and arrived a little early. I wandered around the first floor and poked my head into some conference rooms, but I couldn't find anybody I recognized. I soon wound my way into the main cafeteria. There was a large, open space in the back of the cafeteria that often doubled as a conference room for large audiences. The room was already two-thirds full, and people were still gathering. A group near the front was setting up the video presentation for the Xbox 360 meeting. I almost choked. This was an open meeting room. Many of the Sony and Toshiba engineers from the STI Design Center ate lunch in this cafeteria every day and would most certainly stumble onto this meeting!

I grabbed the first manager I could find, someone from Steve Curtis's organization whose name escaped me.

I gripped his arm and stepped in close, bringing our faces nearly nose to nose. "Are you crazy?" I whispered. I know he sensed the urgency in my voice, because he turned a shade paler. "You can't have this meeting here. You need to find a conference room where you can close the door for privacy. The Sony and Toshiba engineers cannot be exposed to this!"

The manager stammered, "Don't you think you're overreacting?"

That pushed me over the top and I marched to the front of the conference room area. With a little yank, I unplugged the overhead projector. I pointed to the gape-mouthed manager and said, "You. Grab that projector." I faced the crowd and waved my arms until I got everyone's attention. "Folks, we're moving this show to another conference room. Follow me."

I led the way to the second floor and (luckily) found a large, empty conference room. The bewildered group of engineers tagging along behind me grumbled and whispered, but I ignored it. I assigned people to collect more chairs, arrange the room, and set up the projector, all before our Microsoft guests entered. The meeting was a success, but I made a few enemies among the IBM folks. There were a lot of "who do you think you are" stares, but I couldn't let it bother me. I had to protect IBM's interests as well as those of my Japanese friends.

The grapevine grew heavy with rumors shortly after the appearance of a subtle, no-fanfare public announcement about IBM and Microsoft's partnership on the Xbox 360 development. That's the kind of juicy stuff an ambitious junior engineer would find on the Web just seconds after it was posted. One of the Toshiba managers who worked on the PowerPC core brought a printout of the announcement to me, and asked me what chip was to be used for their competitor's box. Of course, I feigned ignorance, but made sure he understood that even if I had known, I wouldn't have shared the information with him. "We don't share customer confidential data." At that point, we were under strict secrecy orders.

The now-suspicious Sony and Toshiba engineers on my team began to decipher the whispered gossip they were hearing from an unhappy team's hall talk. When new features necessary to support the Xbox were added to the design, they struggled to understand our (IBM's) mysterious motivations for changes that Sony didn't need for the PlayStation 3. They gathered intelligence, scooped up tidbits of information and rumors, and built their own understanding of the real situation, finally seeing that they were all working on the very microprocessor core that would help their fiercest competitor, Microsoft—the "other customer" Kahle had mentioned when he convinced them to accept the common core. They went straight to Suzuoki and Masubuchi with this news, who, I'm sure, were on the phone to Kutaragi within minutes. Soon, I saw many Sony-only or Toshiba-only meetings as they attempted to explain to their own employees what they thought was happening.

As our Japanese partners came to grips with this unexpected dilemma, a new tension in the STI partnership developed. The Sony and Toshiba engineers working on the core exhibited very uncharacteristic outbursts of anger and became much more vocal in the design process. They were wary, and a general air of mistrust hung in the STI Design Center. Friendships floundered in the midst of this turmoil. I felt especially disloyal to some of the Japanese engineers who were also my friends, like Hiroo. It was hard for me to look him in the eye during this dark time.

Amazingly, Sony and Toshiba stuck with the program. I guess it was the only choice, given how much money had already been spent.

Even after all this pain and agony, even after all the difficult and controversial decisions, we still didn't completely resolve the staffing shortfalls. In addition, we had a new PowerPC core design that was still in the concept phase. We had lots of ideas about how to meet Apple's high-performance needs and lots of ideas about how to meet Microsoft's expectations. But our design ideas had not converged yet on a buildable solution that we could take into a high-level design phase. With the short amount of time remaining on the schedule and with a huge amount of difficult redesign work still ahead, drastic action was required to reduce the risk to Microsoft's and Sony's 2005 product launch plans.

At this point, the workloads were almost unbearable. Mickie and her three first-line managers were providing dinner every night of the week to any PowerPC engineers who were willing to keep working through the evening. Then they started delivering lunch on Saturdays and Sundays. It was a monumental effort to keep this going, especially when they began including the other teams (Synergistic core, software, convergence, etc.). Mickie finally rounded up all the other first- and second-line managers in the Design Center and started a rotation scheme to help with fetching and delivering meals, giving her three first-line managers a little relief. One enterprising manager, Gilles Gervais, launched a custom-designed program on the Intranet that allowed the teams to sign up for meals and even place specific food orders from menus. I can't say it made up for all the lost time with our families, but it certainly helped to have a good hot meal instead of chips and cookies from the vending machine.

As if I didn't have enough stress in my life, the new PowerPC core created yet another processor war in IBM. Our friends at Intel and AMD, who already completely owned the PC space, had spent the last few years busily working their way up the computing food chain with a new breed of microprocessor targeted at low-end servers. They enabled companies like Dell and Hewlett Packard to develop inexpensive servers and sell them for ten to twenty thousand dollars. This intrusion into the server business represented a huge threat to IBM, who made most of its hardware profit from selling big expensive servers. Their machines used PowerPC cores like the Power4 that Kahle and I designed, and cost anywhere from several hundred thousand dollars to over $1 million. IBM failed to react quickly and lost a lot of market share in the low-end server space. They feared that Intel and AMD would eventually replace even the more expensive IBM servers. Some reporters who followed the technology trends predicted that these dinosaurs were in the death throes of extinction.

In true form, IBM created a low-end server task force and directed Kahle and me to serve as members. Kahle took the opportunity to push his own agenda to proliferate the use of Cell chips, but most of the other IBM folks were not willing to swallow the software overhaul that would be required to use the Cell chips this extensively. However, there was some interest in using the as-yet-unrealized six-gigahertz version of my PowerPC core to take on this new threat from Intel. It really came down to cost. Traditional server chips are very costly due to their low volume usage. Intel and AMD reduced the cost of their devices by leveraging higher volumes of the chips in other products. My PowerPC core was small and inexpensive. We could use

Apple's higher volumes to keep the cost low, and Microsoft's Xbox 360 project covered most of the engineering cost to develop it. However, many old-time IBMers in the Server Group still had a "Not Invented Here" mentality. They didn't want this renegade bunch from the STI Design Center to upstage them.

The culmination of the task force took place in IBM vice president Vincent Jennings's conference room in Poughkeepsie, New York. The plush room oozed with lavish luxury, carrying the look and feel of a megacorporation's exclusive board room. Rich wood covered the walls, and a large mahogany conference table filled most of the floor space. Jennings strolled in with all of his bravado. The last ten years at IBM had been good for him. He rose to the level of senior vice president at a very fast pace, riding the coattails of his first management success in mainframe servers and following that up with the ultrasuccessful Unix server, the GigaProcessor. However, he was out of touch with the emerging client side of the business, and he completely missed the emergence of cheap X86 Intel and AMD low-end servers that were rapidly devouring his precious server volumes.

I hadn't seen Vincent in several years, but rumor had it that he was not a big fan of engineers who left IBM and then later returned. We had been good friends in my Power4 processor design days, but times were much different now.

Vincent took his seat at the head of the massive table, rested his elbows on the tabletop, and folded his hands under his chin. I thought for a minute that he was going to lead us in prayer. "So, what do you have for me?" he asked.

As the senior IBM Fellow on the task force, Kahle rose to summarize their conclusions. "Basically, Vincent, it boils down to cost. How should IBM attack this new threat from Intel and AMD? Should we attack it with cost-reduced versions of the current Power4 and Power5 style server chips or go with a smaller, cheaper PowerPC chip like the one being designed for STI or Microsoft?"

Vincent interrupted. "First of all, I would have never signed the Microsoft deal. But that's history now. What I want is one PowerPC core that covers both the low-end server space and the game space. I want the Power5 to be the base for this new core."

Trying to keep from rolling my eyes at Vincent's ludicrous suggestion, I jumped into the discussion. "That may be what you want, but that is not what our customer Microsoft wants. They have given us their requirements for frequency, features, and cost, and what you propose makes no sense. The only solution for Microsoft is to enhance the PowerPC core we designed for Sony." I was tired and frustrated, and even I could hear the edge in my voice.

Vincent leaned back in his chair and looked at me as if it was the first time he had noticed I was in the room. He heaved a dramatic sigh. "So, Mr. Shippy, I heard that you were back at IBM. You sound like you could use a sabbatical within our Research Division. You seem stressed."

With that thinly veiled threat, he turned his attention to his favored server team and virtually ignored me for the rest of the meeting. Kahle and I spent half the day arguing the merits of my PowerPC core, but at the end of the day, we adjourned with no real conclusion. I thought it was typical of an IBM task force, a lot of wasted time and energy and still no clear direction.

While Vincent could choose what chip to use in the IBM servers, it was not in his power to change the direction for the Microsoft game chip.

Meanwhile, back at the Design Center, we still needed to make some tough decisions about the content of the common PowerPC core to be used in the Sony and Microsoft game machines. Jim Kahle, still boiling about the signing of the Microsoft contract and the resulting common core decision, demanded an official review of our PowerPC core and Memory Flow Control concept designs before allowing us to proceed into detailed design. It was a cold day, but the crowded conference room was overheated, so I was already sweating. Numerous IBMers from around the world telephoned in to participate in the conference call. Technical leads from all areas of the chip filled the chairs around the huge conference table, and a few invited guests from the server team across the street took seats along the back wall. I nodded to my old server buddies, but was nervous about their presence here. I knew they were biased, resentful of the fact that the Server Group wasn't in charge of this design. I also sensed that Kahle was out to exert some authority over the PowerPC team and over me, and this review presented him with the perfect stage. His Server

Group friends were his backup. I wasn't known for my submissiveness, and this had caused some ripples with Kahle lately. Akrout sat next to Kahle at the head of the table, as usual. All this attention just for us—I was quite honestly a little intimidated even though Jim Van Norstrand, Tony Truong, and I were well prepared with detailed presentations to show the status of our high-level design.

Jim Van Norstrand worried me some, and I glanced at him to gauge his mood. He was concerned that we were rushing into the next phase. He would have liked more time—wouldn't we all?—to flesh out the problematic areas, to make sure we had the right approach. But if we didn't move on and get into the meat of the design, we would not have a product for Sony's Christmas 2005 launch of the PlayStation 3, so I was willing to take some risks. I hoped Jim would respond to questions with some uncharacteristic optimism, but my confidence on that was pretty low.

The meeting was long and dynamic, with lots of questions and feedback from the audience. Mostly it was going well, but I kept an eye on Kahle. By his hard-nosed questions, I could tell he was preparing to veto our attempt to move on with the design. My temper was barely in check, but I had to wait until the final verdict.

At the end of Jim's and Tony's status presentations, Kahle rose and assumed command. "I want to thank the PowerPC team for the tremendous amount of work you've accomplished in such a short time, but I am deeply concerned about your ability to complete the job on schedule given the degree of complexity in this design."

I quickly responded, "I'm cautiously optimistic. Yes, we've got big challenges ahead of us, but I'm confident we can overcome them." I glanced at Akrout as I said this, and he smiled and nodded his head in approval, which just strengthened my resolve. Mickie Phipps sat at my side, and I already knew that she was supportive of my position.

Then Jim Van Norstrand agreed with Kahle, which pissed me off. Tony sat quietly at the back of the room, looking at his shoes, and that pissed me off even more. Why was it so difficult for the three of us to walk in there and speak with one voice? Our core just had too many cooks in the kitchen.

I took my turn at the podium then and presented the expected performance of the PowerPC core. I based my conclusions on the software performance model that the Rochester team maintained.

It didn't take Kahle long to show his hand. "Schedule is our top priority," he said, pounding a fist on the table for emphasis. He glanced around the room, and then focused on me. "Not performance or frequency or power or area. What are the tradeoffs that can help reduce the schedule risk?" He walked to the whiteboard and with big bold strokes wrote: Remove Out-of-Order Processing.

I was still standing at the podium when Kahle turned away from the whiteboard and quickly scanned the room for support. He was obviously waiting for me to make an argument for keeping this high-value feature in the design. Maybe I should have, but I was so tired of fighting. I just wanted to move on.

I sighed and addressed the audience. I didn't see too many happy faces out there. "We've been trying to satisfy too many customers with one product, and now I worry that they will all be unhappy with the final product. I agree that removing out-of-order processing will reduce the level of complexity—and therefore, risk—in the design, but it will also likely cause Apple to abandon the project. If you can live with that consequence, then go ahead."

Surprisingly, Akrout allowed Kahle to have his way. Maybe he thought he could still persuade his friends at Apple to accept a compromise. But as I predicted, Apple executives Jon Rubenstein and Bob Mansfield were furious with the design changes and the proposed revamping of their roadmap, claiming the lower PowerPC performance would ruin their opportunity to overtake Intel on the schedule they planned. They blamed Akrout for not protecting their interests. To IBM vice president John Kelly, it was all about economics. Though Apple was a treasured customer, the volume of chip business they pushed through the IBM foundry was not big in comparison to the volumes of game chips expected from Sony and Microsoft. Apple simply didn't have the clout to make Kelly reverse this decision. Besides, Sony and Microsoft were both contributing enormous amounts of money up front to the cost of the development of their chips, whereas IBM always footed the bill for the development of Apple's chips. The only money IBM got from Apple was for chip production.

Akrout was fiercely loyal to Apple, and it distressed him greatly to have fallen out of their favor. He remained in his office with the door shut for long periods of time, and when he did come out, his characteristic dimpled smile was absent, his shoulders slumped, he was late to meetings, and he was noticeably distracted. He worked hard to quickly find and present other acceptable options for Apple's future desktop and laptop lines. With a great deal of angry opposition, Apple finally agreed to accept a different core designed by IBM's Server Group. In reality, they were at least temporarily backed into a corner and had no other choice, but I'm sure they immediately started pouring energy and money into scouting for a replacement solution. Akrout still retained ownership of IBM's business with Apple, but his relationship with his favorite customer was forever changed.

My Server Group buddies made a lot of noise about our schedule risk, finally tipping the scales in their favor. John Kelly's optimistic plan (as sold to him by Akrout) had been to use one core, my PowerPC, for new server products as well as for the game consoles. This would save tons of development money and time, and with the current economic conditions, that sounded too good to pass up. Under an onslaught from the naysayers, Kelly backed off and allowed the Server Group to finish developing their own in-house chip for their next product.

Quick as a flash, I was down to two customers again—STI and Microsoft.

CHAPTER 10

Keep Up the Pace

*When time is of the essence, success demands fast
decisions. Move on to the next problem. Trust your
instincts. Limit debate on the decision.*

IN FALL 2003, I PARTICIPATED in the concept phase
for the overall Xbox 360 chip architecture. My role here was the same
as it had been during the PlayStation 3 concept development; however, this time around, I had to be very careful about what I said. I was
"contaminated" with insider knowledge of Sony's programming
model and design philosophy for the PlayStation 3 architecture. I absolutely could not use that inside information to influence the design
of the Xbox 360 solution. Akrout often told me (in Chekib-speak) I was
so contaminated with knowledge of both designs that I was "glowing
green." He knew he'd put me in a very tricky situation, and he tried to
be supportive. I felt comfortable enough enabling Microsoft to solve
tough engineering problems to meet their architecture needs, but I
drew the line when it came to suggesting broad architecture ideas.
The Microsoft team was never aware of my silence on these issues, accepting that I was only there to discuss the PowerPC design.

Microsoft needed to solve all of the same problems as Sony had already done on the PlayStation 3. They needed massive computing parallelism, spectacular vector number-crunching capability, and the ability to overcome the high latency involved in retrieving data from or storing data in main memory. It was déjà vu for me.

A small group of individuals assembled to define the Xbox 360 chip architecture: Jeff Andrews from Microsoft, Dave Luick and Eric Mejdrich from IBM, and me. We held our kickoff meeting in Rochester, Minnesota, on Dave and Eric's turf, where I was to meet all the players involved.

Even with my IBM badge from Austin, I couldn't just walk into the IBM facilities at Rochester unescorted, so I signed in at the front desk and then sat down on one of the plush lounge chairs to wait. Being very short on sleep, I quickly found myself struggling not to nod off. My plane had arrived late the night before, and by the time I got to the hotel, ate dinner, and checked my e-mail, it was well after midnight. When my escort pushed through the security door and strode across the lobby, I stood and tried to stifle a yawn, but without much luck.

"Eric Mejdrich," he said, introducing himself and giving me a crushing handshake. It was evident he pumped a little iron in his spare time. "Why don't we wait here in the lobby until our Microsoft guest arrives?" he suggested, indicating that I should sit back down. "It's a time-consuming walk from here to the cracker-box conference room I've reserved for us, and we don't want to do it twice."

"Sounds good to me. I'll just go back to my nap," I joked.

The Rochester site consists of a series of long, rectangular, boxlike buildings laid end-to-end, but with each one offset just a little bit so that no single hallway runs the full length of the structure. It's handy when the snow is deep outside, because you don't have to go outside and face the weather to get to the cafeteria, but it's terribly disorienting for visitors with all the twists and turns in the maze. I'd been there before; but without an escort, I am always completely dependent on the maps that hang at each dogleg hallway where one building joins another.

Eric plopped down in the chair across from me and started talking as if we were long lost friends. Very unpretentious and easy to get to know. My first impression was that he was a hardware engineer who moonlighted as a software guy. I think he was a computer hacker by nature, because he'd rewritten a lot of software on his own personal computer. He was an expert in graphics software, the kind that games require; he was a real heavy hitter. The more we talked, the happier I was that he was on the team. We chugged through the normal chitchat about my uneventful trip up north and the surprisingly cool weather, and transitioned into talking about our backgrounds when Jeff Andrews entered the lobby.

I recognized him straightaway from the Xbox 360 kickoff meeting, though we'd had very little chance to talk back then. Eric and I stood to introduce ourselves. Probably in his late thirties, Jeff was about my height, around six feet tall. He wore his light sandy-red hair in a fashionably long style and dressed in a black leather jacket, faded blue jeans, and tennis shoes. Not exactly what I pictured for Microsoft's technical lead for the Xbox 360 chip. My kind of dress code.

Jeff and I hit it off immediately. He was soft-spoken and bright, with a good sense of humor. He was also very passionate about the Xbox 360 project. His children were about the same age as mine, so we had lots in common as we talked about schools, dentists, and childcare issues.

Dave Luick, who joined us in the tiny conference room, was a veteran IBMer with over thirty years in the company. He'd made significant contributions on IBM's AS/400 minicomputers. He was a smart cookie, and he'd spent many recent years pontificating on cool new design ideas. Dave had lots of innovative ideas of his own, some practical, some not. You just had to weed through them to find the jewels.

After another round of introductions, I quickly settled into my place, eager to work. Obviously all alpha types used to taking the lead, we three IBMers fidgeted, darted glances at each other, bit our tongues, and waited for our customer to speak first. Patience is not one of my virtues, and I was antsy to get the dialog going. Meanwhile, Jeff shrugged out of his jacket, slowly set up his laptop, sipped his coffee in between responding to a few e-mails, and then finally looked up at us.

"Okay," he said. "Let's get started."

He was quiet and his movements were spare, almost as if he was conserving energy, but Jeff had no trouble taking command. I appreciated his directness, his no-nonsense approach. He went straight to the main issues as he wrote his primary must-haves on a whiteboard:

- As many vector processing units as possible on the chip

- Vector units with a large scratchpad memory (register file) to hide the deep pipeline

- Vector units which can handle dot product well (important mathematical operations for graphics processing)

- Wider issue width to feed the vector units

- Memory subsystem to feed the vector units

- Mechanism to hide the main memory latency and lock data in cache memory so it doesn't get cast out

In short, they needed to move a lot of data around as fast as possible, manipulate the data with number-crunching vector operations, and then blast it out to the video screen to wiggle all of the pixels to wow the gamers. I envisioned fluid race cars whipping around turns, lifelike football players scoring touchdowns, and *Halo* action heroes conquering new worlds with bold new movements.

Back in 2001 during the high-level design phase of Sony's original PowerPC core, Jim Kahle and I had argued about keeping the wider dual instruction issue in the design. I had told him then that he would regret removing it in favor of single instruction issue. Sitting there looking at Jeff's list of must-haves, I could see that my prediction had been right on the money. If only the PowerPC core had dual-issue, I could shave hundreds of hours of engineering time off the Microsoft project. The base PowerPC core for the Xbox 360 architecture would have been complete, and we could focus all of our effort on the new vector units. Instead, we made plans to rip up the guts of the PowerPC pipeline to widen everything to allow two instructions to be issued. It was indeed nearly a start-from-scratch design. And we only had eleven months to perform an eighteen-month task! My head ached. Why had I accepted this assignment?

The items on Jeff's list were pretty much the same problems we had solved for the PlayStation 3 using a single PowerPC core and eight Synergistic cores. Jeff attacked the problem with a more traditional homogeneous structure with multiple PowerPC cores. He wanted four cores which, if each core had two threads, would give the game code the same horsepower as eight vector processors all working in parallel. I thought it was interesting that there were also eight vector units (Synergistic cores) in the PlayStation 3. The similarity was uncanny but, of course, I kept my mouth shut. I was probably glowing green again. I also thought back to those infuriating Sony patents exposed on the Internet just a few months before. No doubt, Microsoft had crawled through those patents in great detail and learned valuable insider information, but again I kept my mouth shut.

In the months that followed, my worries about contamination subsided, because fortunately Microsoft had some very capable engineers, like Jeff, who were able to develop a new concept in a completely unique way which did not infringe on any of the PlayStation 3 ideas. By the end of the concept phase, Jeff had cut the design down to just three cores to stay within the area and power budgets of the Xbox 360 console. I was relieved; I really did not want to end up in a court of law explaining similarities between the two designs.

I was amazed at how the two projects used similar building blocks to attack the same problems, but came up with two completely different solutions. Sony solved main memory latency and read streaming with fancy DMA operations in a heterogeneous multiprocessor system. Eight Synergistic processing elements handled the Cell chip's number-crunching duties. Microsoft solved memory latency and read streaming with new prefetch operations in a homogeneous multiprocessor system. New vector units embedded in each PowerPC core handled their number crunching. I was proud that I contributed to the overall architecture of each game machine without polluting either design with my insider knowledge.

Going from the single Intel processor core contained in the original Xbox machine to multiple cores with multithreading was like turning a four-cylinder engine into an eight-cylinder, turbo-injected engine. Programs like *Quake* or *Halo* or *Madden NFL* required millions of complex mathematical vector operations. With each processor core running two parallel threads of computer instructions, the new chip could subdivide the game code and put each core (or car cylinder) to work in parallel on the complex physics that made the games so realistic. One thread might be calculating the movement of a blade of grass blowing in the wind, while another thread would be running calculations to generate the reflection of the moon on a nearby puddle of water in the road. Meanwhile, one of the other processor cores could be calculating the physical forces that would determine the next movement of one of the game players. Having all of these things going on in parallel is what makes the games look and feel so real. It takes a hell of a lot of silicon horsepower. On the original Xbox machine, the new generation of high-definition games would run as slow as elephants through tar pits.

In subsequent meetings, we dug deeper into the design and refined the new vector unit architecture. This included defining a new set of vector instructions to enhance Microsoft's graphics code. From an engineer's point of view, this was a big deal. While many engineers may get the opportunity to design a new processor in their careers, defining a new instruction set architecture was rare. It allowed the greatest amount of engineering freedom.

In the fifty-year history of processor design, just a few major instruction set architectures were created. There was the original IBM System 360 processors, the Intel X86, various RISC processors like PowerPC, MIPS, and Sparc, and, of course, the instruction set architecture created for the PlayStation 3's Synergistic core. To be involved with inventing new instructions was a rare treat. It also gave me a new appreciation for how the Synergistic core team architects must have felt as they invented their new architecture.

We conducted many of these architecture meetings via telephone conference calls between Jeff Andrews on the West Coast, IBM engineers in Rochester, and me in Austin. These teleconferences were usually quite lively and always interesting. Jeff, Dave, and Eric wanted the world. They were busily inventing new vector instructions to make the game code "do the dance."

"Jeff, you're killing me," I said after yet another request that seemed to come from outer space. "We just can't implement a new instruction that complex at these bleeding-edge frequencies." It was my job to bring their requests down to earth with the reality of what we could build in hardware. I listened to my customer, but I also paid attention to the nagging voice in my head that ticked off the numerous things that could go wrong. It was a delicate balance.

My life was a zinging ping-pong between the PlayStation 3 chip and the Xbox 360 chip, and I got tired of running up and down the stairs from the STI floors to the IBM-only area on the sixth floor every time I needed to discuss something related to Microsoft. One day, to conserve my energy, I used one of the breakout rooms inside the STI Design Center for a quick teleconference. Balancing my laptop on my knees and a hurriedly grabbed sandwich in one hand, I used the speakerphone to call Jeff Andrews and his team. We all wanted to talk at once, and the conversation quickly escalated. Everyone, including me, had to yell to be heard.

Mickie Phipps stuck her head into the little room and said, "You know the whole floor, including our Japanese partners, can hear every word of your conversation." She gave me a dark look before backing out of the room.

I quickly silenced the speakerphone while I thought about how many Sony or Toshiba engineers might have passed by.

During one architecture meeting, we attacked the problem of read streaming and reducing the main memory latency. Jeff Andrews asked, "Is there any way we could use some sort of prefetching mechanism to get data into the processor before it was actually required?" This would be like calling ahead to have your limo sitting at the door waiting for you.

I had an "aha moment." I said, "What if we use the data cache block touch instruction to prefetch data and add some new control bits to steer the data into either the L1 cache or the L2 cache? We could then use the L2 cache locking mechanism to pin it near the processor." This method allowed the game code to prefetch data in advance, well ahead of the time it was required, and then hold it there so that it would be available at lightning speed the instant the core called for it. It effectively removed the long latency to memory.

Jeff agreed, and I wrote down the instructions for us to review at the next meeting. We added an additional swizzle to data prefetch around the L2 cache and put data directly into the L1 Data cache. This brought the data as close as possible to the vector processing units where all the heavy lifting was done.

Before I committed to the idea, I wanted to talk to Farmer Dave (David Ray). It was going to be his job to implement this feature in the load/store unit. I found him huddled with a couple of other members of his team, helping them work through a tricky bug. With some reluctance, he followed me into a breakout room. "I have a new feature I'd like you to size up for the load/store unit."

Dave grumbled, "Every time you come to me with a so-called feature, it just means more work for me."

"True, but name one thing I asked you to add to the design that wasn't worth the effort," I prodded.

Dave didn't have an answer, but that didn't mean he was any happier with me. I talked through the details of the new operation.

"We'll have to increase the size of the load-miss queue from four entries to eight," he said with a sigh. (The load-miss queue holds the loads until data comes back from memory.)

We talked some more about the details of the work. Once I was convinced Dave was comfortable with the idea, I sent him on his way and called Jeff Andrews. "It's a go. We'll commit to that design change."

This prefetch idea became the fundamental mechanism that the Xbox 360 used to stream in massive amounts of data in parallel and to reduce the high memory latency.

We next tackled speeding up the data flow from the central processor back out to the video screen. The original PowerPC design from the PlayStation 3 included a few features that aided this function, which is the write streaming. First, the L1 caches in our PowerPC core were write-through caches. Every time the core wrote data to the L1 cache, it automatically forwarded the data to the next level of cache. The second feature was L2 cache locking. With this mechanism, sections of the L2 cache could be set aside for write streaming buffers. While the streaming data was locked in the L2 cache, the graphics processing chip could then read the data directly from the L2 and write it out to the video display.

Sony, relying heavily on their eight Synergistic cores to provide the muscle, wanted to stay with the older vector unit found on the original PowerPC design. The vector unit was not something they intended to use much anyway, and they had agreed to its inclusion in the first place only because IBM wanted to use the Cell chip in other products where the vector unit would be an asset. Kutaragi and the Toshiba executives felt upgrading to the new vector unit (VMX128) would add unnecessary risk. This difference in vector units was the only distinction between the PowerPC core planned for Microsoft and the one planned for the Cell chip.

However, there were significant technology differences between the Sony machine and the Microsoft console that went far beyond the PowerPC core, such as the choice of input/output (I/O) interconnect and memory technology. Because of a highly successful partnership with Rambus on the PlayStation 2, Kutaragi insisted on a repeat performance on the PlayStation 3 by selecting Rambus's interconnect I/O and memory system. He justified this choice by claiming Rambus offered high-performance solutions with a low overall cost for the package, board, and system, and he refused to listen to Chekib Akrout's concerns about added risk. That decision put Rambus right in the critical path of silicon release, which put it directly in Keryn Mills's crosshairs, too. IBM was forced to rely on getting the processor bus and memory interface intellectual property blocks from Rambus rather than designing them internally, so this was a huge point of contention. Akrout knew IBM possessed competing technologies and fought tooth and nail with Kutaragi to keep Rambus out of the design, but to no avail. Kutaragi was bound and determined to have his way on this. And he did.

That decision came back to haunt him. The Rambus technology added risk to the completion of the STI chip, something I first heard about in one of Keryn Mills's weekly status meetings.

Frustrated and tightlipped, John Keaty berated his Rambus counterpart over the phone. "Your product release methodology is too loose. I told you exactly how I wanted you to demonstrate timing closure and final deliverable quality. Though you agreed at the time, you later chose to ignore our rules. And now, we have no idea where you are on timing. Based on what I have seen, you are way over the budget, and I have no confidence this stuff will ever work!"

Rambus's methodology did not follow IBM's tried and true final release criteria and best practices that produced quality chips time and time again. Keryn Mills pounced on Keaty's bandwagon and initiated daily phone calls with Rambus to track progress on the timing front and to instill in them a sorely lacking sense of urgency. She also convinced the Sony director to use his influence to sway Rambus. Under severe pressure, Rambus finally conformed and received Keaty's blessing on their design.

Microsoft did not have this risky dependency on external intellectual property. They chose a more traditional processor bus, the Front Side Bus, architected and uniquely designed by IBM specifically for the Xbox 360. This processor bus interconnected the central processing chip to the graphics chip. IBM controlled the design without relying on an outside source. Additionally, Microsoft chose to incorporate the same memory used in most PCs, which was very stable, reliable, and available from many sources. A traditional memory interface attached the main 512-megabyte memory block to the graphics chip.

In another major decision, the Microsoft design team chose to stick with a tried-and-true programming model for the game console. In a simplistic view, game machines use two major hardware components for processing. One is the central processing unit and the other is the graphics processing unit. Traditionally, the graphics unit is a separate chip. Sony's central processor was the heterogeneous Cell chip, which had eight Synergistic cores and one PowerPC core. Microsoft's homogeneous central processor included three PowerPC cores on a single chip.

Sony believed they could push a lot of the graphics software execution into the eight Synergistic cores on their Cell chip, which meant they didn't really need a powerful graphics chip. They thought they could save some cost with a scaled-down design that their own Sony engineers could develop. The two major graphics chip makers at the time, NVidia and ATI, would most certainly have asked for top dollar to design a specialized chip for the PlayStation 3.

Microsoft stuck with a more traditional symmetric three-way multiprocessing model and offloaded the graphics processing to a powerful ATI custom graphics chip. This approach was similar to the original Xbox software model. Microsoft knew there was already enough risk in the new game machine hardware that they didn't want to add additional risk by changing the programming model or shifting the balance between the central processing unit's workload and the graphic chip's workload.

Microsoft was burned miserably on the original Xbox due to delays in the graphics chip delivery schedule and the high price Nvidia charged for that chip. This time around, they decided to go with ATI. This decision took the graphics chip out of the critical path in the product launch, and all of the Microsoft team's effort focused on the new central processing chip and the fancy new game software.

All of these corporate giants were busy wheeling and dealing, arguing and negotiating, strategizing and planning. So one might think that the IBM executives, who were right in the middle of everything, had enough to deal with, but apparently not. They screamed for a new name for the modified common PowerPC core, as they were already tired of calling it the PowerPC+, PowerPC2, or the "new" PowerPC. With all the other pressing demands, renaming the design wasn't at the top of my list, but Mickie pushed me to do something to stop the persistent nagging and the inevitable confusion with the original core.

I met with Jim Van Norstrand and a handful of other PowerPC core leaders from IBM and tossed around various ideas. None of us wanted to be there, but it was a break from the routine. There was a lot of laughter as we conjured up the perfect name. We quickly discarded PUS (PowerPC Unit Supercharged) and PAMPer (PowerPC Amplified). The idea we liked the very best was PlayBox, a not too subtle combination of the PlayStation and the Xbox names. I knew this wouldn't fly with the executive types, so I shortened it to the PB core and told everyone this stood for PowerPC-boosted core.

No one above us liked the new name much, but they didn't want to risk an uprising, so they let it go. They knew how touchy we were right then. This new name added a little light-hearted fun to our days, and it was hard not to grin every time anyone used the term "PB," because my team and I knew it really meant PlayBox.

With the chip-level concept solidified, we were then ready to start the high-level design of the new PlayBox core. We went back to the beginning of the process to construct the fundamental architecture of the design. We needed to draw a new set of blueprints similar to those we had created for the original PlayStation 3 PowerPC core. The low-level implementation phase followed, in which we once again carefully layered the bricks and mortar (millions of silicon transistors) in a very specific order to build the new house we called the PlayBox.

We needed enough time during this high-level planning stage to draw up a quality blueprint, an effort that typically took six to twelve months. I occasionally worked on projects that spent less time on this stage, but not often. There is always great temptation to shortcut the process; however, this is nearly a guarantee that the later phases will be more complicated. If you're an architect building a two-story house, you don't draw only the first floor, and then start construction.

I feared the cost of accepting shortcuts, but to meet this particular schedule, we only had two months to spend on the high-level design. I planned to spend December 2003 through January 2004 on the blueprint and then February 2004 through November 2004 on the detailed chip design, leading to a release of the design to manufacturing just before Christmas 2004. It was the most aggressive schedule ever attempted at IBM.

From ten thousand feet, the new design changes didn't seem that difficult but, of course, the devil's in the details. The performance a microprocessor can achieve is a combination of the frequency (measured in gigahertz) and the length of time each game code instruction takes to execute on the hardware. Think of the cartoon character Wile E. Coyote. When he takes off running, his feet are moving at such a high speed that all you see is a swirl of dust—but it takes a couple of seconds before he actually starts moving down the road to catch the Road Runner. You can have high speed (high frequency) without making any measurable progress. The game code needs to go fast, but it also needs to get to the endpoint without any wasted effort. It's all a matter of efficiency in the design.

Game developers write code in a high-level programming language, which a compiler reduces to a series of simple instructions in the hardware. Each instruction initiates a series of calculations that determine the color and shade of a pixel on a computer or TV screen, combining to paint each scene in such a way as to give the impression of action. Our goal was to feed these game code instructions to their final destinations as efficiently as possible. First, we had to create wider paths for data and instructions coming from memory, then we had to create wider paths to feed these instructions to the new turbocharged vector units.

So here we were, ready to start the high-level design activities, and my mind was on Christmas vacation. With the past year-long, nonstop work schedule on the original PlayStation 3 PowerPC core design, my team was exhausted. Just less than a month ago, we had handed off that design to the chip team to prep for manufacturing. Few people took time off during the summer months because of the intense schedule demands, so numerous members of the team still had weeks of vacation on the books. I had nearly a full month left over and was just as ready as anyone for a long break, but I accepted that it just wasn't in the cards for me this year. IBM doesn't allow us to rollover our vacation into the next year, but even if they did, there's only so far we felt we could push this team. They really needed a break. I scrambled to find a key subset of the team who were willing to join me in getting the high-level design activities started while everyone else enjoyed the holidays with their families.

I claimed a tiny, empty, windowless conference room on the sixth floor because that was one floor where the Sony and Toshiba partners were denied access. And also because it was all that was available. Our pink palace was bulging at the seams with people as IBM attempted to consolidate and sell off old buildings on the massive campus across the street. Whiteboards covered three walls of our War Room; two old tables formed something resembling a conference table; and a dozen mismatched semifunctional chairs I pilfered from other rooms provided uncomfortable seating.

In our first session in the War Room, I sketched on the whiteboard the basic pipeline of the new PlayBox core. "We need a way to feed more instructions to the vector unit here," I said, turning to the board to mark the spot. "That's where the adders and multipliers for the graphics software are located. How can we make the instruction fetch and issue wider?"

This was similar to widening a pipe to increase the flow of fluid through it.

My lead circuit designer, Bob Philhower, leaned back in his chair and locked his hands behind his head. "At these frequencies," he warned, "if you widen the instruction issue width, that's just going to make the pipeline deeper."

Bob was one of the top circuit designers in the company and worked out of the Yorktown Research Center in New York. We had run through the fire together on the Gigaprocessor design, where I gained a huge amount of respect for his technical depth. Bob was great to have on the team, but he was very conservative. I had to consider the "Philhower factor" every time he offered his opinion or advice. He reminded me of Scotty on the old Star Trek series—"Captain, I've *got* to have more time to fix the engines."

I nodded my head, carefully thinking through my response. "It's a valid concern, Bob. Increasing the issue width does mean we have to increase the number of stages in our pipeline, which then causes the graphics instructions to take longer to get to their destination in the vector unit."

Remember the analogy of the automobile assembly line.

"It's a vicious cycle," Jim Van Norstrand added, shaking his head.

"So we just have to invent other mechanisms to make up for this performance loss," I said. "That's our challenge."

Jim and Bob glanced at each other, and it was easy for me to interpret the unspoken message that passed between them. They really did not believe we would win that challenge. I ignored their misgivings, hoping that they would gain confidence as we went along.

Each day we made complicated tradeoffs between schedule, performance, power, and physical design, often sacrificing one for the other. I constantly asked myself, "What additional problems could this decision cause?" I knew from experience the executives and the formidable Keryn Mills would explode over some excuse about "unanticipated problems" that blew the schedule. The success of the project depended upon farsighted leaders who could spot trouble a mile away, who could react early enough to keep the schedule on track. The executives would hold our feet to the fire on this point. As Jim Kahle frequently reiterated, schedule was our number one priority.

My small band of IBMers spent much of the next two months locked in that War Room solving problems such as this. It was vitally important that our Sony and Toshiba partners didn't get wind of our design changes for Microsoft, but they began to question why we were never in the Design Center anymore. Among ourselves, we IBMers often talked about the difficulties of keeping secrets from the Japanese engineers who had worked side by side with us for the last two years, but talking about it was nothing compared to actually doing it. It didn't feel right to any of us—and that included me.

About that time, I held a series of meetings with the Raleigh design team to architect the blueprint for the new vector unit for the Xbox 360. The Raleigh team seemed capable, but they had never designed such a high performance beast. And a significant number of their engineers were fresh from college with very little design experience. For some of the meetings, I was physically in Raleigh, but I conducted many of them over the telephone. Some of my more painful experiences with the original PowerPC core were still fresh in my mind, so I began with the end in mind. The first thing we needed to do was to rearrange the floorplan to reduce the length of the wires so that we didn't sacrifice any speed; we called this a short-wire architecture. I made suggestions, then left the Raleigh team to try out the many possible permutations and fit each of the functions together like a complex jigsaw puzzle. They narrowed down the selection from about ten possible floorplans to the top three. After much spirited discussion on the pros and cons of each, I selected what I believed was the best solution. We were short on time, and it was necessary to make a quick decision and move on.

I also directed their circuit designers to create small cross sections of the most complex parts of the design to ensure we could meet the frequency and area targets. There was some resistance, because their team had never before carried out this much rigorous checking during early phases of a design.

"Look guys," I said, "this is a tried and true method that I've successfully used for years. Trust me, you need to do it." My temper was short, and I resorted to commanding the troops like a dictatorial general. With a more veteran design team, maybe I could have delegated many of these decisions, but with the short schedule and the relative inexperience of the team, I saw no other choice. I'm not sure the Raleigh team ever completely warmed up to my abrasive leadership style. I thought about Jim Kahle and my own resentment over his domineering leadership style. I smiled as a sweet little slice of shared experience appeared on my plate like an unexpected dessert.

Since the Xbox 360 chip design called for multiple PowerPC processors all requiring access to a single memory subsystem, we needed a fancy new crossbar switch to handle the dynamic exchanges of data. I handed off that design work to Tony Truong, who was on a temporary assignment in Raleigh to design the new Xbox 360 memory subsystem. Back in Austin, Alvan Ng took over Tony's old Memory Flow Control team which continued work on the Sony PlayStation 3 design. Alvan was a quiet, highly skilled engineer who led by example. His work ethic was as strong as Tony's, so I'm not sure when either of these guys slept or saw their families.

Tony drew from crossbar concepts used in high-performance IBM server chips to solve the design problems, and I was very glad to be able to rely on him during this stressful period. Even here, we pushed the state of the art in multiprocessing, for neither IBM nor Intel had attempted more than two cores on a single chip before this time. We created a screaming, streamlined, on-chip three-way multiprocessor.

Just as I predicted, with all of these changes, by the end of high-level design phase we touched virtually every part of the core. The new PlayBox core was practically a complete redesign. Even the Memory Flow Control unit was completely redesigned to incorporate flexibility to function with the Xbox 360's three PowerPC cores.

Fear mongers within the Server Group who were still mad about losing the turf battles at the beginning of the STI Design Center slipped through the back door with concerns about insane schedules and designs that were far too complex. They whispered of potential failure, and Steve Carter, Akrout's new boss, listened. Adding insult to injury, he brought in an independent audit team from the Server Group to assess the feasibility of my PlayBox team's completing the design by December 2004, which was the last possible date that might still support a Christmas 2005 product launch. My team and I spent many hours preparing for this review—hours that should have been spent working on the design—and I spent hour after hour in a stifling hot conference room crawling through all of the design changes with the audit team, many of whom were former coworkers and buddies. They didn't seem so friendly then. It was worse than having my teeth drilled at the dentist's office.

The audit team, led by Ralf Fischer, concluded that the best-case scenario was that it would take the PlayBox team until February or March of 2005 to complete the detailed design work. They claimed the task was impossible without an extension of three to four months added to the current schedule.

There were some on my own PlayBox team who secretly agreed with the audit team. We were all exhausted, and I couldn't blame them for wanting a little relief. They just wanted someone, anyone, to extend the schedule and stop the eighty-hour work weeks.

The audit team relayed this grim news to the executives. Everyone had a sick feeling, but felt trapped into sticking with the existing schedule. An extension was unacceptable to Sony or to Microsoft. As for me, I claimed "victory or death."

To stay on schedule, it was time to transition from high-level design to the detailed design phase—these are two distinct phases in any IBM project, with each having defined guidelines to structure the work. This move meant that we believed the blueprints were complete and the bricks (transistors) were ready to place. Any downstream changes to the blueprints would require ripping up the design and starting over. It would be like forgetting to run a plumbing pipe to the kitchen and having to rip up the slab later to put one in.

Jim Kahle opposed exiting high-level design this early, but he was conflicted with the hope that the Cell chip, which was now committed to using this common PlayBox core, could still achieve the Christmas 2005 launch. Any delay in moving on to the next phase meant that we would most likely miss the sacred launch date. There simply was no slack in the schedule.

My team leads reluctantly gathered for an internal vote on whether or not to exit high-level design and start the detailed logic and circuit design. It was a chilly day, and everyone was sniffling from colds picked up from their kids. The winter temperature hovered in the mid-thirties—cold for Austin, Texas. We were frazzled and overworked. We all wanted more time to complete a thorough study and simulation of the basic design before we started adding in the details. But I knew we needed to move on.

Mark Morrison, the PlayBox verification lead, was the most vocal about what he considered a premature and foolhardy transition. He wasn't a cheerful man on his best days, but the purpose of this meeting set him on edge. He sat in the corner of the room with his normal glowering expression. I completely trusted Morrison's verification skills and his vast knowledge of microprocessors, but he and I had often butted heads over his tendency to sandbag. It was sometimes difficult for me to tell if we were really only halfway through with a verification task, nearly through, on schedule, or in trouble. Morrison liked to play things very close to the vest and then declare victory at the last second—and never never one second too early! He certainly didn't want to give those pesky project managers a new precedent that could be used to whip his team into an even shorter schedule on the next project. Morrison's constant negative attitude was wearing me down.

Morrison and his team were busily building software models based on the modified logic design, running test cases through the model, and finding bugs, which he handed back to the logic designers to fix. Bugs are design flaws accidentally coded into the logic, which cause it to misbehave. Generally, this means that an instruction computes the wrong answer, like $2 + 2 = 5$. Once we exited high-level design, as Morrison well knew, the design would take on more depth, more complexity, and the bugs would become both harder to find and harder to fix. On top of that, when fixing one problem, we always faced the chance of introducing another bug into the design. It was exactly the situation he wanted to avoid.

As I polled my team leads, all were struggling with the decision, but they agreed we needed to move on.

Only Morrison continued to voice his unwavering opposition to exiting high-level design. "If we proceed, we're at very high risk of finding a major bug so late in the project it will be catastrophic to both Sony's and Microsoft's product release schedules. This could cost millions of dollars. Worse yet, in our rush, a major bug might slip by and find its way into the product. That would be very embarrassing and perhaps extremely costly to all companies involved." Morrison most certainly would have taken that as a personal failure.

On the other hand, time to market was absolutely crucial for these game consoles. All of our customers—had we given them the opportunity to voice an opinion about this decision—would have wanted us to take the risk; Microsoft more so than Sony. Microsoft was the underdog, the one fighting to topple the giant. Risk-taking was part of their strategy.

"Mark," I said, "I understand and respect your opinion, but we have to move on. I'll take responsibility if we fail. The only way we have a shot at success is to dive into the design."

Morrison grumbled, "It's just stupid."

I made a mental note that I had to replace Morrison before his pessimistic attitude contaminated the team.

CHAPTER 11

Be Proactive, Anticipate Problems

There are two kinds of problems in the engineering
process: the complex puzzles that demand
innovative solutions and entice the best from an
engineer, and the potentially avoidable mistakes
that drown the engineer's creative spirit.
Anticipating those nasty problems before they
occur is an art form which comes from rigorous
tracking of design deliverables. Engineering
accountability is key.

TWO THOUSAND FOUR, the year following the signing of the
Microsoft contract, will be forever etched in my mind as one of the
most painful and most joyful periods in my life. We had a monumental task ahead of us—to design a complex new microprocessor core in
record time. It hurt my head trying to predict all of the potential problems we would encounter. The trick was rooting out the showstoppers.

And then there was my unruly team. They were constantly fighting
and acting up, reacting poorly to the tricky situation we were in as we
balanced Microsoft and Sony's demands. We all hated the compart-

mentalized secrecy we were forced to accept. Mickie and her first-line managers spent more and more time dealing with the team's temper tantrums and anger issues.

Further, there was that damned blinding spotlight. All eyes seemed to be on us, and the pressure was intense as all those watchers expected us to make major, sweeping changes to the PowerPC core design, effectively starting over, and still meet the same end date we started with two years earlier. With less than one year to go, the clock was ticking! But in spite of it all, I was having a blast as the creative juices flowed like a river through my team. We were inventing. Creating. Walking where no engineer had set foot before. To say the least, my emotions were waging a full-scale war inside me.

I knew from the very beginning that it was a huge risk for IBM to commit to such an insane schedule, where even tiny hiccups resulted in huge repercussions. I could see what had happened—a megamillion dollar deal turned our executives' hearts to stone. The money we made on our design work was chump change to Big Blue, who made its real profits from chip manufacturing, not development. The revenues generated by the tremendous volume of chips that would run through IBM's foundry for Sony's and Microsoft's game machines far outweighed the executives' concerns about team burnout. They would have no qualms about making us casualties of IBM's income statement. That actually sounds a little more bitter than I mean it to, because even I had voted to go for it. But I often felt expendable.

The date and time banner winking from the corner of my laptop screen was a constant reminder that time was flying. Programmed from years of training on other high-pressure projects, I automatically went into overdrive. I wouldn't have known how not to.

We moved on to the detailed design phase with Mark Morrison's noted objections and started the long grind of logic and circuit design. The logic designers were responsible for taking the architecture blueprints and translating them into a lower-level set of detailed mathematical equations called "Boolean expressions," which represented how the microprocessor executed the game software. Just as they had done on the original PowerPC design, they performed this translation with a very high-level design programming language called VHDL. The circuit designers started entering their low-level transistor schematics and wires to match the logic. The results of their work would eventually be handed over to the chip integrator (Mr. Keaty, in this instance) to incorporate into the full chip design which would then be fabricated in silicon.

The designers put their heads down and cranked out the design, often working seventy to eighty hours per week. The initial focus of the logic team was to write several hundred thousand lines of logic in VHDL. In some cases, there was quantity but very little quality, which kept Morrison and his verification team in constant swirl as they fought their way through layer after layer of design bugs. In the first months of low-level design, it appeared the logic design team was mostly on track. They wrote VHDL at a record rate, and the corresponding circuit schematics kept pace.

As we moved into this high-pressure design environment, I knew I needed to take a hard look at my verification team, maybe do some fine-tuning. There was so much at stake, and we needed to run like a well-oiled machine. Morrison, as verification lead, had done an admirable job on the original PowerPC design, but it was obvious to everyone that he liked hands-on verification work much more than he liked to lead. His team needed more guidance. Like most high-tech companies, IBM tended to promote the best engineers into leadership positions, but those highly skilled techies don't always make the best leaders. Morrison was definitely one of the best verification engineers in the company, and I needed him cranking out verification code and finding bugs. I could find another strong leader to coordinate the efforts of the team more easily than I could find another top-notch verification engineer. Besides, with both of us being stubborn and strong willed, Morrison and I butted heads on this project far too often. It was time for a change.

I called my old friend Andy Petruski. Andy and I joined IBM at the same time in Endicott, New York, back in the mid-1980s. When I transferred to Austin, I recruited Andy to come work with me on the Power2 processor. Later, when I left the IBM mother ship to join the satellite Somerset Design Center, Andy followed. We also both tried our luck together at a small startup in Austin. He was still at the startup when I reached him. Having worked together off and on for nearly twenty years, I knew Andy was exactly what my team needed. He was a sharp engineer and a proven leader with an easygoing attitude and a specialty in verification.

I met Andy over beer at the Dog and Duck Pub, a bar near the University of Texas campus that truly represented what I love about Austin. It was a laid-back rustic place where you could sit outside in a beer garden and choose from a large selection of quality beers. In a more youthful past, Andy and I had spent many evenings closing down the place.

He suspected I had an ulterior motive for our little reunion, so I didn't need any preamble. I just jumped right in. "Andy, isn't it time you give up on the startup riches dream and come take a real job?" I went on to explain the high-stakes project we had. "It won't be easy, but the rewards could be nice. Plus it will involve some really cool leading-edge engineering work."

It took a couple more beers, but I finally got Andy to agree, although somewhat reluctantly, to meet with Mickie to talk about the position.

The next day, I escorted him through the security process and left him in a small conference room with Mickie. She gave him all the hype about how wonderful it would be to work for IBM again, and discussed the pay and other benefits. Andy still wasn't convinced that he wanted to work for a big bureaucracy again. A smaller company, where each individual is highly valued and made to feel like family, offers so many intangible advantages. Andy knew he would not enjoy such warm fuzzies at IBM, but the work was truly hard to beat. He took a couple of weeks to think about it, then he called me and accepted the lead verification job.

Andy's first major assignment was to be a good listener. His team had a lot to get off their chests, and Andy was patient and steady as a rock. I came to check on him several times during his first couple of weeks and almost always found him in a breakout room with a disgruntled engineer. In a month or so, the team accepted him, and he brought peace to the group and gave them much needed direction. Maybe best of all, he and Mark Morrison, the indispensable backbone of our verification team, found the right balance in skills and roles. Miracles never cease.

The first major milestone was "VHDL entry complete," set for March 31, 2004. This milestone signified that the basic architecture blueprints now lived in a set of complex logic equations. However, by no means was that the final set of equations, ready for manufacturing. There were probably still hundreds of designs flaws for the verification team to uncover. Therefore, with no quality assessment from the verification folks attached to it, "VHDL entry complete" was a fairly useless metric. Unfortunately, in an effort to soothe the worry mongers, Mickie led the project managers from the STI Design Center and from Microsoft to believe this milestone could be the first indicator of whether or not the audit team's predictions for a schedule slip were true or not. So everyone attached unwarranted significance to this milestone.

A few weeks before the deadline, Jim Van Norstrand cornered me in the hallway. "We aren't even going to hit the first damn milestone. The designers are spread too thin, and there are still a handful of logic blocks that have not been coded into VHDL."

I was probably irritable from lack of sleep, which is no excuse, but I was so tired of whiners. I yelled, "Jim, come to me with solutions, not problems!" I think the whole floor heard me. As I stomped off, I growled, "I'll code the friggin' blocks myself."

Despite having the responsibility of running the day-to-day technical operation of the design team and the demands of countless time-consuming status meetings, I cleared my calendar and wrote VHDL code for several weeks. In my mind, the urgency of the situation demanded "all hands on deck." Also, I was staying focused on the end result despite the obstacles.

Actually, I loved it. It was fun to be writing logic again, and it was good for me, too, to be experiencing all the travails my logic designers were going through. I loved getting my hands dirty again with some of the low-level details of the design, the tedious and time-consuming work of sketching and testing the logic flow of the machine. These equations had tremendous cumulative importance. They translated into millions of transistors that all connected together in logical harmony.

I was uneasy about the lack of a quality metric, but as I went from designer to designer on the last day of March, each one nodded and said their VHDL entry was complete. In some cases, I think it was almost like grade school with some of the designers nodding their heads but secretly having their fingers crossed behind their backs. It appeared this first task was complete.

Hubcap was one of the last folks I talked to that day. He owned the biggest block of VHDL, the most complex part of the design. I often worried it was too much for a junior engineer, but he attacked the VHDL so aggressively that we kept piling more on him. I approached his cubicle. He had two 21-inch computer screens full of open windows containing schematics, calculations, and chat sessions with other engineers whose work dovetailed into his own. There were at least ten open windows on each screen. Talk about multitasking! Under normal circumstances, I would have challenged any junior engineer and crawled through his designs to check for completeness. But that deadline day, all I did was cheerfully ask, "How's it going, Hubcap? You have your VHDL all entered?"

He smiled and winked, "All done."

In those crazy times, I let it go and patted him on the back. "Good job!"

Somewhat reluctantly, I raised my arms to signify victory and loudly announced over the top of our little sea of cubicles, "The 'VHDL entry complete' milestone has been met, and I'm buying beer!" Everyone cheered, and the team broke early and fled to the Waterloo Ice House for beer. As I drank with the team that night, I wasn't sure if we were celebrating a success or the fate of a sinking ship, but I kept my worries to myself. Congratulatory notes from executives across IBM, Sony, and Toshiba flowed in for the on-schedule completion of this major milestone. Microsoft was very happy.

The good mood was short lived.

With an ever-increasing number of disturbing, difficult-to-solve bugs, I grew concerned about a section of the instruction unit. My gut told me that there was a major design flaw. If my instincts proved true, it sure was good to catch a potentially fatal problem now, but I kicked myself for not heeding the warning bells that had been ringing in my own head these past few weeks. I pulled Jim Van Norstrand into a breakout room about the size of a closet. Inside were two comfy armchairs and a big whiteboard. One partially frosted glass wall allowed everyone in cube city to see who was inside, even if they might have to struggle a bit to actually see something written on the whiteboard. If Jim and I were in one breakout room together, it usually meant trouble. We called this room the "Cone of Silence," referring to the old *Get Smart* sitcom. We used it for privacy, but it wasn't very private. Sound carried through the walls far too easily.

I quietly told Jim my fears about the instruction unit design. "We need to dig into the bugs. Crawl through the VHDL and try to understand what the designers have done."

Not only was I concerned about the nagging bugs, but I was also concerned about the inexperience of the junior level engineers working on the logic. As my second in command, Jim had leadership over the entire microprocessor core at this point.

After some discussion about the problem, I said, "Jim, as much as I hate to do this, I think you need to step down as the core lead and take over the instruction unit. The current unit leader is good, and he has tons of potential. But he's just too inexperienced to catch these complicated bugs and to make the tough decisions to move the design forward. He wields no power. I want you to hold a series of design reviews and get to the bottom of what's wrong here. This could be a project showstopper. We need to also look at moving more experienced designers over to help these junior level guys."

Jim agreed with my conclusions, so we spent another hour discussing possible reassignments and potential impacts, and then fell into some general venting. By then it was pretty warm in there, and I was ready for some fresh air.

As we stood to leave, Jim said, "Are we having fun yet?" But he wasn't smiling.

While Mickie bluffed to keep Keryn Mills and Jim Kahle off our backs for a few days, Jim Van Norstrand quietly scheduled a series of semi-secret architecture review meetings in a third-floor conference room. Luckily, it had a window across one whole side, so we at least got a view of the outside world. I would almost have preferred to jump out that window than to step back into high-level design to update our architecture blueprints.

Jim Van Norstrand set the tone of the meeting. "We're in deep shit, and we need answers quickly. I want the vector instruction queue designers front and center at the board explaining how this bloody thing works."

With that tone in his voice, he didn't need his baseball bat to get his point across.

We listened for about an hour, and then I caught Jim's eye. I knew we were thinking the same thing. I held up a hand to stop the feeble presentation, and said, "Guys, you've been up there for an hour, and I still don't get it. If you can't make us understand your design in about ten minutes, then it's too damn complicated."

It was a tangled design with muddy outputs. I likened the problem to a juggler with too many balls in the air at the same time.

After a couple more days imprisoned in intense microarchitecture reviews where we filled whiteboards with diagrams, fought over ideas, and shot down theories, we finally uncovered the root cause of the design problem. By that point, the resolution was obvious, but it was a bitter pill to swallow.

Frustrated and exhausted, we got back to work (with a few changes in roles and assignments again), but not before we missed a few of the early milestones in the schedule. Some of the managers and even some of my own team accused me of jumping the gun by announcing on March 31 that we'd met the "VHDL entry complete" milestone.

Jim and I steeled ourselves for the flogging we would receive when we announced to management the discovery of these new problems. Fortunately, we had a well-thought-out recovery plan in hand that we hoped would help ease the pain. While I was very disappointed in the near-term schedule hiccup, I knew this design change was the right thing for the long run. It's like the auto repair commercial slogan: "You can pay me now or pay me later." At a far higher cost, paying for this later in the design cycle would have been a disaster.

In April 2004, Akrout invited Mickie and me to attend a conference call with Steve Carter, where we would break the news that we were going to miss some of our near-term project milestones.

After some painful strategy planning and preparation for the call, Akrout said, "Okay, we're ready." He took a deep breath and dialed Steve Carter's number in New York.

My first interaction with Carter earlier in the project had been favorable. He was tall and slender, and at 45-ish, he was a fairly young guy for an IBM vice president. Carter joined IBM in 1979 after receiving his bachelor's degree in electrical engineering from the New Jersey Institute of Technology. He earned his master's degree in electrical engineering from Syracuse University in 1987. He talked of enjoying many outdoor activities such as mountain climbing and long-distance biking, and he seemed like a nice guy. I'll never forget the day I changed my mind about him.

"Are you thinking this is going to be a bloodbath?" I asked. My palms were sweating.

Akrout shook his head and smiled. "No, of course not. We just need to present the recovery plan in the right way."

As he dialed the phone, I experienced a moment of utter panic. Akrout's optimism was legendary. He always thought everything was going to be okay. He possessed complete confidence in his own ability to lead us out of any hole we could dig for ourselves, and he was convinced that the upper echelons above us would trust him to do just that. They almost always did. But in that moment, I sensed a train coming at us.

Akrout started the discussion with his smooth "used car salesman" song and dance. He pointed out the schedule slip, but quickly moved to the recovery plan.

Carter's reaction was not what we had hoped. He nearly ripped Akrout's head off from several thousand miles away. "This is crap! Why am I paying for all of those project managers to track the schedule? Where were the headlights to indicate we were falling behind? How is it possible to fall off the cliff after we just successfully passed our first major milestone?"

There was a long pause when no one said anything. We were too stunned, and I guess Carter was just too mad. No longer shouting but still gruff and unforgiving, Carter said, "Don't you dare try to dump this in my lap. I want a full-scale review immediately, and I want detailed daily status reports highlighting every move these guys make."

He abruptly hung up without a goodbye.

Akrout regretted having invited us to the conference call. I walked out of his office with my tail between my legs. Mickie was wounded by Carter's comments about ineffective project management, which was her job. We both wondered how we could have done better.

Akrout, Carter, and John Kelly (the senior vice president above them) were already watching the project very closely but, at this point, they moved to intense scrutiny and micromanagement. A new era in IBM project management was born. Vice presidents started driving our weekly status meetings. On a more realistic schedule, many problems encountered in the normal course of design work would never have made it to a vice president's desk. There would be enough room in the schedule to handle bugs, errors, or miscommunications. On a normal schedule, no one but the immediate manager and technical lead would be aware that a key designer was absent for a day or two to get married, have a baby, or recover from a cold. But on this hell-bent schedule and with this level of scrutiny, the vice presidents were seeing every minor issue as it arose. We felt completely exposed, with every decision we made questioned and second-guessed, and every mistake we made spotlighted and probed. Morale fell to an all-time low.

The vice presidents called for numerous investigations and audits, sometimes called "deep dives," into various parts of the design. A deep dive is a detailed design review that also includes schedules, risks, and issues. These were extremely time-consuming and added yet another layer of pressure on my team. We were already working to an unrealistic schedule, yet the management team couldn't leave us alone long enough to do the work. Project managers browbeat the team to work smarter, harder, longer, and to recover a day here or another day there. Vacations were put on hold.

To make matters worse, the Raleigh team fell further and further behind in the design work for both the vector unit and the Memory Flow Control. They were failing on all fronts, including timing takedown and bug fixes. Timing takedown is an engineering discipline focused on tuning the slowest parts of the design in order to achieve the final frequency goals. I flew to Raleigh about every other week to get a handle on the problems. Mickie even brought some of the managers and technical leads from Austin to see if they could help. What I finally came to realize was that there was a shortage of strong leadership and sound engineering practice at the Raleigh site because so many of the seasoned veterans were now at Qualcomm. I decided enough was enough, and I pulled together all the first-line managers and the technical leads, and laid it on the line.

"Look guys, you're not getting the design done doing it your way, so from now on you're going to do it my way," I said. There I was being a bullheaded control freak again, but working as Jim Kahle's protégé on several products, I had learned that a certain series of meetings and a certain set of methods can drive team behavior in the right direction for success.

I went to the whiteboard and started outlining those required meetings and methods. "I want biweekly timing takedown meetings to identify the top problem timing paths and assign owners to fix them." The Raleigh team grumbled behind me, and I turned to look at them. I stared them down and continued. "You have to have the entire team there. It motivates an engineer to make fixes when his name keeps showing up on the top of the timing takedown list.

"Secondly," I said, turning back to the board, "I want daily bug swat meetings for logic designers to meet with the verification team and discuss the latest showstopper bugs. Similar to the timing takedown meetings, this forces engineers to get their bugs fixed when they become the reason we're not making verification progress. And by daily, I mean Saturdays, too." The grumbling turned to a low roar, but I ignored it. "I'm coming back in two weeks, and I want to see significant progress."

I closed my notebook computer, ended the meeting, and raced to the airport to catch my flight.

I came back two weeks later to find that they had followed through on the daily verification meetings. Pete, the first-line manager, pulled me aside and said, "You know, that was a good idea. We've made a lot of progress on the bug front since we started tracking them your way."

I discovered, however, that the timing takedown meetings were not having the same success. I pulled in the team lead of the vector unit and gave him an earful. He started arguing with me, but I cut him short. "If you can't drive these meetings, then I'll put someone else in your job. It's that simple. Now pull your team together. I want a timing takedown meeting right now." That was the last time I had to do that.

The timing meetings became a regular occurrence and the vector unit's timing started to converge.

During that same visit, I went to see my friend Tony Truong. The Memory Flow Control team was having the same problems as the vector unit team. Tony had successfully defined the new architecture of the unit, but he was having less success actually driving the day-to-day activities of the team. He complained, "There's a strange culture here that won't let me in. I could use your help."

I knew immediately it was the same old Raleigh versus Austin competition again. I talked to the first-line manager in charge of the Memory Flow Control unit, stressing the point that Tony was the overall lead and the team needed to follow his direction. I asked for immediate compliance, and I think he got the point. Over time, things smoothed out under Tony's soft leadership.

Back in Austin, status meetings with the vice presidents consumed what little breathing room Mickie and I had left over in our exhausting schedules. We participated in no less than five weekly status meetings and numerous technical reviews. Each meeting required extensive preparation and sometimes even dry runs up the chain, depending on the final audience. This meant the tough daily engineering problems the team faced were not getting adequate attention from me or the rest of the leadership team. Mickie barely had time to do anything other than gather data for the next day's status reviews.

I also required the Austin design team to hold all the same engineering meetings I had insisted on in Raleigh. We held daily swat meetings to review the current list of bugs, assign owners, and track status. Weekly timing meetings forced the engineers to study the bottlenecks in their designs and find ways to speed things up. I struggled to attend as many of these meetings as possible. I knew it was important to keep the executives happy, but in the long run, what would make them happiest was if we could finish the design on schedule. That's what I focused on. This required rigor in beating down the bugs and beating down the timing. I knew my presence in these engineering meetings helped keep the heat turned up to finish the design in a quality manner. I had no qualms about taking a hard line when necessary and keeping everyone accountable.

Midway through the design, I realized we were in trouble. We couldn't do it all—hold the schedule, achieve the ultimate frequency target, and deliver a high-quality design. I went straight to Akrout's office. Akrout was less and less accessible these days, and he was in a sour mood much more often than in the past. Justifiably, I was uncomfortable broaching this subject, but I knew I had to do it.

"Chekib, something's got to give. I think we can hold our schedule, but we need some relief on the timing target. I propose we reduce the timing target by several hundred picoseconds for the first-pass spin of the design. We will make it up in the second-pass revision." I braced myself for the flogging. With a change like this, the initial chip would run slightly slower than the current frequency target.

Akrout looked tired as he leaned his head back against the top of his chair. That restless energy that kept him in constant motion seemed to have deserted him. He gave a big sigh. "Okay, Dave. Let's make the proposal to the Xbox project management team."

We conducted weekly conference calls with the Xbox project managers in Rochester, and most weeks Albert Randall joined the call. Randall was IBM's director in charge of chip development for the Xbox 360 project. He was a new director, brought into the new Technical and Engineering Services Division specifically to run the Microsoft project. I first encountered Randall in an IBM task force where I gained respect for his technical ability. He came to IBM from Intel and, unfortunately, he brought with him Intel's "in your face" management style. His nature was to be confrontational about just about everything. He enjoyed arguing, but he did it with no humor, and it was painful for those who had to work with him. My relationship with Randall was already on shaky ground because of previous visits he had made to meet with my team. Supposedly, he came to boost morale and show executive support, but his confrontational style often angered the team. Mickie and I scrambled to do damage control after he left, so it got to where we dreaded his visits to Austin.

In my usual get-it-over-with style, I jumped straight to the timing issue at the start of the meeting. "I want to make a proposal. I don't see any way my PowerPC core team can hold the schedule and also make the frequency target. I propose we relax the timing target by several hundred picoseconds for the first pass and make it up in the second pass."

Randall lashed out immediately. "Your team is out of control. You have no idea where you are on timing, do you?"

The hair on the back of my neck bristled, and I countered gruffly, "We know exactly where we are, and I can show you a plan to deliver the first-pass silicon on schedule with a relaxed timing target. We will then beat down the timing in the second-pass silicon drop. Isn't schedule still our highest priority?"

The original, agreed-upon strategy did indeed include two passes of silicon; however, we planned to incorporate only minor must-have bug fixes on the second pass. Keep it light and simple. So much was riding on completing this design in just two passes, and it was risky to push a lot of change into that last design phase. Too much could go wrong and thus drive a third pass. Nevertheless, I believed the only way to hold schedule and have any chance at making a Christmas 2005 launch was to make this alteration in the plan. I took a big gamble, but my gut told me it was the right thing to do for the project.

Randall grumbled something about discussing this off-line with Akrout, and abruptly hung up. That was the last I heard on the subject, so I proceeded with my adjusted timing takedown plan.

Out on the West Coast, Microsoft's Xbox team was also very busy and facing multiple challenges with designing the console, developing the graphics chip, and getting games ready to launch alongside the new Xbox 360. They asked IBM for a hardware solution that would allow early game code development even before completion of either the triple PowerPC chip or ATI's graphics chip.

Akrout called his leadership team into his executive conference room and presented Microsoft's challenging request. "Surely there's some PowerPC-based hardware we can kluge together into a game developer's kit. Let's get creative, think outside the box—pun intended."

Most of us laughed at Akrout's little joke, but Kahle grumbled something under his breath, distracting me. He seemed particularly put out by this request. It wasn't too difficult to figure out why. Sony had no possibilities for a similar early solution for their game developers because of the radical new Cell architecture in the PlayStation 3. There was no such Synergistic core–based beast in existence. The PlayStation 3 early game code development would have to be accomplished on much slower software emulators that could never provide insight into the real-time behavior of the code. So most of the game development would have to wait until we delivered the Cell chip prototypes. Furthermore, there was a limited supply of available game developers in the world, and they operated on a first-come, first-served basis. If we could devise a development platform for Microsoft, they would gain the upper hand in securing any talent not already committed to PlayStation 2 or Xbox work.

I turned my attention back to the problem at hand. For Microsoft, we needed a PowerPC solution that most closely matched the Xbox 360 configuration. An inelegant kluge, as Akrout suggested, could be a patched-together configuration of relatively mismatched components, as long as this new mutt resembled three PowerPC cores working in concert. We discussed the pros and cons of combining multiple copies of the original PlayStation 3 PowerPC core that we designed for Sony. We could throw some glue logic around it to make it look like the three-way Xbox 360 chip. This conglomeration would come closest to the new design, but it would require a lot of invention. We had neither the manpower nor the time for that work.

A second proposal was to cut and run with the new PlayBox core, releasing something early even though it was certain to have bugs.

"Chekib, that's not an option!" I quickly interjected. "It will be garbage in, garbage out. The chip won't work when we get it back from the fab, and it will pull the whole team down! We'll end up spending all our time chasing down bugs on multiple fronts."

Akrout spread his big hands out on the table and leaned forward. He smiled at me. "Dave, calm down. We're exploring all options."

He was trying to placate me, but I had to make doubly sure no one thought for one instant that we could be successful with that idea. I didn't want to debate it. I fired back, "I need to make it clear. That option stinks. It will just require more work from my team, putting us further behind schedule, and risking the launch date for both projects."

Jim Kahle stepped into the fray. "Maybe we can use the IBM 970 chip we're designing for Apple."

Now that was a sweet idea! I looked at Kahle in surprise. I guess he did still know how to put on his IBM hat. This 970 chip, with its two

PowerPC cores, was still in production, and Apple had not publicly released it in a product yet. It made a nice compromise. The 970's PowerPC core was a modified version of the Power4 core that Kahle and I had worked on years before, and we were both intimately familiar with this design. It would only give about one half the frequency of the new Xbox 360 chip, but it still had a lot of processing power. The 970 chip, when paired with an off-the-shelf ATI Radeon 9800 graphics card, would allow game coders to experiment with subdividing their code into multiple tasks. It wouldn't be exactly like the Xbox 360 design, but it would be close enough. And best of all, it didn't require any work from my team. The Microsoft team could handle all the integration and testing.

Akrout went to Microsoft and sold them on the plan.

This allowed game developers to start writing code and porting it to hardware almost a year before the actual Xbox 360 prototype hardware was available. They made major progress on their artwork, because they got a taste of the quality and speed the real hardware would bring to their animations.

The bug swat meetings I had insisted on called for my Austin team to demonstrate a little bit of acting and a lot of patience. We broke them into two meetings. The first one I called the "double top-secret bug meeting." It was an IBM-only meeting where we discussed all the bugs found in both the PlayStation 3 and the Xbox 360 simulation environments and those that were unique to the Xbox 360. We invited the Sony and Toshiba engineers to a second meeting where we discussed (usually for the second time that morning) all the PlayStation 3 bugs. The most difficult part was acting as if it was the first time I heard the verification engineer describe the bug. I repeated the questions I'd asked during the earlier meeting and pretended I didn't know the logic designer's response. It was time consuming having two meetings but a necessity, given the secrecy of the projects. There were times when we found a bug in the design using the Xbox 360 simulation environment, and the responsible engineer happened to be a Sony or Toshiba employee. We couldn't just hand the bug over to the designer without first re-creating it in the PlayStation 3 environment. This was duplicate effort that angered some of the IBMers, especially our verification engineers, but it was unavoidable. I yearned for our simple life, when our only goal was to deliver the PlayStation 3 PowerPC core. These were strange times, and everyone felt the pressure of all the secrecy between the projects.

The executives' greatest fear was that one of the competitors, either Sony or Microsoft, would successfully launch on schedule and one would not, and it would be IBM's fault. With this intertwined development activity where Sony and Toshiba engineers were unknowingly working on a chip destined for their competitor's product, the potential liability for IBM was unthinkable. Steve Carter still demanded detailed daily status reviews so that he could have the earliest heads-up of impending disaster, which he obviously thought was inevitable. He placed extreme pressure on Akrout, Mickie, and me, and ultimately onto the team, often resorting to bullheaded shouts and accusations. The stress wreaked havoc on our team, for no matter how much Mickie and I tried to shelter them, we still had to get information from them. They reacted poorly to this level of scrutiny, viewing it as a sign of distrust.

Even though the team racked up history-making achievements as the project progressed, they felt no one recognized their accomplishments. They began to wonder why. Would all of their hard work go unrewarded? Why wouldn't the executives trust them? When they didn't get profoundly believable answers to those questions, they made up their own. I heard many variations of comments like: "We're being set up for failure," and "They spent the reward money to bring in the Microsoft contract," or "Our managers and executives are too stupid to recognize the jewels we hand them." People cut back on their hours, called in sick, slowed down, and made up excuses to avoid work on weekends. As the unhappiness rapidly rose to a crescendo, I panicked. I had to do something before this expectation of failure strangled the whole project.

"And why shouldn't we cut back?" they asked when I challenged them. "We can work our butts off, and fail. Or we can enjoy life a little, and still fail. What difference does it make?"

"We're not going to fail!" I stated passionately. "We still have a chance to pull this off. You're doing fantastic work. Don't stop just short of the goal line."

We all tried to tone down the rhetoric, to use encouraging words, and to remember to say thank you every once in a while. Perhaps this moved the team a little bit away from the edge, because the work pace actually did pick up. We began to see progress again.

Whew! We had avoided a major catastrophe.

Maybe the team just felt so sorry for their misguided leaders that they shrugged their shoulders and decided to keep plodding along. Besides, the whole industry was in a slump. Where else were they going to go?

Mickie and I were on a first-name basis with stress. We rode the roller coaster as our careers first seemed to skyrocket, then nose dive. We called Akrout's executive office the "torture chamber" where he and his staff examined each core design decision and every design bug in excruciating detail before it was taken up the chain for Carter's review. It was the most overexposed design ever created in the IBM Corporation. Tempers flared in tough in-your-face cross-examinations. Jim Van Norstrand and I often felt we were on the witness stand in a court of law. I cautioned Jim to think very carefully before speaking, because who knew what they would use against us later.

In one intense IBM-only session, Akrout summoned his leadership team, which included all the STI project's second-line managers, project managers, and technical leads. Mickie, Jim, and I were the first to enter into the torture chamber, where we waited in glum silence and tried to prepare ourselves for yet another assault. Soon, the rest of Akrout's invitees and his direct reports, including Randall, joined us. In this particular torture session, they were once again questioning whether my team had any prayer of completing the design by the end of the year with an acceptable measure of quality.

Akrout asked, "What level of confidence do you have that the Xbox 360 will be able to boot its game kernel? Are our chances of success thirty percent, sixty percent, ninety percent?"

I looked at Jim and we both shrugged. "Chekib, it's way too early in the design cycle to make an estimate. It would just be a baseless guess," I said.

Akrout wouldn't give in. "Come on, what's your gut feel? I need a number."

I felt trapped. It didn't matter what I said, I was going to be grilled and criticized for my opinion. I was so sick and tired of everyone accusing me of being too optimistic. "Less than thirty percent," I fired off, to get Akrout to back away.

I heard the initial synchronized gasp, then the room went silent. Oops.

I looked down at the table in front of me, but I could still feel everyone's eyes on me. The next thing I knew, Randall leaned forward in his chair and fired a direct shot at me. "You have no idea what you're doing, do you? I lost trust in you when you recommended that we relax the timing target to meet the schedule. Now this!" He punctuated his angry spate of words with a loud slap of his big hands on the table. He shifted his fierce glare to Akrout, his nonverbal communication clearly demanding my execution.

For me, this was the last straw. I folded my arms across my chest to keep myself from taking a swing at Randall. "Albert, what answer could I have possibly given to that loaded question that would have met with your approval? Never mind!" I flipped up a hand to halt the vicious response that seemed ready to flame from his mouth. "Don't answer that. I don't really give a damn what your opinion is, and I don't think anyone else in the room does either." We both looked around the room, a silent poll.

No one looked away—the drama was just too raw and riveting. But no one stood up for him—or for me.

Randall stormed out of the room like a hurt child. My declaration was probably a career-limiting move, but I was stretched to the limit and wasn't going to take crap from anyone else, executive or otherwise.

The meeting ended soon after that outburst, and my forecast spread quickly to our Microsoft customers, who unexpectedly responded by calling it what it was . . . duress. Mickie and I spent hours coaxing the IBM executives back from the brink, but the Microsoft team never wavered. They continued to believe that their goals were achievable. Whatever we messed up in hardware, they reasoned, they could fix in software.

The Sony and Toshiba executives, fed continually with inside information from their own engineers on my PlayBox team, already knew as much as anyone about the problems we faced. They didn't know about my Xbox 360 predictions, of course, but they formed their own assessment of the potential for our success, and they quietly pressured Kahle and Akrout. Trust, the backbone of the triad that led the Design Center, eroded into a sham.

The months that followed were painful. The daily scrutiny continued, and we became a little more hardened to the public floggings. Mickie tried to cheer up the team with some fun events, including one really nice party-boat ride out on Lake Travis, a luau with a roasted pig and a margarita machine, a few Happy Hours at our favorite bar, and birthday celebrations with cake and ice cream. But it was simply a gloomy time. Tempers were short, smiles were scarce, and the friendships we had worked so hard to form dissolved in distrust. Any hope we'd had for an enjoyable work environment disappeared like vapor on the wind. No, we were not having fun.

IBM executives allowed, and maybe even supported, the narcissistic construction of fiefdoms and internal empires. They seemed far less interested in doing the right thing for the company—or maybe they simply didn't recognize the right thing when they saw it. Vincent Jennings was a perfect example of this. A major reorganization at IBM suddenly placed all processor development, from server chips to game chips, under Jennings. This was the beginning of the end for the rising star Chekib Akrout. He and Jennings had never been the best of friends, and now, with this move, Akrout found himself working for Jennings. It should have been the other way around, and it was a slap in the face for Akrout. I think this move had something to do with the disappointing changes to Apple's roadmap, which IBM's server elite still held against Akrout even though he was so successful with the game chips.

Jennings was disconnected from the convergence of consumer electronic devices (such as game machines) with the home computing space, and the introduction of the low-end blade server space. I remember meeting with him right after the re-organization and telling him about our incredible accomplishment of designing a supercomputer on a chip. My words fell on deaf ears. He asked why we hadn't used one of his prized server microprocessors. He just didn't get it. We achieved twice the frequency of those server chips within a power budget that was an order of magnitude smaller. We're talking 10 watts compared to 100 watts! Our customers would have walked away if we had not come up with something to compete in the consumer product space, which his server chips did not do. He should have been jumping up and down about our record-beating chip but, instead, he seemed to view it as a one-time shooting star. It wasn't a server chip, and his beloved Server Group hadn't developed it, so it didn't seem to warrant any of his attention. I was extremely disappointed. While I was disappointed in Jennings, I could certainly hold fast to the many lessons learned under Akrout's tutelage. There was a strong similarity in the way that he and Robbie Bach looked at risk, and that's what I wanted to emulate. I aggressively tackled a difficult design on a short schedule, and I tried to be proactive and anticipate problems before they snowballed. I tried to think like my customer. That's what it took to deliver on the Microsoft schedule, so *I changed*. And this may be at least partly what contributed to my falling out with Jim Kahle. He felt I had betrayed him.

In spite of all that, my phenomenal team continued to do their best work that unforgettable summer of 2004, ignoring the tumultuous leadership storms that raged above them. Miraculously, our recovery plan worked. Remember that plan we tried to tell Steve Carter about before he exploded, the plan we'd worked up *before* the shocking news broadcast about our little hiccup? Quietly, behind the scenes, my team had trudged ahead with that recovery plan gradually making up for lost time. Step by step, we moved closer and closer to hitting our targets.

Against all odds and expectations, the PlayBox team finished both the Xbox 360 and the PlayStation 3 PowerPC designs a few days ahead of schedule at the end of September 2004, and we exceeded our frequency target. We passed our first hurdle, but still had a full second-pass revision to complete before production.

We really wanted to celebrate this victory, but we were just too tired. We found it easier to thumb our noses at the naysayers, and then go home. Home to renew our relationships with the families we had so long neglected, to tackle those ever-growing piles of chores, and to perhaps sleep through a full night.

Having met our major design goals, Mickie chose this particular juncture to leave IBM to pursue an opportunity as a small business owner and a writer, and to have time to ride her Harley, travel, and play. I knew, though almost no one else did, that her departure came just one year earlier than she had planned. The brutal experience we'd just been through together made her take a hard look at the value she expected to gain from giving one more year to IBM. I guess the desire for a change won out.

When our PlayBox team released *both* the Sony core and the Microsoft core to the chip's physical design teams, there was still much work ahead to meet a December 2004 manufacturing date. As John Keaty and his team of integrators laid out the physical design for the whole chip, my team continued to work. It would be fantastic to have enough time to wring out every last bug in a design before it went to fab, but I don't expect that will ever happen, and it certainly did not happen on this lickety-split schedule.

My verification team continued to probe, hunting for those remote bugs triggered only when certain conditions occurred in exactly the right sequence. Andy Petruski (our verification team leader) had his team automate a lot of this to run overnight or over weekends, but whenever a bug was uncovered, we jumped through hoops to investigate it. The earlier in the process we found the bug, the easier it would be for John Keaty to absorb a repaired piece of circuitry without a schedule hit. Hopefully, that's all the fix entailed, because anything more could set the integration process back by weeks.

It was imperative to isolate any showstoppers as quickly as possible because if we were going to redesign, we needed to do it before the money has been spent in fabrication. Though we were way past the point of anything like a cheap fix, millions of dollars could be lost if a catastrophic bug was found after the fabrication process actually started.

"What's up?" I asked, as I approached Clark O'niell's desk to review the list of bugs uncovered during the previous night's run. Every morning, my first stop (after coffee) was at the command center where we tracked all bugs.

With all the energy of a hyperactive kid, Clark responded, "Three bugs. Two are probable test case problems. One could be a problem in the IU." He tapped his pencil against his knee, rat-a-tat-tat-tat-tat.

"Who's the logic designer and the circuit designer? Let's get 'em in here so we can determine if it's fixable without a major rip up," I said. I sipped my coffee and tried to remember when we'd last had a major bug. Awhile ago.

"Sure, we can do that," he replied, bobbing his blond head up and down. "But . . . maybe I better explain something first."

Clark was a brilliant engineer, one who would go far in the company. I trusted his instincts, even if he was a little excitable. "So explain," I said, sitting down on the desk next to him.

"If I'm right, the PlayStation can probably tolerate this bug, but the XBox absolutely cannot. And the logic designer is a Sony engineer who will recognize that there's no valid reason for him to fix it. Especially at this late date."

"Oh, shit," I said. I took another sip of my coffee and tried to stay calm. I looked around the sea of cubicles to make sure there were no Sony or Toshiba engineers nearby. "Okay, let's do this. Get Van Norstrand in here to review the bug. I want his opinion on whether or not we have to fix it." Jim had more experience with IU designs than just about anyone in the company.

An hour later, Jim stopped by my desk. "We dodged a bullet," he said quietly.

"What happened? Did it turn out it wasn't really a bug?"

"Oh, no, we weren't that lucky. But I talked to the designer about it. He agreed to get it fixed."

I thought he seemed to be avoiding something, so I decided to be more direct. "Are you telling me that he knows he's making a fix for Xbox?"

Jim raised his eyebrows. "We didn't discuss it, but I'm sure he understood. Let's just leave it like that. I can verify that the fix is done correctly."

"Wow," I whispered.

He nodded in agreement. There didn't seem to be anything else to say. We shook hands, and Jim walked away. He had considerable influence with the team, and I guess he just proved how much.

There was never another word spoken about the problem.

Sang Dhong's Synergistic core team delivered their final drop on time, but there were others not so prompt. One of the components being designed in Rochester failed to meet the timing goals, so they continued working to bring the timing down, even though Keaty and Keryn Mills were sweating bullets about the deadlines. The whole chip would only run as fast as our slowest component.

Missing our manufacturing deadline was a very big deal, because we were trying to hit a tiny window of opportunity just before Christmas. If we ran late, all the manufacturing engineers who performed the up-front work on the chip before sending it to the fab would be off on vacation. And we would be set back at least three weeks. There was also the potential for other chips to take the slot away from us. This could add weeks or even months into the schedule while we waited for another slot to open up. IBM's primary profits come from selling servers and manufacturing chips. They won't tolerate idle manufacturing facilities, so they always have chips in the pipeline. When one is delayed, which is not uncommon in this business, they do everything possible to move another chip up. One project's problems become another project's gain.

It was touch and go right up to the last moment, but Keaty and his team delivered both the PlayStation 3 chip and the Xbox 360 chip to the manufacturing team on time. With a collective sigh, we all went home for Christmas.

CHAPTER 12

Celebrate Success!

Take every opportunity to celebrate success. Even when you don't feel like it. Even when you're tired and stressed out. Even when the accomplishment was accidental. Put thought and energy into your celebrations. Be creative. Let your team see the sincerity in your praise. Let your words ignite a new spark of energy and vitality in the team.

WITH MICKIE GONE and Jennings running the show, it was a little lonely for me as we waited for the fabrication effort to spin out the first chips (known in the industry as "first silicon"). I considered leaving then, too, but I had this burning desire to be here with my team when they crossed the finish line. I wanted to be here to celebrate our undeniable victory, for I was certain that both Sony and Microsoft would succeed. I needed to know that all the pain was worthwhile. So I stayed.

Unfortunately, IBM encountered problems at the foundry that delayed delivery of Sony's first Cell chips and the first Microsoft chips by six weeks. Microsoft revealed that they had a backup plan—a second manufacturing source, Chartered Semiconductor. Chartered received the chip design at the same time as the IBM foundry and processed the silicon in parallel. This kind of insurance policy was very expensive, but it paid off in spades when Chartered managed to deliver parts more than a month earlier than IBM. Sony had to restart the manufacturing process, and so they failed to meet the committed schedule for delivery of first prototypes to the game developers, who were already destined to be in a crunch.

I still remember the dismayed look on Keryn Mills's face when she heard Microsoft would receive chips before Sony. Keryn prided herself in her project management skills, but despite her best efforts, she could not improve the schedule for Sony. Keryn was nothing if not a true-blue IBMer, so IBM's concerns were her concerns. She called meetings, she grilled people at the fabrication facility, she grumbled, ranted, and raved, but nothing could be done. The IBM fab failed all of us.

The scariest and possibly the most exciting time of all design work is the day the manufacturing team delivers the first real chips. I prayed we'd already discovered and resolved all catastrophic bugs before fabrication. On previous projects, chips sometimes came in DOA, meaning they couldn't even be fired up and checked out. That always made it infinitely harder to determine failure causes and, of course, it also meant another costly run through the fab once the bugs were corrected.

I assigned two engineers from my design team to head up the PowerPC core debug effort. Chris Abernathy and Ron Hall were up-and-coming hotshot engineers, who aspired to fill my shoes some day as chief architect. Ron worked in the Sony lab, and Chris worked in the Microsoft lab.

I got to know both of them well over the last couple of years on the project. Ron organized a weekly poker party for the design team, wisely finding a way to have it at someone else's house. He convinced James McClurg, a verification engineer, to let us trash his bachelor pad. James didn't really like to play poker, but he liked to drink a lot and heckle from the peanut gallery. Ron got me hooked on Texas Hold 'Em. This latest craze in poker stormed the country, even receiving coverage on ESPN. In our little private poker parties, we each threw in twenty dollars and played until one person captured all the money, even if it took all night. The game involved both the luck of the draw and each person's tolerance to risk. With the words "all in," any person could bet all of their chips and take the game or go down in flames with nothing and bow out.

I was terrible the first few times I played, but as I watched experts like Ron win game after game, I eventually developed my own strategy. The first time I took the pot was a real head rush. Luckily, the games never got too serious and the beer-drinking never got too out of hand.

Before their lab assignments started, I pulled Chris and Ron aside to give them a pep talk. I thought they might need some incentive, because lab work can be grueling. "You have to work in a debug lab at least once in your career," I said. "The environment is intense and the work is tough, but it's a fantastic learning experience. You can't duplicate it anywhere else. Upper level management and executives will get to know you by name, and they'll learn what you're capable of doing. You won't always like that level of exposure, but it can have a significant impact on the rest of your career."

I went on to tell them about my first experience in the lab. I was a young engineer in Austin debugging the Power2 processor. We worked night and day when we got first silicon back, and we worked around some tough bugs and got the kernel to boot up in the first week. This accomplishment was exactly what every design team desires—to have working silicon on first-pass hardware. I told Chris and Ron how much I learned about the interaction between software and hardware.

"Sometimes it took every bit of engineering skill I possessed to resolve some tricky bugs," I said. "Lab debug is like solving a complex murder mystery." Old reruns of *Columbo* flashed through my head. I said, "You start with very few facts. You gather as much information as you can. You head down false rabbit holes more often than you'd like, but you keep asking questions and keep searching for answers. Then one day it all clicks, and you solve the mystery bug."

Ron and Chris charged off to the lab, full of purpose and energy mixed in with a little bit of dread. I sort of envied them. They were embarking on a journey that would change the rest of their careers, just as it had mine. There's no other engineering experience quite as rewarding as seeing your design come to life in hardware.

I was there in the secret laboratory on the sixth floor above the STI Design Center when the first Xbox 360 chips arrived in January 2005, hand-delivered by Microsoft's alternate fab, Chartered Semiconductor. The room was crowded with sweating engineers and technicians. A technician plopped the first chip into a prepared console. I held my breath while he checked for proper voltage levels and signals. These first tests seem ever so trivial, but they are sometimes the most important. A fundamental bug in the input voltage could result in a fatally smoked chip, and we only had a handful of chips to work with at that point. They were as precious as gold. The technician sent a few bits of information into the chip to see if it would respond, like checking for a beating heart on a newborn baby.

Success! The signals wiggled, we had a heartbeat. I gave a big sigh of relief. The part was not DOA. The biggest challenge, however, still lay ahead. Would we be able to boot a Windows game kernel and would we be able to run real game code? Failure here would mean Christmas 2005 was out.

The next couple of days were intense. No fewer than thirty managers and project managers wandered into the lab and asked for progress. I often thought we had more project managers than engineers. My typical response was, "Go away, stop bothering us." If it was an executive, I said the same thing, except with a smile.

Finally, the team was ready for the acid test. Could the chips boot the Windows game kernel? We got a code dump from Microsoft with the latest and greatest kernel.

"Let it rip," I said.

On the first attempt, the processor made it well into the kernel code but then hung. We all groaned in unison.

It was time to unleash the big dogs—our top-notch debug team. Several teams worked in shifts, 24/7, both in Austin and at the Microsoft facility in Redmond, Washington.

Eric Mejdrich was the Xbox 360 chip bring-up lead at our Austin facility. On Superbowl Sunday, he was stuck in the lab with a hung kernel. He tried several work-arounds, but kept getting stuck. Finally, he called his buddy Dinarte Morais from Microsoft in San Jose and begged for help. Morais nearly single-handedly wrote the game kernel himself, and he knew it like the back of his hand. Morais was at a

Superbowl party but was willing to help debug the problem over the phone. Between the beers and the Cheetos, he listened to Eric describe the symptoms of the bug. Finally, he snapped his fingers.

"It's the memory configuration driver," he said excitedly. "It must not be enabled properly."

He quickly suggested a few minor code changes and Eric was off to the races.

On Superbowl Sunday, the kernel booted.

Eric had been there for thirty-six hours straight. He slumped in his chair in relief and called me. "The friggin' thing booted!" he shouted over the phone, with his last burst of energy.

I shouted right back, pumping my fist in the air and doing a little victory dance in the end zone at my own Superbowl party.

Only Eric and a couple of undergraduate interns happened to be in the lab at the time, so there was not much celebrating. However, when everyone came in the next day, word traveled fast and the partying began.

Once the kernel booted, Microsoft sent in their swat game code team. They were anxious to get the first games running on the hardware. My most exciting moment on the project came a few days later. The lead Microsoft game engineer handed me the joystick, surprising me with the honor of playing the very first game on the Xbox 360. I have never had so much fun racing around a castle and swinging a bloody sword to slice the heads off everyone in my path.

The near-instant success—from delivery of the chip until we were playing games on it was only a matter of a couple of weeks—in the Xbox 360 lab meant champagne celebrations everywhere. The excitement inevitably spilled over to the STI Design Center where the PowerPC core designers "lived." This led to some awkward situations, some conversations that Sony and Toshiba engineers shouldn't have overheard.

"Have you heard? *Quake 2* is running on an Xbox 360 in the lab!"

It was hard for my IBMers to contain their excitement, and they felt guilty for not being able to share the success with our Sony and Toshiba partners who participated in the design of the common core.

The Xbox 360 chips were working so well so quickly that by the time Sony's chips arrived a few weeks later, in late February, I could afford to devote myself completely to bringing up the Cell chip. Couriers hand-delivered the precious first chips late one evening. I went on home, thinking it would be awhile before the lab team completed the initial "does-it-have-a-heartbeat" tests, but they went so much further. Astounding us all, the Cell chip booted in the middle of the night.

Jim Kahle called me at home and said, "Get your ass out of bed! The kernel booted, and we're celebrating in the lab."

Kahle and I showed up at IBM in pajamas, and we toasted champagne with the team. Akrout was there, too, in the same clothes he'd worn all day. He'd worked very late, and just about the time he was ready to go home, someone raced down the hallway to tell him (and anyone else who was still around) they were very close to success in the PlayStation 3 lab. So he stayed . . . and stayed . . . and stayed. It took longer than they thought it would, but I think he was very happy to be there when it finally happened. That first night, the chips ran at speeds over five gigahertz, blowing away every known processing speed record. Somebody came in with a camera and took pictures of all of us wearing our goofy grins.

I was really dragging the next day, but I managed to make it into the office before noon. As I stepped into the elevator, it dawned on me that all four companies—Sony, Toshiba, IBM, and Microsoft—were represented in the people sharing the car with me. A sign above our heads stated, "Do not discuss confidential information in this area." Boy, you had to see the irony in that. It was totally quiet. We darted furtive glances at each other. We weren't talking about anything, but we were disclosing confidential information just by being in the same elevator in the same building. At least, that's how it felt. The Microsoft engineers proudly sported black and neon-green Xbox T-shirts, never really understanding why that presented such a conflict for me.

The elevator doors opened onto the STI floor first, and the Sony and Toshiba engineers and I exited. I glanced back to see the Microsoft guys looking out at the prohibited domain of the PlayStation 3 team, their eyes glistening with the momentary thrill of a spy. Then the doors closed, and the car ascended on to Xbox land on the sixth floor.

February 14, 2005, Valentine's Day, was another memorable day. The IBMers on my team joined a champagne celebration in the Xbox 360 lab on the sixth floor in the morning, and then joined the entire STI design team in the afternoon for a PlayStation 3 celebration on the third floor. That's when it finally sunk in for us—all of our hard work in 2004 had paid off. Both the Xbox 360 chip and the PlayStation 3 chip were high-quality designs. The common PowerPC core was a huge success.

Of course, there were still bumps and bruises along the way. We were a long way from releasing final chips for product launch. In the Cell lab, the chips came to life rather nicely. However, we noticed some strange performance problems. Some of the performance benchmarks were running dog slow. A performance benchmark is a piece of software that has a well-known behavior when run on other processors and allows us to calibrate our processor's performance. It was as if our race car's turbo eight-cylinder engine was running like a minivan's four-cylinder engine. It needed a tune-up. A sinking feeling crept over me. Had we missed something fundamental in our verification?

A normal functional bug usually manifests itself by giving the wrong answer like $2 + 2 = 5$. However, performance bugs are often the hardest to trace. They often require manual testing and tediously crawling through timing diagrams to look for devious behavior. This was my specialty. I prided myself in coming through with designs that delivered on their performance claims.

On a previous project, the Power4 microprocessor, I held the title "performance czar." We took performance testing to a new level on that project, writing specific software test cases targeted at detecting deviant behavior in the chip. I spent hours crawling over timing diagrams and comparing the behavior to the spec.

On the Cell project, we hadn't been quite as rigorous on performance testing along the way, but we applied a lot of the learning from the Power4 project. I was worried we had gotten sloppy and missed something, so I parked my butt at a lab station and vowed not to leave until we uncovered the problem. It was like trying to find a needle in a haystack, only we weren't even sure which haystack to start with. We had to collect loads of data and then crawl through it carefully. I sat in that seat all afternoon and well into the night, demanding run after run from the engineers operating the station. They thought I was a slave driver; I just wanted answers.

About a day into the debugging process, I spotted a problem. Was it "the" problem? The processor was consistently falling into what we call a "slow mode." We implemented a slow mode as a debug tool to help us understand livelocks. A livelock occurs when the processor keeps looping back through a known sequence and can't make forward progress. It's like the movie *Groundhog Day* where Bill Murray's character wakes up and relives the same day over and over again.

"It's the damn slow mode," I said, "but why do we keep jumping into it?"

I kept digging until I found the glitch. Our processor supports two threads, a hardware technique called multithreading. Under certain conditions, like bootup, one thread can be put to sleep while the other remains active. This particular bug was causing the sleeping thread to force the active thread into slow mode. It was like a person with a split personality, but the deviant side only took over during nap-time. It was extremely hard to isolate the problem. We almost hadn't looked for it there. It was a bad nightmare gone awry. The sleeping thread had an internal counter that kept track of interrupts on either thread. When the counter reached a certain threshold of interrupts, it kicked into slow mode. So it wasn't fully asleep.

Luckily, we had a "chicken switch" to work around the problem. A chicken switch is an internal mode bit purposely inserted into a tricky part of the design, or into a part of the design that is difficult to verify. It allows us to revert to a fallback position if we run into a bug in the chip, thus saving us from another run through the fab to correct the problem. Eventually, we do fix most of these bugs, but the chicken switch allows us to keep making forward progress. We can then accumulate all the fixes into one re-spin of the silicon.

Sure enough, we flipped the switch and boom, the processor started performing as expected. There were high fives all around the lab. I knew this wouldn't be the last tricky bug we would come across.

The next bug we encountered was also a multithreading bug. I was starting to wonder if the decision we made early in the project to add multithreading was a good one. This bug had a much more serious consequence than the previous performance bug. It caused the entire Cell chip to hang. If you've ever had a computer freeze up right when you were working with important data, and you lost all your unsaved material, then you know how frustrating that can be.

The multithreading function allowed the programmer to select the priority for each thread, either high or low. It was like Cinderella and her mean stepsisters. The stepsisters were granted high priority to live the good life while Cinderella slaved away in the basement. Similarly, the high-priority thread got almost all the available processor resources, and the poor second thread had to fight for leftovers.

The high-priority thread got greedy and took over all of the processor resources; however, without allowing the low-priority thread to set a certain register, it couldn't make forward progress. The greedy high-priority thread didn't realize it couldn't survive without giving some time back to the low-priority thread. Therefore, it killed itself and the other thread by hanging the system.

We had a software work-around for this that set both threads to equal priority. The mean stepsisters would just have to learn to live with an equal Cinderella. Once again, a work-around saved us. I wondered how many of our nine lives we had already used, and after nine bugs, would we self-destruct?

I bounced back and forth from lab to lab so often that some days I forgot where I was. I caught myself babbling about PlayStation 3 bugs in the Xbox 360 lab and vice versa. It was a crazy time. Sometimes, under my breath, I cursed the day I agreed to take on both projects simultaneously. What was I thinking?

We found the next bug in the Xbox 360 lab. It was a bad one, and it had no work-arounds. Fortunately, we only saw it with Xbox software, and it rarely occurred. It was the nastiest of bugs, which showed up when we moved lots of data around in our load/store unit. For this problem, we called on David Ray (Farmer Dave), since that was the unit designed by him and his team.

David spent more and more time in the lab, and he was very willing to help solve any problem that arose. However, this one wasn't an easy one to pin down. The machine often ran for up to twelve hours before the bug manifested itself. This alone made it very difficult to pinpoint. Over the course of several weeks, David and his team collected enough data to develop a theory about what was going on. They set up a trap to catch this nasty bug.

It turned out that a queue entry was reallocated before the previous operation finished. An analogy: You're watching TV in your hotel room when another hotel guest barges in and kicks you out. And they got the key from the front desk! We fixed this bug in a later revision of the hardware. It was an isolated problem that occurred so infrequently that it didn't slow down our debugging activities.

Slowly but surely, we experienced fewer and fewer "Oh, shit" moments in the lab. It actually was as quiet as a library, with all the technicians and engineers methodically plowing their way through the test plan with meticulous attention to detail. With every passing moment, we gained confidence that our first-pass silicon was a huge success.

CHAPTER 13

Plan Ahead, Be Persistent, and Be Patient

*Planning, persistence, and patience—the three Ps
of survival in the high-tech world. Think ahead, do
your homework, and develop the best plan. Don't
give up when things get rough. Take a breath.*

THE FINAL MONTHS OF THE PROJECT in early 2005
were fast and furious. We proved we could deliver high-quality, first-
pass silicon, but could we deliver final production silicon with only
one more revision of the chip? This final revision had to be bug free,
meet the frequency goals, and provide high manufacturing yield. With
each bug we fixed, we risked inadvertently introducing another one
into the design. Our designers took extra care to do a perfect repair
job, but our verification team continued to find errors they'd made. It
was difficult to spot every way that a fix could affect this complex design. That was okay, just so long as we found them all and understood
them all before the next silicon run.

To complicate things, we had different requirements and priorities
coming in from the two projects. To navigate our way through serving
two masters with one core, Chekib Akrout established an all-IBM
Common Core Committee. The goal of the committee was to commu-

nicate and prioritize every change considered for Rev2 (final production) of the core.

Jim Kahle took the lead for the PlayStation 3 side, and Jeff Brown took the lead for the Xbox 360 half of the committee. Jeff was the overall technical lead for the Xbox 360. I had run into Jeff on and off over the years, though it was only on this project that we really got to know each other. He reminded me of a big Labrador; on the outside, he seemed soft and cuddly, but he carried a big bark if you happened to be on the wrong side of the fence. Jeff's claim to fame came from the early days on the AS/400 mid-range computer development, when he'd led the memory subsystem design effort.

The Common Core Committee held weekly teleconference meetings in Akrout's stark sixth-floor conference room, the dreaded torture chamber. Typically, I started the meetings with a summary of the contemplated design changes and bug fixes of the week, sometimes with help from the owner of the logic in question. Then Kahle, Jeff, Akrout, and I would vote on whether the changes should go into the core or not. If we couldn't reach agreement, Akrout was the final decision maker.

Akrout's conference room suddenly turned into a courtroom. Kahle and Jeff were opposing attorneys; Akrout was the judge. I was always on the witness stand. Albert Randall often joined the teleconference, playing the role of the surprise hostile co-counsel for Jeff. He was a wild card, and I never knew what he might do or say. Some days he went with the flow, some days he made wild, over-the-top statements. His indiscriminate hostility was just as likely to spew out at Jim Kahle, but most often he targeted me. He accused my team and me of siding with the PlayStation 3 contingent. He believed that because we were physically in the STI Design Center and our first love was the project we started with, we were ignoring actions that were in the Xbox 360's best interests. There was probably a small grain of truth in what he said. A few folks on the project did let their project prejudices get the best of them, but I really wanted to do the right thing for both projects. Despite my telling Randall this on many occasions, he continued to accuse me of playing favorites. He had difficulty taking a global view of the projects himself and stayed primarily concerned only about the Xbox 360 project, so he couldn't see why the rest of us wouldn't behave in a similar fashion.

Even Jim Kahle and Jeff Brown tried to be good corporate citizens and do the right thing for the company, but they did have their own set of priorities. I was the guy in the middle, squeezed on all sides. Sometimes, if my patience wasn't completely depleted, I took the role of mediator and tried to get both sides to come to consensus. It was certainly to my benefit if I could keep everyone working and playing well together.

Every change in the core went through the Common Core Committee including timing, performance, and bug fixes. The problem came when there were conflicting requirements. For example, a bug fix for the Xbox 360 might not be required for the PlayStation 3 due to the different programming models on the two projects. Also, performance bugs in one area of the design might be very important for one project, but not interesting at all for the other.

One of the most interesting items to come through the committee was the request by Microsoft for better emulation support. The original Xbox was based on a standard off-the-shelf X86 microprocessor from Intel. As such, all of the game code for that machine was written for the X86 architecture. This meant the old Xbox game code might not run as efficiently on the new PowerPC architecture since it was not optimized for that purpose. Microsoft wanted us to make the PowerPC architecture emulate the X86 architecture so that the old code would think it was running on an X86 and achieve the same level of performance. For the most part, this was not a problem for us, because what we lacked in identical functionality, we made up for with the massive increase in frequency and the multiple execution threads. The player wouldn't see the differences. However, there was fear that some games that relied heavily on X86 architecture would run slower on the Xbox 360.

To accommodate Microsoft's request, we would have to implement two new instructions as well as add little endian support to the cache control logic. Endianness is the system used to arrange things by order of magnitude. We generally write numbers in a big endian order, with the highest order numbers coming first. The X86 code was all written assuming a binary number system labeled from right to left; in other words, the littlest number was on the right (known as "little endian"). The PowerPC architecture, also a binary number system, was labeled from left to right—in "big endian" format. To switch from big endian order to little endian meant that every instruction and every data element fetched from the memory subsystem had to be swizzled in order.

At IBM, a change of this magnitude would be unheard of for final production silicon for a server. Once again, Microsoft had a much different view of risk. They couldn't understand why we couldn't just "tuck it" into the design.

The meeting to discuss the emulation support took on the air of the O.J. Simpson trial. All the key players from both sides joined the call. I presented the changes and let them hang in the air.

Randall didn't hesitate to jump into the silence. "My customer needs these changes to get good performance on Xbox1 game code. Your team has not delivered the performance you promised, so we need this change. Your design has always favored the PlayStation 3 partners, but for once you need to come through for our side!"

Jim Kahle fired right back. "That's bullshit, Albert. This team has bent over backwards to accommodate you. It would be crazy to put this change in final production silicon without a rigorous test process, which we don't have time to do. The risk is huge, and I can't let you jeopardize the common core for this."

Akrout, ever the peacemaker, stepped in. "This is not productive. Dave, what do you think about the risk of adding this change so late in the game?"

"Personally, I think it's technically feasible. I also think we can make the changes to the hardware in such a way that even if it doesn't work, it won't break anything in the code around it." Even as I said this, I couldn't bring myself to accept the challenge. I was tired and wanted the project to end, so I took a deep breath and continued. "I think we could do it on the schedule, but I don't think it's worth the risk. The other sticky part about this is that it will be hard to sell to our PlayStation 3 partners. Why would they want to accept a significant change like this, to take such a huge risk just so that the Xbox1 code can run better? They have no reason at all to want this change."

We argued some more that day but ultimately could not come to consensus. Akrout decided to defer this and discuss it with other experts. It eventually went to very high places in IBM where it was squashed. I can't say I was sorry.

A fairly significant performance bug came through the committee next. This was one that Microsoft found during a run of their own game benchmarks, and they wanted it fixed. The bug caused the core hardware to create a stall condition in the pipeline. This was like hitting road construction during rush hour traffic, and everything slowed to a crawl. It occurred when a store operation to memory was followed by a load operation to an overlapping memory region. We called it the load-hit-store "feature." The mechanism was intended to stall the load operation long enough for the store operation to write its data to memory. Otherwise, the wrong data would be loaded. However, to improve the timing in the original PowerPC design, the team cut back on the number of comparisons of the memory operation address bits. They imprecisely speculated that the load was hitting a pending store. Because of the lack of precision, sometimes they guessed wrong and stalled the pipeline.

Randall had his usual arguments. "You have to fix this. It is causing a fifteen percent performance degradation in our critical game code. Are you going to do anything to accommodate my customer, or does Sony get their way again?" Randall was still pissed off about not getting the Xbox1 emulation changes he wanted.

Of course, Kahle had his usual arguments, too. "It's crazy to make any changes to production silicon that aren't must-have bug fixes. Will it run without this fix? The answer is yes, so I'm saying we shouldn't touch it."

Prior to the meeting, I did some homework on how hard it would be to fix this feature. Once again, this bug hit David Ray's load/store unit.

Dave grumbled, "Now what do you want, another new feature?"

I said, "No. I just need you to size the effort to correctly fix the load-hit-store bug."

Dave countered with, "I'm tracking down potential real bugs in the debug lab, and you want me to take time to look at this silly performance bug? What's happened to your priorities?"

These were the times I felt very lonely. Pleasing two demanding customers was not easy, and my team had little appreciation for my position. I felt the weight of an $80 billion company on my shoulders. I twisted Dave's arm, and he conceded that it really wasn't that much work.

When it was my turn to speak at the committee meeting, I said, "I think we should fix this bug. We can do it and still have plenty of time for sufficient verification cycles to make sure we didn't screw up something else." I felt Kahle's glare burning a hole in the side of my head. I got no acknowledgment from Randall that I had done him a favor. The committee voted to fix the bug, and I left the room with a bad taste in my mouth.

Sony and Toshiba also got into the act. They requested we fix a parity error recovery mechanism in, you guessed it, Dave's load/store unit. It turned out that the caches in the core were susceptible to alpha particle bombardment, which could flip bits in the memory. As technology dimensions shrink, this becomes more of an issue. We had cut some corners in the original design, and we didn't fully recover from these errors. I met with Kahle before this one got to the common core committee. "I guess we'll have to throw Sony a bone here, since we fixed other Microsoft bugs."

"You bet your ass we will. You go into that committee meeting and convince them this is an easy fix." Kahle's bitter reply stung.

But it was exactly the support I needed. With the behind-the-scenes negotiations and manipulations accomplished, this one sailed through the committee. Even Randall was quiet on this one.

Other interesting performance and functional bugs came before the committee. If the bug favored PlayStation 3, then Kahle argued for it. If the bug favored Xbox 360, then Jeff Brown and Albert Randall argued for it. I was weary and felt I'd been put through a meat grinder one too many times. Luckily, the schedule dictated closure, and it all eventually did end. We locked down the changes and sent the design to the fab for the final silicon spin. Even so, there were still constant scares from the lab, where testing of the first silicon chips (Rev1) continued. I attended a daily lab meeting for both projects, once again running from the first floor to the sixth floor. Any time I heard of a potential logic bug, I cringed but demanded the details. I either classified it as a potential real bug or wrote it off as harmless. I didn't sleep well when it appeared to be a real bug. We were spending millions in the fab, all of which would be lost if we were forced to step back to re-solve a serious bug. Time and time again, the hardware proved true, and we found no showstopper bugs. Despite the sleepless nights, I was more optimistic than anything else. I believed in my world-class team, and I was confident that our design would stand the test of time.

Whenever I heard fearful voices in the hallways as my team dis-cussed a bug that could potentially set back both projects, I tried to re-main calm. "It's probably nothing but a problem with the test case. This is a solid design," I told them. I know this positive attitude helped me, but I also think it helped the team around me.

Against the advice of IBM with their decades of experience in sili-con foundries, Microsoft decided to begin fabrication of their chip with what is known as a "risk ramp." That means they activated a manufacturing plan on a design that was not fully verified in the lab. Usually, clients wait until the final spin of a chip has been rigorously proven in the hardware lab before proceeding with their manufactur-ing plan. But Microsoft lined up hundreds of thousands of silicon wafers in the fabrication facility so that they would have a shot at hav-ing the volumes needed for a Christmas 2005 launch of the Xbox 360. With several millions of dollars at risk, Microsoft was living on the edge. It was just like the motto that drove their Windows software business: "Get it to market first at all cost, worry about the bugs later." In the early spring of 2005, the final revision (at least we hoped it was final) of the chip was still undergoing intensive testing in the labora-tory, and it would not have been a big surprise to uncover an obscure bug that would force Microsoft to trash all those chips in the line. It could happen.

Chekib Akrout strongly urged them to reconsider. I couldn't help but think, the old Chekib would have sided with Microsoft and said "Go for it!" The new and weary Chekib, beaten down by Vincent Jennings, sided with his conservative IBM peers. It was an almost un-heard of risk, one that neither IBM nor Sony would have taken. But everyone knew Bill Gates had very deep pockets. A failed risk ramp would cost millions of dollars. On the other hand, beating Sony to market was worth hundreds of millions of dollars. The amount of money Microsoft would make from game software would dwarf their earnings from many of their other software products.

Microsoft's Larry Yang just smiled and said, "Microsoft is used to taking big risks."

The first production-level chips from this risk-ramp arrived in May 2005, and once again I held my breath while the technicians fired them up. My momentary fear passed quickly, for the chips booted up smoothly and were running games in the lab within mere hours of receipt—Microsoft's gamble paid off. They would have the volumes for a Christmas 2005 launch!

As witnessed repeatedly during the course of this project, risk-taking is a Microsoft characteristic that enabled them to take giant steps forward. Sony and IBM's strategy in the lab was to play it safe, to be very thorough, and to slowly and methodically work through every test plan. Although very different from the Microsoft strategy, history proved that this test strategy was also very successful.

At that same time on the PlayStation 3 side of the house, things were not so rosy. It took a long time to recognize the blunder in Sony's choice of graphics chips. Keryn Mills ran weekly status meetings with the leadership team, which included reports from Sony's onsite deputy director Suzuoki-san, even though IBM had nothing to do with the development of the PlayStation 3 companion graphics chip. Keryn extended her reach as far as anyone allowed, because she thought she could make a difference. When she spotted an area of risk that threatened the Christmas 2005 launch of the PlayStation 3, she didn't hesitate to take ownership. Each week Keryn pounded on Suzuoki-san as he reported that the graphics chip designed by the Sony engineers was slipping schedule. Sony had designed simple graphics chips in the past, but it was clearly not their area of expertise.

After many months of schedule slips, it became obvious that Sony could not deliver the promised graphics chip. They turned to NVidia for help; however, it was too little too late. It was the final straw, piling up on the already heavy burdens of past mistakes. The game developers, having started late due to hardware delays, probably would not have time to complete a sufficient number of hot games to bundle with the PlayStation 3 for Christmas '05. The IBM silicon fabrication facilities, faltering right out of the starting gate, were struggling to deliver sufficient volumes for even a limited launch. In combination, these three problems were insurmountable.

Emotions ran high when Sony, Toshiba, and IBM all realized that the product would not meet the Christmas 2005 launch. Sony announced that they were slipping the date to spring 2006. What a blow to everyone! It saddened us to know that we busted our butts to meet the schedule, but in the end we couldn't do one thing to change the outcome. The 2005 launch had been the entire team's vision and goal from day one. The loss of this dream was a huge blow to all three companies in terms of lost chip revenue, but it was also a double whammy for Toshiba, because they had counted on being the only manufacturer to produce the Sony-designed graphics chip. The Sony and Toshiba relationship took an unexpected turn for the worse at this point.

The solidly backed STI project, with its two-year head start, actually missed the target while Microsoft succeeded!

After all the bad blood following the introduction of the new common core into the PlayStation 3 chip and all the finger pointing, the PowerPC core was not the cause for the missed product launch. My team and I were relieved we weren't the stumbling block, but we were very disappointed that despite all our hard work, the product would not be announced until 2006. Our only consolation was that the Xbox 360 would launch on time.

The project had been a wild ride. We all agreed it was intellectually stimulating and fun pushing the leading edge, but nobody on my team, including me, wanted to participate in such a project ever again. Serving so many masters left us all a little crazy. With the demanding hours, the browbeating that passed as managerial, motivational technique, we all felt IBM had violated many of its own company and business practices in jockeying both horses in this particular race. There was a slogan bantered around over the years by IBM managers called "respect for the individual." I thought about our ride on this roller-coaster project. Where was the respect this time?

I was proud of my team. We delivered even through the face of extreme adversity. We also delivered on a record schedule unheard of in the industry.

I suffered one more blow that final year. In April 2005, my dear friend and mentor Chekib Akrout resigned from IBM, leaving after more than twenty years. He had endured enough under the harsh rule of Jennings and the shifting politics of the company leadership. Immediately after Akrout gave notice of his resignation, he took a few days off. I still don't know whether that "vacation" was voluntary or not, but regardless, he never did come back to work. IBM's practice is to get people out the door as quickly as possible, especially executives, before they have a chance to contaminate the rest of the team or draw others along with them. Jennings assigned someone else to clean out Akrout's office and retrieve his badge, so we never had the chance to give the big send-off that he so deserved. His record at IBM is legendary. It gives me great pleasure to know that he found a home at AMD, where he is creating a new central engineering organization. His leaving IBM was devastating to me. Akrout was the one person who maintained integrity and calm through the storm, and I hated to see him go.

Earlier in the project, Chekib Akrout had a high level of self-confidence and charisma, like Robbie Bach and Ken Kutaragi. He was a risk-taker. As IBM's vice president of entertainment and embedded processor development, he was the one who strongly pursued other customers for our PowerPC core, who balanced the demands of two archrivals and brought success to both, who fought hard to keep the Apple business, who tried to break away from the traditional IBM conservatism. He was a well-respected visionary with the spirit of a warrior. But over the course of the project, he was so beaten up by the more conservative server-centric senior IBM management that he surrendered. In a different company, Akrout will be a shining Robbie Bach.

The final celebration party for the Xbox 360 was anticlimactic. Microsoft rewarded everyone who worked on the project with an Xbox 360 game machine. We had an offsite celebration at a local Mexican restaurant, and I remember Vincent Jennings strolling through the crowd shaking hands and making small talk as if he'd been there all along. He couldn't even spell game machine just a few months before. I missed my friend Chekib.

I was extremely proud of my team. I walked around the restaurant and tried to find everyone on my team, look each one in the eye, and thank him or her from my heart. I was fortunate to work with the hundreds of talented engineers who made this development effort a success. Despite all the corporate battles that swirled around us, we delivered! We successfully created the common microprocessor core that became the heart and soul of the 234-million-transistor PlayStation 3 Cell central processor chip and the 165-million-transistor Xbox 360 central processor chip.

I was disappointed that the Sony and Toshiba partners could not participate in the Xbox 360 celebration. I often think of my friends Hiroo-san and Masa-san and all the other Sony and Toshiba engineers who worked on the common core. They were phenomenal. Even knowing that their work would lend power to their competition, they never held back on innovative, quality engineering. They were true to the work. I would work with them again in an instant. They are truly heroes.

EPILOGUE

Is it ever really over?
Your past is the bridge to your future.

S O , D I D W E R E A L I Z E Ken Kutaragi's grand vision for the Cell chip? The answer is not simple. Although there were many technological inventions (generating over 500 patents), IBM never adopted the Cell chip as their one-size-fits-all solution for products ranging from mainframes to embedded solutions. They are, however, working with Los Alamos National Laboratory to develop a supercomputer, a hybrid code-named Roadrunner, based on sixteen thousand Cell processors running in combination with sixteen thousand AMD Opterons. And IBM did introduce a blade server based on the Cell chip. They offer a software development kit for potential users of the Cell broadband engine chip, so I guess Mike Day and his software team finally did get some funding. That's good, because that will allow the Cell technology to make inroads in many areas, including seismic image processing, medical imaging, financial analysis, aerospace system development, and anywhere else where there's a computationally intensive workload.

IBM is also working with several universities, including MIT, Georgia Institute of Technology, and Washington University, to develop competence in programming the Cell chip and to experiment on new applications. They recently announced plans for a $3.8 million center for developing Cell-based products and applications at

Indiana University-Purdue University Indianapolis—the first such IBM facility on a college campus.

Toshiba introduced a new laptop, the Qosmio, which is loaded with four Synergistic cores from the Cell chip. They call this new co-processor chip the SpursEngine, and the laptop is touted to have very high capabilities for image processing (like face recognition). At the Consumer Electronics Show in 2008, Toshiba also showed a prototype television running on the Cell chip. The demonstration of this proto-type showed how easy it would be to navigate a number of video channels simultaneously—Toshiba actually showed forty-eight thumb-nail television clips running on the screen at the same time.

At the SIGGRAPH conference in 2007, Sony introduced a Cell-based product, the Cell Computing Board, which allows faster image processing and rendering. Sony collaborated with several software companies to develop complete package solutions based on this prod-uct for movie studios, animation houses, and graphic design compa-nies that require the creation and processing of high-quality images. Sony already sold their stake in the manufacturing plants to Toshiba for a reported $835 million, trying to recoup some of the money they had invested in Cell technologies.

I would be remiss if I did not at least mention this secondary battle fueled by the game console war. Despite serious technology chal-lenges, Sony insisted on providing the PlayStation 3 console with the ability to play Blu-ray discs. Blu-ray is a new high-density optical disc format for storage of digital information (like movies). Sony desper-ately wanted their PlayStation 3 to be the first consumer Blu-ray de-vice in the U.S. market. Sony engaged in a "to the death" battle with Toshiba over who would own the market for movie discs. Sony lost out during the Betamax versus VHS war thirty years ago, and they do not intend to do so again. Blu-ray was Sony's invention, while Toshiba developed the competing technology for the HD-DVD format, which has been out on the market longer. Blu-ray discs are more expensive, but they hold more data. To Sony's benefit, the PlayStation 3 is one of the cheaper Blu-ray players on the market. There is some debate about whether or not the addition of this feature had a negative im-pact on PlayStation 3 sales—it did raise the price to an unacceptable level for many gamers' pocketbooks—but there is no doubt that sales of the console had a strong influence over the Blu-ray/HD-DVD war. Of the top fifteen major motion picture companies, all but four said that they would move their titles from HD-DVD to the Blu-ray format. This marked the beginning of the end of the war, but Toshiba's announcement in February 2008 that it was pulling support for the HD-DVD format officially ended it. Toshiba said they would cease production of the HD-DVD players. Sony won, and with that win, the PlayStation 3 has one more point in its favor for those game console buyers still trying to make up their minds.

So while Sony did not fully realize Kutaragi's dream to take over the home computing and entertainment space yet, all three STI partners continue to make deep strides into that territory.

Microsoft seriously upped the ante on the battle for the living room with the Xbox 360 and its powerful online following. In retrospect, I see even more clearly the stark differences in my two masters, Sony and Microsoft, and I marvel that we survived. They attacked the game market in quite different ways, both from a business standpoint and from a technical standpoint. Both central processing chips contained the same common foundation, the PowerPC core, but Sony and Microsoft each developed well-defined strategies for product differentiation. Both game consoles flexed powerful (but different) muscles to perform all those millions of floating-point computations required for realistic graphics. Sony had their "eight is beautiful" Synergistic cores, while Microsoft had their new vector unit, one on each of the three PowerPC cores providing six parallel threads. Each also had a powerful graphics processing chip. With the combination of the central processing chip and the graphics chip, each console boasted significant horsepower. However, the Xbox 360 used a more traditional multiprocessing model, which helped them with simpler game code development and system bring-up.

Sony's more risk-averse business style was in stark contrast to Microsoft's double-dare-you attitude. Microsoft was overly focused on the end result, a Christmas 2005 product launch, so much so that the date might as well have been tattooed on the forehead of every Microsoft employee. It was a "victory or death" attitude. Sony, on the other hand, was much more reserved and unwilling to make compromises and tough business decisions to ensure an early launch at all costs. Microsoft was willing to accept risk with regard to time to market, product testing, tolerance for error, and bug resolution. They were willing to live with some significant hardware bugs if it meant they could stay on schedule, a very aggressive approach to risk. I repeatedly advised them of the danger of encountering a major bug that simply couldn't be worked around in software, but they just smiled and waved it off. Microsoft is, after all, a software company, and they exuded confidence. They projected a more cavalier attitude about the bugs than did Sony or I. Sony, consistently more cautious, was less willing to accept problems in the hardware and more willing to spend money for an additional run through the fabrication facility to correct them.

The management style that allowed Microsoft to succeed in meeting the Christmas 2005 goal clearly started at the top. Both companies had dynamic personalities at the executive level. For Microsoft, that was Robbie Bach; for Sony, Ken Kutaragi. Additionally, Bach seemed to have succeeded in pushing his forward-thinking management philosophy down into the lower ranking managers who were actually running the day-to-day operation of the project.

In 2004, at the height of the PlayStation 2 era and in the midst of PlayStation 3 development, *Time* magazine named Kutaragi as one of the world's one hundred most influential people. Accordingly, everyone assumed Kutaragi was the heir apparent for the CEO position, destined to assume control over all of Sony. However, in a surprise move in 2005, Sony announced a new CEO, the Welsh-born Sir Howard Stringer. He was the first non-Japanese executive to run the company. Kutaragi was demoted from the board of directors and from his place as head of consumer electronics, though he retained his position as head of Sony Computer Entertainment Division. Many thought his demotion was a direct result of his outspoken criticism of some of Sony's policies and product strategies. As time moved on, Kutaragi seemed more and more removed from project execution and, in 2007, he retired.

In spite of these differences in strategy, style, and leadership, both Sony and Microsoft were extremely effective at achieving their goals.

They took these revolutionary chips we built, each having the power of a turbo-boosted supercomputer, and blasted the gaming experience into a new realm.

Did Intel end up where Peter Hofstee predicted? After all, that was the driving force behind our aggressive goals. Well, Intel has certainly moved closer, but the Cell chip still holds the highest frequency trophy of 10 FO4. Intel introduced their new dual-and quad-core Penryn-based set of 45 nanometer chips in late 2007, taking Intel products well beyond three gigahertz in frequency. However, their best-of-breed design today is 16 FO4 compared to the Cell's 10 FO4. The Penryn includes a larger cache and an integrated graphics core. AMD is also offering new computer chips with an integrated graphics core, so it's one more sign to me that the game industry has had a major impact across the board in the computing and entertainment industries. In August 2007, AMD introduced its highest frequency processor to date—the 6400+ Black Edition—which operates at 3.2 gigahertz, but is still slower than our record-smashing 10 FO4 design. This chip targets users of digital media applications and photo editing. Actually, IBM itself came the closest to beating the Cell chip's speed record with the Power6 processor. It tops out at 13 FO4, just slightly slower than the cell design. At least for now, our cell chip holds the planet's speed record.

As for Apple, they left IBM behind in 2005 in favor of Intel, and they seem to be making deeper inroads into the PC market with this change. Though Apple is well known for keeping their roadmap plans secret, it's easy enough to look at Intel's roadmap to see what's in store for them.

Chekib Akrout pushed us to go beyond Hofstee's predictions for Intel's chips, and we did. We took on the dark side and won, a glorious victory even without trumpets blaring and fireworks showering the skies. I think the end to this part of the story is still somewhere out in the future.

Both game consoles, Xbox 360 and PlayStation 3, have done exceedingly well in the market, but being the latecomer this time, Sony had to work harder to attain the level of market share they wanted. With a price cut and the favorable outcome of the Blu-Ray/HD-DVD war, they were able to boost their sales considerably at the end of 2007. Cumulatively, Sony sold over ten million PlayStation 3 units worldwide by the end of 2007, compared to over nineteen million of Microsoft's Xbox 360 consoles and over twenty-one million of Nintendo's Wii. I think the Wii's underdog success has been quite a shock for our two Goliaths. When you look at the attach rate (number of games purchased with each new console), the Xbox 360 is clearly in the lead with an attach rate of over seven (the highest ever for the industry), while the Wii has about five and PlayStation 3 has a little less than five. That higher attach rate translates directly into more dollars for Microsoft. In the bigger picture, sales of gaming hardware, software, and accessories hit $4.7 billion in the year ending March 2008. It's expected to reach $68.3 billion by 2012. That's a very tasty growth rate for investors.

I like knowing that my fingerprints are on all three major games consoles, the PlayStation 3, Xbox 360, and the Wii. The Wii used the base PowerPC G3 microprocessor that I helped create so many years ago in the Somerset Design Center. At least for that moment, I ruled the game hardware industry. I am also proud that in round two of a head-to-head fight with Intel, we locked them out of the high-volume market for game chips.

According to Robbie Bach in an address at the Consumer Electronics Show on January 6, 2008: "From January to November 2007, the console Microsoft Xbox 360 generated $3.5 billion in revenue, which . . . was over $2 billion more than the PlayStation 3 and $1 billion more than the Nintendo Wii." In 2007, at least 45 million families in the United States owned game consoles, of which 4.4 million were connected to the Internet. As of mid 2008, Xbox Live surpassed twelve million members, almost doubling in the past year. It is now the largest community in the connected console game sector.

The games themselves are a huge source of revenue for Microsoft. There have been well over eight million *Halo3* games sold since its launch in September 2007, generating just under $500 million. Microsoft announced that the launch of *Halo3* broke all previous records for game sales, with an estimated $170 million in sales in the United States alone in the first twenty-four hours. *Halo4* is slated for release in late 2008.

Both Microsoft and Sony are well positioned for a stellar future with their game consoles and are selling hundreds of thousands of them every month.

Throughout this project, we got lots of things right, but sometimes the most significant lessons came from our mistakes. Success is so much sweeter when achieved through a little blood, lots of sweat, and even a few tears. I learned and applied important life principles that helped us succeed as a team and that help me still today. It made me proud to be an "optimist" according to the IBM management. Optimism and positive thinking are much underused tools that can help teams through high challenge and adversity. A can-do attitude is contagious. I believed that my team could meet the project goals and schedule, and I never gave up.

It takes a bold vision to inspire a high-performance team to create, to take risks, and to stay focused on the goal. The rewards that fell into our laps when we got that "vision thing" right, and the misfortune that befell us when we got it wrong, taught us how crucial that first step really is. Building the right vision with achievable milestones and realistic boundaries is kind of like divining the future. It's that powerful. It's the map. Sony's Kutaragi was strong enough to make us believe his world-conquering vision was achievable, and even though we endured a few bumps and revisions along the way, we kept our eyes on the goal. Revise the map as you go along if you must, but realize that it creates work and the opportunity for confusion. Better to start right and minimize the effects of change.

I also learned that team dynamics are tricky, slippery, and full of treachery. All the old adages—one bad apple can spoil the whole basket, oil and water don't mix, the chain is only as strong as its weakest link—are so true! Putting a bunch of geniuses together to work on the same project will not guarantee success unless some level of agreeableness and acceptance exists between them. Minimize turmoil and maximize the desire to excel by carefully juxtaposing the right skills and personalities on your team. People work best around people they like and respect, and it's often easier to create that perfect mix from scratch than to correct an imbalance in an existing team. My advice is to pay at least as much attention to the team dynamics as you do to the individual skills. Work very hard to make the right choices up front.

Make it a rewarding environment, and your team will respond. Celebrate every success, no matter how small. Encouragement doesn't cost much and it can go a long way, but eventually, you'll have to put your money where your mouth is. Your budget should always include delivery of tangible benefits for performance.

There's no substitute for an accurate understanding of the competition. It takes time, knowledge, and work to create a thorough assessment but, in the end, you'll respond faster to changes in the market. Your product will have those winning characteristics that consumers want, and you'll be more likely to overachieve than to miss the mark.

Last words of advice: work hard, play hard. In my experience, that translates to "victory or death" whether I'm working or playing. I'm very competitive and winning is everything. Mickie prefers to look at this as having the correct work-life balance. I guess I can live with that, as long as it's intense. We couldn't always afford the luxury of "balance" during the project, but we both aspired to that philosophy.

I still see Mickie sometimes, and it's been fun and maybe cathartic for us to write our story. We always did work well together. Following a particularly stressful or bizarre day at the STI Design Center, we often teasingly said to each other, "We should write a book about this." The more we talked about it, the more we decided we actually did have an exclusive story to tell. Being on the inside of this complex business of chip design, we were uniquely positioned to shed light on the corporate-level challenges and intrigues, as well as the day-to-day life of these talented engineers. We wanted to inspire other young people to embrace technology and seek out challenging careers. Our own leadership skills were certainly put to the test in the midst of cultural conflict, extraordinary innovation, and fierce pressure to work harder, faster, better. We felt we had some leadership lessons to share that might benefit others. Mickie says she has never been happier than in the years since she left IBM for a simplified life, and I believe her. She is enjoying having time to write, which has always been a passion for her.

Keryn Mills, Pam Spann, Kathy Papermaster, and Linda Van

Grinsven, the other members of the women's coalition of which Mickie was a part, all remained at IBM. So have Peter Hofstee and Mike Day. Sang Dhong left to pursue a career at AMD, and Dac Pham ended up at Freescale.

I left IBM early in 2006 to return to the small startup company where Jim Kahle found me five years before. My job is not stressfree, nor is it without some drama—but nothing on the scale as that which I encountered at the STI Design Center. I enjoy time with my family, and I'm very happy as I sit on the floor playing *Halo3* on my Xbox 360 with my two boys. The graphics are incredible, and I'm proud of this awesome computing engine I helped create. We race around a fantastic futuristic planet and blast aliens that are so real they scare me. Vivid scenes actually place us there on that distant planet. The movements are fast and fluid, and I become one with my character. We've come a long way in the last twenty years, but it's not a stretch for me to imagine that I have been zapped into an electronic world similar to the computer in the old Tron story.

I put it all on the line to make it happen, and I'm glad I held nothing back. However, I never again want to try to serve so many masters in such a high-stakes undertaking, and I hope I can make that resolution stick. The price was entirely too steep. The team suffered from the constant scrutiny and hammering; the work suffered from having so many opposing decision makers involved; and I felt hollowed out in spite of the phenomenal technical successes.

Jim Kahle remains the chief evangelist for Cell technologies at IBM, and Chekib Akrout is doing extremely well at AMD, where I hear he is very highly regarded. In spite of huge corporate successes, Chekib, Jim, and I were casualties of war. Still friends? Possibly, given enough time to heal. Did we gain the fame and fortune we expected? The jury is still out.

NERD WORD ALLEY

Cell broadband engine architecture (CBEA)—The microprocessor developed by the Sony/Toshiba/IBM coalition in Austin, Texas, for the PlayStation 3.

Central processing unit (CPU)—A microprocessor that executes a sequence of stored instructions called a program; typically thought of as the brains of a computer.

Circuit design—The transistor and physical implementation of a computer microarchitecture. At this stage, the physical layout and electrical connections of each component are also decided. This layout commonly takes the form of artwork for the production of a printed circuit board or an integrated circuit.

CISC (Complex instruction set computer)—A microprocessor instruction set architecture (ISA) in which each instruction can execute several low-level operations, such as a load from memory, an arithmetic operation, and a memory store, all in a single instruction.

Dual instruction issue—A measure of the instruction width of a microprocessor. Two instructions are issued on each single thread in parallel.

Execution unit—A part of the CPU that performs the operations and calculations called for by a program.

Fanout-of-four (FO4)—A measure of the number of gate delays in a processor pipeline. More specifically, the number of simple inverter gates connected in series, each having a fanout or load of four gates connected to them. A smaller FO4 gate delay translates to a faster frequency. It is a way to compare processor speed across multiple manufacturing technologies.

Floating-point numbers—Real numbers that have a decimal point that can be placed anywhere relative to the significant digits of the number; a computer realization of scientific notation. The advantage of this representation is that it can support a much wider range of values than fixed-point numbers.

Floorplanning—The step of creating a basic chip-map showing the expected locations on the chip for logic gates, power and ground planes, I/O pads, and hard macros. (This is analogous to a city planner's activity in creating residential, commercial, and industrial zones within a city block.)

Instruction set architecture (ISA)—The part of the computer architecture related to programming, including the native data types, instructions, registers, addressing modes, memory architecture, interrupt and exception handling, and external I/O. An ISA includes a specification of the set of opcodes (machine language), the native commands implemented by a particular CPU design.

Instruction unit—The part of a CPU responsible for maintaining the fetch pipeline and for dispatching instructions. It stores the instructions required to process the data.

L1—Level 1 cache is a block of on-chip memory that provides fast access for the CPU by keeping frequently requested data in close proximity.

L2—Level 2 cache is a secondary block of memory that resided off-chip from the CPU in older computers, but with today's integrated circuit technology, is usually included on-chip: The microprocessor first checks its internal cache (L1), then the L2 cache, and finally main memory (off-chip Dynamic Random Access Memory, or DRAM) for instructions or data. Because cache memory is faster than DRAM, it can be accessed more quickly, thus helping keep the pipeline full.

Logic design—The logical specification of a computer microarchitecture. Register transfer level (RTL) abstraction is used in hardware description languages like VHDL to create high-level representations of a circuit, from which lower-level representations and ultimately actual wiring can be derived.

Memory Flow Control—The memory subsystem associated with the Cell chip's PowerPC core; includes many of the arrays and the L2 cache.

Microarchitecture—The set of processor design techniques used to implement the instruction set; the internal hardware architecture of a computer. Computers with different microarchitectures can share a common instruction set. For example, the Intel Pentium and the AMD Athlon implement nearly identical versions of the X86 instruction set, but have radically different internal designs.

Microprocessor core—A self-contained processor which is a major embedded component of a larger chip.

Multithreading—Running multiple computation threads in parallel on a common hardware base.

Out-of-order execution—A paradigm used in most high-performance microprocessors to make use of cycles that would otherwise be wasted by a certain type of costly delay; requires more design complexity and more silicon real estate to implement.

PowerPC core—The embedded high-performance RISC processor included on the chip used in the PlayStation 3 and the Xbox 360.

RISC—Reduced Instruction Set Computer, represents a CPU design strategy emphasizing the insight that simplified instructions, which "do less", may still provide for higher performance if this simplicity can be utilized to make instructions execute very fast.

STI—Sony/Toshiba/IBM partnership.

Synergistic core—The embedded floating-point processor that lives on the Cell chip (first introduced on the PlayStation 3); the Cell chip includes eight instances of this core.

Throughput—The aggregate performance of a processor running multiple programs.

VHDL (very high-level design language)—VHSIC hardware description language—a fairly general-purpose programming language used to simplify the design of digital circuits. The key advantage of VHDL when used for systems design is that it allows the behavior of the required system to be described (modeled) and verified (simulated) before synthesis tools translate the design into real hardware (gates and wires).

INDEX